teach yourself...

Windows NT 4.0 Workstation

teach yourself…

Windows NT 4.0 Workstation

Aaron Hoffmeyer
Hy Rao

A Subsidiary of
Henry Holt and Co., Inc.
New York

Associate Publisher: *Paul Farrell*

Managing Editor: *Shari Chappell*
Editor: *Laura Lewin*
Copy Edit Manager: *Karen Tongish*

Production Editor: *Gay Nichols*
Copy Editor: *Betsy Hardinger*

CONTENTS IN BRIEF

CONTENTS

What's Special About Windows NT 4.0 Workstation

Since the advent of DOS, Microsoft has dominated the operating system market for personal computers. Although this market was large enough to propel Microsoft to the top of the software company ladder, other markets were almost untouched by Microsoft's presence. These markets included network operating systems (owned by NetWare), application servers (the realm of UNIX) and high-end graphics (dominated by Apple and Silicon Graphics). In 1992, Microsoft released its answer and challenge to these markets—Windows NT.

At first, response was mixed. Wags dubbed the system "Windows Not Today" and "Windows No Takers." (NT stands for New Technology.) However,

Microsoft has gradually improved the product through three generations to arrive at a world-beater: Windows NT 4.0.

One of Microsoft's smartest decisions was to start fresh and not build Windows NT as an evolutionary form of Windows. That decision has lead to a wholly original operating system that takes advantage of the latest technology without being weighed down by years of baggage. Although Windows NT has not edged out NetWare or UNIX for the lead in total system installations, the industry consensus is that Windows NT will grow to become a dominant force.

Currently, Windows NT comes in two variations: Windows NT Server and Windows NT Workstation. Although we are more interested in NT Workstation, it might be helpful to talk a bit about NT Server. NT Server that it is aimed at heavy-duty networking, such as connecting hundreds of computers or providing information on the Internet. This system is designed to be a shared resource and not a personal computer system. NT Workstation, on the other hand, is designed for use by a limited number of people. It has some of the networking capabilities of NT Server but on a more personal level. If you bought Workstation to serve more than 10 people, you might want to give NT Server another look. Both products share a 32-bit architecture, the ability to use more than one processor, multitasking and multithreading, and compatibility with a wide array of processors.

In this chapter you will learn about the following topics:

- The motivation for creating Windows NT
- Features of Windows NT
- Client/server architecture
- Multiprocessing
- Security
- Internationalization
- Integrated networking and messaging facilities
- A comparison between NT and UNIX

WHY WINDOWS NT?

The Windows family came into existence in 1985 with the introduction of Microsoft Windows. Windows has come a long way since then, dominating the graphical user interface market for Intel-based personal computers and compatibles. Thousands of software titles run under Microsoft Windows and Windows 95, and Microsoft operating systems run on a majority of the computers sold worldwide. Ideally, any new operating system will be able to run applications from the rich and diverse universe of Windows software. Windows NT does just that.

Enabling Groupware, Internet and Intranet Communications

With the introduction of networking technology for PCs, computers can share files and resources in workgroups and across domains. Groupware applications, such as Lotus Notes, have gained wide corporate acceptance. *Groupware* is software that enables groups of users to work together more productively. Two themes dominate groupware development: sharing information and efficient messaging.

Because of the explosion of resources available on the World Wide Web and the Internet, corporations have recently discovered the virtues of creating their own *intranets,* enabling them to share resources within their internal networks. These company networks, also called local area networks, or LANs, can support access to resources through browsers, such as Internet Explorer and Netscape Navigator, and HyperText Markup Language (HTML) documents. The significant advantage of these intranets is that their high bandwidths enable users to access resources and to communicate quickly and efficiently. They can also be exciting to use.

To develop increasingly powerful groupware, Internet, and intranet applications, a new and more powerful operating system was needed that would integrate networking and messaging technology as part of the operating system.

Using Hardware Capability

Although engineers made enormous strides in increasing the capability and performance of hardware in the last 20 years, operating systems did not keep pace until recently. Intel Corporation introduced a 32-bit microprocessor in the 386 generation of microprocessors in the mid-1980s, but it took Microsoft almost five years before it released its own 32-bit operating system, Windows NT. Even Windows 95 still contains 16-bit code and is not a true 32-bit operating system, although it supports 32-bit applications quite well.

The Intel Pentium microprocessors have increased the raw computing power of the desktop as well as the sophistication of the hardware. Microprocessors now have features found only on mainframe computers five years ago. An operating system that takes advantage of these advances will usher in a new generation of sophisticated software applications.

Breaking Down the "Glass House"

A transformation is taking place in the way corporations handle the millions of bits of data that were the foundation of business transactions. Corporations store mountains of data in databases, and they need quick and efficient access the information. In the traditional arrangement, huge, expensive mainframe computers—lodged in so-called glass houses—are used to run the database server as well as run database application programs. The database server is the centralized program that responds to requests for data, and database application programs are used by various people in a company to manipulate the data—for example, performing calculations or entering employee information. Because a large number of users must share a single computing resource, this process is inefficient.

The advent of networked workstations and PCs has expanded the computing power of users' desktops, allowing for a new kind of database system: The database lives on one machine (perhaps a mainframe computer), and the applications that use the data (called *client* applications) reside on users' machines. The database server is a shared resource, but users spend most of their computing time (and computing resources) on their own machines, thereby limiting the load on the server and making data access faster and more efficient. Enabling this architecture, called *client/server* computing, was one of the key motivations for developing Windows NT.

FEATURES OF WINDOWS NT

Now let's look at a few of the key features of Windows NT.

Hardware Independence

Until the release of Windows NT, Windows software has run exclusively on Intel x86 microprocessor-based PCs. Windows NT broke that mold: It's a highly portable operating system that's capable of being run on other hardware platforms based on other microprocessors. Digital Equipment Corporation's 64-bit

Alpha microprocessor, the MIPS RISC (reduced instruction set computer) chip, and the PowerPC chip have been tested as platforms for Windows NT. Although Intel's processors are likely to continue to dominate the PC market, the emergence of other hardware platforms for Windows NT will ensure that you can get a variety of solutions to suit your budget and hardware palate. Moreover, because the line between the workstation and the PC is disappearing, workstations and PCs built by such companies as IBM/Motorola, Digital Equipment, Sun Microsystems, MIPS, and others should all be able to run Windows NT and therefore be able to network easily with rich applications in corporate computing, CAD (computer-aided design), and high-end desktop publishing.

Although UNIX software has penetrated both the high and the low ends of the PC market, no common form of UNIX is available for all hardware platforms. In fact, you can find many types of UNIX for a given hardware platform. Software for each of these types cannot be run on a different type, even for the same underlying hardware. Windows NT will be a common thread—from basic Intel Pentium systems to high-end Digital Alpha servers—and will solve the problems associated with UNIX infigting.

32-Bit Operating System

Windows NT uses a 32-bit operating system—that is, it moves data and addresses around in 32-bit chunks. *Addresses* are numbers that represent places in memory for data storage and retrieval. Because Windows NT supports 32-bit addresses, you have larger numbers to represent addresses. The larger the address you can use, the more memory you can make use of. Because memory is the food of programs, this means that you can run highly sophisticated programs that devour memory. NT's 32-bit capability also improves the efficiency and speed of data operations on 32-bit quantities. Given the same hardware, an application optimized for 32 bits will generally run much faster in Windows NT than one optimized for 16 bits will run in Windows 3.1 or Windows 95. For 32-bit microprocessors, applications written for Windows NT will be faster and more efficient.

Virtual 32-bit Linear Address Space

As far as memory addressing is concerned, the Windows family of software has closely tracked the capabilities of the Intel x86 microprocessor line. The first IBM PC with the 8088 microprocessor used 20 address lines, thereby supporting physical addressing of 2^{20} or 1,048,576 bytes (1 megabyte). The physical address is what the microprocessor or CPU (central processing unit), uses to access memory. Software applications use a logical address, which for the 8088 microprocessor is a segmented memory addressing scheme. *Segmented* memory addressing involved two quantities: a 16-bit segment and a 16-bit offset. These two quantities would be combined together after the segment was shifted four bits to form a 20-bit physical address. This complicated scheme enabled the addressing of a 20-bit space. With the Intel 80386 microprocessor, it became possible to present a 32-bit address directly to the CPU. You use what is called *flat* or *linear* addressing, in which there are no offsets or segments to add. You take a 32-bit address and present it directly to the CPU. A process, a task that is running in Windows NT, can address a virtual linear address space of 2^{32}, or 4 gigabytes (4 followed by 9 zeroes).

When an application starts in Windows NT, it has its own memory address space. Each application in Windows NT believes it has 2 GB of RAM to use. Windows NT uses an additional 2 GB of RAM for system files and drivers. You surely don't have 2 GB of RAM on your system. You might have 32 MB. So why and how does NT think that it has all this RAM? Windows NT uses a virtual pagefile on your hard disk, called **pagefile.sys**, to simulate 4 GB of RAM in the system. A process called the Virtual Memory Manager controls the access to the pagefile.

A virtual memory addressing scheme is a way for you to use more memory than is actually available. Memory is divided into *pages*. Virtual memory uses pages that are swapped into a swap space on your hard disk to create the illusion of having a memory of a much larger size. Pages are the blocks of memory passed between RAM and the pagefile. Every time a 32-bit address is used, your computer first searches its memory to see whether the address is already present. In the CPU, there is a *page table*, or a list of available pages in memory. If the page is not present in memory, then it must be brought in from the swap space. The swapping of pages into and out of memory is handled by the Virtual Memory Manager and the CPU.

Portability of Windows NT

The designers of Windows NT have localized all platform-specific operating system code to the hardware abstraction layer, or HAL. This isolation of non-portable code makes the Windows NT operating system portable to a very large extent. Processors as diverse as MIPS R4000, Intel's Pentium, and DEC's Alpha are all able to run Windows NT, making a strong case for portability.

Windows NT Architecture

Windows NT is composed of a *microkernel* operating system surrounded by a few protected subsystems. The subsystems are called "protected" because their interactions with one another and with the microkernel are highly regulated. This arrangement prevents one subsystem from destroying data that belongs to another. The microkernel is responsible for much of the task and resource management in Windows NT.

The Microkernel and Multiple Threads

The microkernel is responsible for scheduling activities and allocating resources. A program that runs on Windows NT is called a *process*. Each process is made up of more than one thread of execution. A *thread* is a portion of a program that performs a task. If you wrote a word processor, you might make the **Save** command into a thread. The microkernel specifies time slices for these threads on a processor. It also allocates resources for each process, including memory and input/output (I/O) device access. For the word processor example, your **Save** command would use up I/O resources to save a file to the hard disk. The microkernel is the indivisible core of the operating system and therefore is always running.

Protected Subsystems

Windows NT allows you to execute several types of programs: Windows 16-bit applications (such as Windows Write in a Windows 3.1 system), OS/2 character mode applications, POSIX applications, DOS applications, and Windows NT 32-bit applications, such as Microsoft Word for Office 97. On top of the microkernel are several subsystems, each of which implements the environment necessary for the application types listed. An *environment* is the user interface and resources that you expect in a particular mode. In other words, when you run a DOS application, for example, it is as if you have a DOS computer allocated to run your application. At the same time (and on the same screen), if you have a Windows NT application running, it is as if you have a different Windows NT computer available to run that application. Each subsystem is protected in the sense that built-in safeguards ensure that the subsystems don't interfere or collide with one other. This arrangement sounds like a lot like *multitasking*, which is the ability to do more than one thing at the same time, but NT carries it one step further. Not only can you do many things at the same time, but you can also execute them in different operating-system environments.

When a POSIX application (a kind of UNIX application) runs, it expects certain behavior from the operating system—for example, dealing with I/O. Windows NT emulates that behavior and encapsulates it in the POSIX protected subsystem. With UNIX, you have certain facilities to which UNIX programs expect to interface. The Windows NT architecture gives you those facilities in a protected subsystem. It's like re-creating Italy in Little Italy and China in Chinatown. Both Little Italy and Chinatown are like protected subsystems for New York. You expect different environments in both places.

Extensible Architecture

You can have Little Italy and Chinatown. What prevents you from having a Mexican Village in the Big Apple, too? The encapsulation of functionality along with an entire set of policies, or ways an operating system interacts and expects interaction makes it easy to add a new subsystem without affecting existing subsystems. You could add a Macintosh-like operating subsystem to Windows NT. The programs that were run in this new subsystem wouldn't affect other subsystems. Thus, you can add subsystems in a modular fashion.

Client/Server Design

The interaction between the protected subsystems and the application running on the machine is an example of client/server design. We've discussed how Windows NT targets the client/server computing market. It turns out that the Windows NT design uses the same model. Each protected subsystem is a server, a self-contained entity that processes requests. The application acts as a client, a requester of information or services. There is a well-defined partition between the two. This arrangement has several advantages:

- Data and services are accessible only through the client/server boundary. A client requests data or service; the server responds only after validating that the request is proper with all necessary parameters. The client never has access directly to the data or services and therefore cannot corrupt global data inadvertently.
- A client/server model lends itself well to distributed computing. Clients and servers don't have to run on the same machine. Client requests can be serviced locally or by a remote server through the network.

Multiprocessing

Multiprocessors are workstations with more than one CPU: they have a common memory and other resources. You can expect a significant performance gain by having more than one CPU, because each CPU can potentially work in parallel with the other CPUs. This is true, however, only if the operating system and application software can take advantage of this technology. To take advantage of a multiprocessor, your operating system must support multiple threads of execution. This capability allows you to run one thread on one CPU and other threads on other CPUs, thereby achieving parallel execution of your program. Multiprocessing technology gives Windows NT powerful hardware scalability for application programs that are written to take advantage of more than one processor. A large portion of the operating system code for Windows NT can be run on more than one processor.

SMP, or *symmetric multiprocessing*, is the type of multiprocessing used by Windows NT. In a symmetric multiprocessor, applications and the operating system are executed over several processors. An *asymmetric* multiprocessor would run, for example, only the operating system on one particular processor; other processors would act as coprocessors in their function. Such an arrangement is not portable across hardware platforms and manufacturers. Windows NT is readily portable, however, to any manufacturer's symmetric multiprocessor. Windows NT 4.0 supports SMP.

Security

Windows NT incorporates several features that implement security:

- A file system, called NTFS, that has definable access control.
- Access control for all resources.
- User passwords for logon.
- A special account for each computer, called an administrator account, with special privileges for maintenance of a Windows NT computer and its resources.

Like the UNIX operating system, Windows NT has definable access control for files. If you protect a file from other users, you can set its access control appropriately. Let's say that you have important files that you don't want others to write into or modify; on the other hand, you need to allow others to look at the data in the files. You make such files read-only for other users. In addition to readability, you can define a variety of other categories of access. In addition to files, all resource objects in Windows NT go through the security subsystem for validation before being allocated to a requester. Examples of resource objects are processes, communication ports, and files. A communication port is a hardware device on your PC that lets you exchange information with another hardware device such as a modem or a mouse. Each resource object has a small database attached to it called an access control list (ACL). It specifies which processes are allowed to access the object and which operations can be performed on it.

Controlled User Access

You can't access a computer running Windows NT without having an account and a password. A special account called administrator sets up accounts. The administrator account is the most privileged account on the system. As administrator, you can control and configure a Windows NT computer and service users by creating new accounts, among other things. All other accounts have limited access to the system and resources.

Internationalization

Windows NT uses Unicode, an international standard for representing characters. This capability allows Windows NT to design applications in any language and script of the world. Unicode uses 16 bits to represent a character, letting you represent 65,536 possible characters, compared with 256 characters in the ASCII character set. All the world's languages used in computer commerce are included in Unicode, and there's room for future expansion. You can write a program in Japanese or French as easily as you can in Sanskrit or English. This is an important step in making Windows NT an international operating system.

Integrated Networking and Messaging Facilities

Windows NT supports peer-to-peer networking integrally. Files and resources (such as printers) can be shared across a network. Users can also use other machines that are present on a network. In addition to using resources on your computer, some applications may use applications on other computers on the network. Some programs may use the client/server model; other, specialized applications may use distributed computing. Windows NT has a mechanism called RPC, or remote procedure call that allows one computer to request and use resources on another computer. RPC is a formal structure for communication between networked computers.

Windows NT comes with a mail application, called Microsoft Exchange, that permits communication with other Windows NT machines in an installation. E-mail is useful for group communication. E-mail can even be used as an ingredient in another application. This is exactly how Outlook 97, a schedule-organizing application in Office 97, is constructed. This application uses Exchange facilities to enable communication among members of a group.

 Windows NT is compatible with computer networks such as Novell NetWare and Banyan Vines. You can run applications in Windows NT that use these other networks and at the same time run other applications that use Windows NT's own networking system.

NOTE

SUMMARY

Windows NT is a network-ready, secure, and scalable operating system that runs many different operating system environments simultaneously, including DOS, OS/2 1.x, POSIX, Windows 16 bit, and Windows NT 32 bit.

Windows NT supports multiple threads of execution on multiple processes, so you can perform several tasks at the same time on your computer. Applications can take advantage of multiprocessor support by executing different threads on different processors. Windows NT supports symmetric multiprocessing; the operating system is written to take advantage of the presence of multiple processors, just as applications can. For corporate enterprise-wide computing or for small peer-to-peer networks, Windows NT offers users the ease of the Windows interface and the benefits of a sophisticated and secure operating system.

Windows NT and the flavors of UNIX compete head to head. Table 1.1 shows a comparison of some of the features of both systems.

Table 1.1 Comparison of Windows NT and UNIX

FEATURE	WINDOWS NT	UNIX
Integrated networking	Yes	Yes
Compatibility with NetWare and Vines	Yes	Available
RPC (remote procedure call)	Yes	Yes
Multithreaded and multiprocessing support	Yes	Yes
Multitasking	Yes	Yes
Government security rating	C2	C2 mostly; level B available
Hardware platform variety	Growing; x86, Alpha, MIPS, PowerPC, mainframes	Large variety; PCs to mainframes
Application base	Huge	Large
Cost of applications	Low to moderate	Moderate to high
Database management software	SQL Server and many	Large variety
GUI	Explorer interface introduced with Windows 95	Variety; derivatives of OpenWindows, Motif
Hardware add-ons	Huge	Huge, vendor specific
Age and stability of OS	> 5 years	> 25 years
Ability to run DOS programs	Yes	Yes, with a software emulation package
Ability to run 16-bit Windows apps	Yes	Yes, with software emulation package

continued on next page

FEATURE	WINDOWS NT	UNIX
Ability to run 32-bit Windows apps	Made for it	Yes, with software emulation
POSIX support	Limited	POSIX is UNIX
Online documentation	Extensive	Extensive
User base	Growing rapidly	Large and stable
Cost of a workstation	$2000 and up	$3000 and up

SUMMARY (CONTINUED)

Windows NT and UNIX have similar capabilities and features. However, Windows NT has distinct advantages over UNIX in many areas—notably, its compatability with Windows 3.1 and Windows 95, the most widely used operating systems in the world. Windows NT is also relatively new. It is the only operating system provided from scratch in the last decade. It takes advantage of all the lessons learned in previously developed operating systems, and utilizes the latest technology.

Finally, the biggest advantage Windows NT has over operating systems is that Microsoft has spent more time on the development of Windows NT than on any other OS. You can bet Microsoft intends their investment to pay off.

CHAPTER 2

What's New in Windows NT 4.0 Workstation?

Most people who work with computers are aware that Windows NT 4.0 Workstation and Windows NT 4.0 Server have been changed significantly from previous versions of Windows NT. When Microsoft released the two Windows NT 4.0 products in the fall of 1996, almost everyone noted that Microsoft had changed the interface to reflect the user interface first seen in Windows 95. However, few people are aware of the extent of the other new features included in the 4.0 release.

Chapter 1 focused on the fundamental architecture of Windows NT and discussed why that architecture positions Windows NT as the operating system for the future. This chapter focuses on the specific features included in the 4.0 release that make NT a great choice for an operating system today. In this chapter you'll learn about:

- The Windows NT 4.0 Workstation user profile
- The new features of Windows NT 4.0 Workstation
- What was left out of Windows NT 4.0 Workstation
- The future of Windows NT computing

WINDOWS NT 4.0 WORKSTATION—PART OF THE WINDOWS FAMILY OF PRODUCTS

Microsoft now offers a complete set of operating systems designed to meet the needs of various customers. This family of operating systems includes Windows 95, Windows NT Workstation, Windows NT Server, and Windows CE (for hand-held devices). In the future Microsoft will introduce NetPC, which is a Windows 9x-based network computer, and Microsoft Broadcast PC, which is a version of Windows designed to run on regular TVs. Only a few years ago, Windows was a subset of the PC market. Today, the PC is a subset of the Windows market.

Although sales of all operating systems, including MacOS, UNIX, and OS/2, grew in absolute numbers in 1996, only Windows NT and Windows 95 gained market share. Microsoft has sold more than 70 million copies of Windows 95 since it was introduced in late 1995 and continues to sell three to five million copies per month. Microsoft sold a noteworthy 4 million copies of Windows NT 4.0 Workstation in 1996. That is not bad, considering it was released late in the year.

Sales projections for Windows NT are strong. Dataquest expects Microsoft to ship 50 million copies of Windows NT Workstation in the year 2000. Microsoft has also stated that the release of Windows 97 in the fall of 1997 will be the last release of the Windows 9x version of the operating system. Thereafter, Windows NT Workstation will be the Microsoft operating system for the standard desktop computer. The "standard" desktop computer for the year 2000 is quite a machine. It will probably sport an 800-MHz CPU, 64MB of RAM and a 9GB hard drive—assuming that Moore's law, which has accurately predicted the processing power of the standard desktop computer for 30 years, continues to hold for three years.

Today, Windows NT 4.0 Workstation, with its industrial-strength reliability and security, high performance, and a complete set of remote management tools, is Microsoft's most powerful desktop operating system. Windows NT 4.0 Server is Microsoft's most powerful operating system for servers.

Customer Profile

Windows NT 4.0 Workstation is designed with several types of users in mind: corporate users, developers, technical workstation users, and computer enthusiasts. Corporate business users like NT Workstation's support for popular business applications, such as Microsoft Excel and PowerPoint, and developers will use it because many of them are now developing applications for the Internet and for Windows. In both cases, the backward compatibility with Windows software and the greater reliability of Windows NT are very important. Technical workstation users, such as those who use sophisticated CAD systems and high-end graphics machines, will find that NT Workstation is a natural fit for their powerful applications. Originally, many of these applications ran only on UNIX workstations, but many of them have been ported to the Windows NT platform. Now these users have access to the extensive world of Windows software. Workstations running NT can be as productive as workstations running UNIX, usually for a fraction of the cost. Computer enthusiasts are starting to rally around Windows NT Workstation. Although they like to have the latest, greatest technology available, they don't want to lose productivity by adopting a platform too early. Windows NT Workstation's powerful features and large library of compatible software means that these users get performance without sacrificing productivity.

NEW FEATURES IN WINDOWS NT 4.0 WORKSTATION

This section is an overview of Windows NT Workstation's new features. Many features changed from version 3.51 to version 4.0, and they are organized here by the type of change. The types of changes are related to the following:

- Interface and usability
- The Internet and intranets
- Networking
- Administration and management
- Mobile computing
- Multimedia and graphics
- Windows development

New Usability Features

The most obvious new features in Windows NT 4.0 Workstation have to do with the user interface, but Microsoft also made many changes to improve the usability of the Windows NT operating system. From a simpler installation process to new accessibility options for people with disabilities, the typical user should find NT Workstation 4.0 much easier to use than the previous versions. The following sections look at important new usability features.

Windows 95 User Interface

Windows NT 4.0 Workstation features the user interface first seen in Windows 95. This means that you can enjoy the same user interface for all your Windows 32-bit desktops and servers. The Windows 95 interface includes these elements:

- **Start** button
- Taskbar
- Shortcuts
- My Computer
- Network Neighborhood
- Recycle Bin

After you log on to Windows NT Workstation, you'll see the new desktop with these new components, as shown in Figure 2.1.

Figure 2.1 *The new user interface for Windows NT 4.0 Workstation.*

You will read about the interface in detail in Chapter 3.

Windows NT Explorer

Windows NT Explorer (Figure 2.2) is a powerful tool for browsing and managing files, folders, drives, and network connections. It displays your computer's contents and connections as a hierarchy, or tree. Windows NT Explorer replaces the File Manager that was used in previous Windows operating systems.

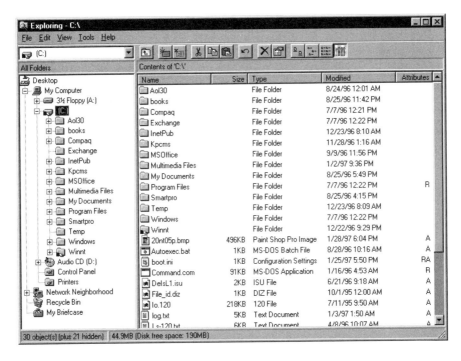

Figure 2.2 *Windows NT Explorer.*

You'll find out more about NT's file management tools in Chapter 6.

Simplified Installation

The new installation process simplifies the setup procedure of installing or upgrading to Windows NT 4.0 Workstation. Enhancements include a new easy-to-use interface, improved hardware detection, installation wizards, and a series of tools that make it much easier for corporate customers to deploy Windows NT Workstation on multiple systems.

Task Manager

The new Task Manager (Figure 2.3) is an integrated tool for managing applications and tasks and for providing key performance metrics of the Windows NT system. Task Manager maintains detailed information on each application and process that is running on the desktop. It also provides a simple way to terminate applications and processes that are not responding, making the overall system more reliable.

Figure 2.3 *Windows NT Task Manager.*

Accessibility Options

Many accessibility options can now be optionally installed. This makes the system easier to use for people with disabilities. These features include:

- Special key functions and support for alternative input devices that emulate the keyboard and mouse for users with limited dexterity.

- Scalable user interface elements, audible prompts during setup, and high-contrast color schemes for users with impaired vision.

- SoundSentry and ShowSounds functions that translate audible cues to visual cues for users who are hard of hearing.

These new features are the result of working with users who have disabilities, organizations that represent people with disabilities, and software developers who create products for this market.

New Accessories

Windows NT 4.0 Workstation now includes a number of additional applications and utilities, many of which first appeared in Windows 95, that are designed to take advantage of new areas of the operating system:

- HyperTerminal, a new 32-bit communications application that provides asynchronous connectivity to host computers such as online services. HyperTerminal is preconfigured to allow easy access to AT&T Mail, CompuServe, MCI Mail, and other systems. HyperTerminal is covered in Chapter 12.

- WordPad, a 32-bit editor that allows users to create simple documents and memos. WordPad is covered in Chapter 10.

- Paint, a 32-bit graphics application that allows users to read PCX and BMP file formats. Paint is covered in Chapter 13.

- Quick Viewers, which enable users to view files in the most popular file formats without opening the application that was used to create the file.

New Internet- and Intranet-Related Features

Microsoft Internet Explorer

Microsoft Internet Explorer 3.0 (Figure 2.4) is Microsoft's easy-to-use Internet browser. Internet Explorer uses existing HTML standards, such as tables, while enhancing HTML with improvements such as inline sound and video, background and animation support, and support for a variety of control and add-on packages. Internet Explorer also features performance enhancements that make it one of the fastest browsers available for even complex Web pages. You can find the latest updates, add-ons, and controls at http://www.microsoft.com/ie.

Figure 2.4 *Internet Explorer 3.0.*

Internet Explorer is covered in Chapter 14.

Peer Web Services

Microsoft Peer Web Services (PWS) enables easy publication of personal Web pages. PWS makes it easy for users to share information on their corporate intranets. PWS is ideal for development, testing and staging of Web applications and is great for peer-to-peer publishing.

Client Support for PPTP

The Point-to-Point Tunneling Protocol (PPTP) enables you to use public data networks, such as the Internet, to create virtual private networks that connect client PCs with servers. PPTP offers protocol encapsulation to support multiple protocols via TCP/IP connections. It also encapsulates data encryption for privacy, making it safer to send information over networks that are not secure. This technology extends the Dial-up Networking capability by enabling remote access and securely extending private networks across the Internet without the need to change the client software.

WINS and DNS Integration

Windows NT 4.0 Workstation now takes advantage of the integration between two Windows NT Server services—Windows Internet Name Service (WINS) and Domain Name System (DNS)—to provide a form of dynamic naming system that exploits the best features of both. With WINS and DNS integration, users can enter fully qualified DNS domain names, making it easier to connect to network resources. For example, using the Windows NT Explorer, a user could gain access to a share via a DNS name such as \\srv1.myco.com\public.

Improved Network Integration Feature: Control Panel

The Windows NT 4.0 Workstation Network Control Panel applet has been improved to provide a single access point where you can install and configure all network settings, such as identification, services, protocols, adapters, and bindings. This new design simplifies system administration and reduces the overall management cost.

Client Support for NDS

Windows NT 4.0 Workstation now includes an improved version of Client Services for NetWare that supports Novell NetWare Directory Services (NDS). This capability enables users to log on to Novell NetWare 4.x servers running NDS to access files and print resources.

Dial-up Networking Multilink Channel Aggregation

Dial-up Networking now provides channel aggregation, which enables users to combine all available dial-up lines to achieve higher transfer speeds. For example, you can combine two or more Point-to-Point Protocol (PPP)–compliant ISDN B channels to achieve speeds as great as 128K, or you can combine two or more standard modem lines. This feature provides increased bandwidth and allows you to combine ISDN lines with analog modem lines for higher performance.

Windows Messaging Client

Windows Messaging Client (Figure 2.5) is a universal e-mail Inbox that you can use with many different e-mail systems. Windows NT 4.0 Workstation includes drivers for Internet Mail and Microsoft Mail. You can use Internet Mail to communicate on the Internet or on any network that has Simple Mail Transfer Protocol (SMTP) or Post Office Protocol version 3 (POP3) services. The Windows Messaging Client includes full support for Messaging API (MAPI) 1.0. You can send, receive, organize, and store e-mail system and file system objects. You can also store e-mail addresses for any e-mail system with a MAPI driver. When Microsoft Exchange Server is installed, the Windows Messaging Client allows you to take full advantage of Microsoft Exchange Server's advanced messaging and groupware functionality.

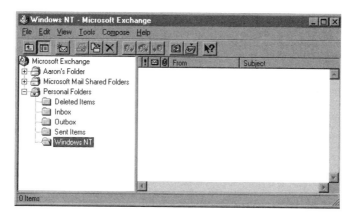

Figure 2.5 *Windows NT Messaging.*

Windows Messaging is covered in Chapter 8.

Improved Management Features: System Policies and User Profiles

System policies and user profiles allow system administrators to easily manage and maintain their users' desktops in a consistent manner. System policies are used to standardize desktop configurations, to enforce behavior, and to control users' work environments. User profiles contain all the user-definable settings for the work environment of a computer running Windows NT 4.0

Workstation. Profiles can be stored on a Windows NT Server so that users always receive the same desktop regardless of their location.

Setup Manager

Setup Manager is a new utility that assists system administrators in creating installation scripts, reducing the time and effort of deploying Windows NT 4.0 Workstation. The new Setup Manager provides an easy-to-use graphical interface for creating hands-free installation scripts that allow system administrators to automate installation for end users. These scripts eliminate the need for users to answer questions during installation, avoiding mistakes that can occur during system software upgrades.

System Difference Utility

Windows NT 4.0 Workstation now includes the System Difference Utility (**sysdiff**), which provides an easy way to preinstall additional applications simultaneously with the operating system. The sysdiff utility allows system administrators to create packages that can be applied to a system during installation and during Windows NT 4.0 Workstation setup.

Improved Windows NT Diagnostics Program

Windows NT 4.0 Workstation includes an updated and improved Windows NT Diagnostics program that simplifies troubleshooting. The new version contains information such as build number as well as data about device driver information, network usage, and system resources such as IRQ, DMA, and I/O addresses. Diagnostics information is viewed in an easy-to-use graphical tool that you can also run remotely on Windows NT.

The diagnostics tool is covered in Chapter 15.

Easier Printer Management

Printer management (Figure 2.6) is simplified by allowing you to manage printers remotely using the remote printers folder on the local machine. Additionally, printer drivers for shared printers can be located on the server for point-and-print automatic client driver installation. Printing performance has also been improved through server-based rendering (spooling) of non-PostScript print jobs. This arrangement results in a rapid return-to-application time. This means that after a print job is initiated, control is returned to the user more quickly.

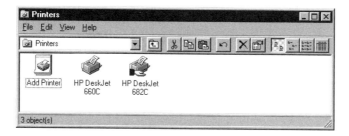

Figure 2.6 *The Printers window.*

The Printers folder is covered in Chapter 7.

Mobile Computing Features: Dial-up Networking

NT Workstation 4.0 extends the functionality of Dial-up Networking and lets you automatically dial a connection. With automatic dialing, dial-up networking is smoothly integrated into the new interface. Whether you are connecting to the Internet or accessing shared files, mobile network access is as easy as network access in the office. Establishing a remote connection works the same as establishing a local connection—you simply double-click the desired network object. For example, you can establish a remote connection to the Internet by simply clicking on the **Internet Explorer** icon.

Hardware Profiles

The Hardware Profiles utility allows you to create hardware configuration lists to meet specific computer needs. For example, if you have a portable computer, you should use a different hardware configuration depending on whether the computer is docked or undocked. At startup, you select the hardware profile to use for the current session.

Briefcase

By tracking relationships between different file versions on different computers, Briefcase allows portable users and telecommuters to escape the hassle of managing document versions. You specify which files and directories you want to track by simply dragging and dropping them into Briefcase.

Multimedia and Graphics Improvements: APIs

Windows NT 4.0 Workstation now supports the multimedia APIs first introduced in Windows 95: DirectDraw, DirectInput, DirectPlay, and DirectSound. Supporting these APIs allows developers to create games and other applications for the Windows 95 and Windows NT 4.0 Workstation platforms simultaneously.

Imaging for Windows NT

The imaging software for Microsoft Windows 95 is now available in Windows NT. This software provides powerful imaging services that enable you to access and control information directly at your desktop.

CDFS Enhancements

Windows NT 4.0 Workstation supports two Compact Disc File System (CDFS) enhancements: Auto-Run and the CD-XA format. Auto-Run allows the operating system to recognize that a compact disc has been inserted into the drive and to start the application immediately. CD-XA is an extended format for video compact discs that contain MPEG movies.

Improved Driver Support

Windows NT 4.0 Workstation includes numerous new video drivers that improve screen quality and are especially useful when you're using multimedia features. Some of the newly supported drivers are WD ThinkPad, Matrox Millennium, Trident, Number 9 Imagine, C&T, and Cirrus.

New Application Programming Interfaces and Additional Features: Telephony APIs

Telephony API (TAPI) integrates the advanced telephone with the powerful capabilities of PCs. By supplying the means for applications to set up and control telephone calls, TAPI provides a level of abstraction for developing applications that are not bound to specific telephone hardware. Through the TAPI interface, communications applications can ask for access to the modem or telephone device and negotiate with applications to share the device cooperatively.

Unimodem (Universal Modem Driver) provides TAPI services for data and fax modems and voice so that users and application developers don't have to learn or maintain difficult modem "AT" commands to dial, answer, and configure modems. Some of the new Windows NT 4.0 applets that take advantage of TAPI and Unimodem support are Dial-up Networking, HyperTerminal, and Phone Dialer.

Cryptography APIs

Windows NT 4.0 Workstation includes a set of encryption APIs that allow developers to easily create applications that work securely over nonsecure networks, such as the Internet.

Distributed COM

The Component Object Model (COM) allows software developers to create component applications. Now, Distributed COM (DCOM) in Windows NT 4.0 Workstation and Windows NT 4.0 Server provides the infrastructure that allows DCOM applications (the technology formally known as Network OLE) to communicate across networks without the need to redevelop applications. An example of a DCOM application would be a stock quote server object running on Windows NT Server that distributes quotes to multiple Windows NT Workstation clients. DCOM provides the infrastructure for connecting and providing uniform communication between client/server objects. DCOM uses the same tools and technologies as those used by COM, preserving investments in training and software.

486 Emulator

The 486 emulator allows 386-enhanced 16-bit applications to run on RISC machines.

WHAT WAS LEFT OUT?

With all the new features and improvements appearing in Windows NT 4.0 Workstation, it's hard to imagine that Microsoft omitted any important features. But that's the case: Some features available in Windows 95 are not in Windows NT 4.0 Workstation. Most, if not all, of these features will be included in Windows NT 5.0 Workstation, which should ship in 1998.

The next section describes some of the features not currently available in Windows NT 4.0 Workstation, but that are likely be included in Windows NT 5.0 Workstation.

Windows 95 Features Not Available in Windows NT 4.0 Workstation

The following list describes the most important features that Microsoft did not include in Windows NT 4.0 Workstation, even though these features were included in Windows 95.

- **Plug and Play (PnP).** PnP is a design philosophy and a set of architecture specifications. The goal of PnP is to make the PC, add-in hardware devices, drivers, and operating system work together without user intervention. To achieve this goal, all the components, including the operating system, need to be PnP compatible.

- **Power Management.** The bane of a portable computer user's existence is short battery life. Although true innovation in battery life depends on physics and hardware engineering, operating systems need to provide power management features that help manage and reduce battery power consumption.

- **Fax.** Windows 95 introduced Microsoft Fax, which provides an integrated set of tools that allows users to send and receive fax messages through the Windows Messaging Inbox.

- **Direct3D.** Direct3D delivers the next generation of real-time, interactive 3-D technology for mainstream PC users on the desktop and the Internet. It is supported by more than 80 leading software developers, hardware vendors, and PC manufacturers.

- **Infrared (IR).** IR communications, based on technology similar to remote controls, offers a convenient, inexpensive, and reliable way to connect computers and peripheral devices without cables. A set of standards for IR communications has been agreed upon by the Infrared Data Association to provide infrared communications for PCs.

THE FUTURE OF WINDOWS NT WORKSTATION

Windows NT Workstation is designed for high-end workstations, and its continuing development will target that same market. As hardware technology advances, the standard desktop computer, which probably runs Windows 95 or even Windows 3.1 now, will advance to the point where Windows NT Workstation will be a better, more stable, and faster operating system choice. In other words, the standard desktop will evolve into a high-end workstation, and then NT Workstation will be the operating system of choice for the "low-end" computer.

But the long-term future is not always easy to predict, so let's look at the near future. Microsoft plans to release Windows NT 5.0 Workstation in 1998. It should follow several months after the release of Windows 97.

Windows 97 should offer some dramatic changes from Windows 95. Plans are that it will include FAT32, a new 32-bit file system designed to boost performance and reliability. This should eliminate many of the problems with the FAT file system, such as the limited number of clusters, but will still be backward-compatible with FAT. Second, Windows 97 will probably incorporate the WebView interface; while you're using Windows Explorer, this interface will allow you to switch to a "site" view of your network. In effect, the left pane of Explorer will display a hierarchical tree of the resources on your site or local network, and the right pane will show the currently selected page of an intranet document. In this view, Explorer will look much like a standard browser. With Office 97, Windows applications should also support live links to other documents on your local network and on the Internet. And Windows 97 will extend that support for links to the operating system and its applications.

Windows NT 5.0 Workstation will probably offer the same WebView interface addition and also support embedded live links in documents. Windows NT 5.0, both Server and Workstation, will also support Plug and Play, and Active Desktop, an extensive set of tools for Internet and intranet development. NT Server 5.0 will in addition support Active Server, which will enable IT managers to publish rich content to Active Desktops over company networks or across the Internet. NT will also pick up the support for some of other features that were included in Windows 95 but left out of NT 4.0, such as fax support, power management, and Direct3D.

SUMMARY

Windows NT 4.0 Workstation is a powerful, reliable operating system that is just starting to come on in the marketplace. It is positioned as Microsoft's operating system for mid-level to high-end desktop computers, but, as hardware technology evolves, it will become the operating system for the low-end desktop computer.

Windows NT 4.0 Workstation includes so many new features and improvements that it was the most significant update of the operating system since the original release. Microsoft revamped the interface to reflect the interface of Windows 95, and it threw in many new 32-bit applications. Microsoft made significant changes under the hood, too. Networking, intranet, and Internet support applications and wizards were included, along with support for mobile computing and high-end graphics. Microsoft extended support for multimedia and added new diagnostic and system management tools.

However, the 4.0 release of NT Workstation and NT Server did not include several useful features that Microsoft included in Windows 95. The most significant omission was support for Plug and Play, the standard that enables software to recognize the hardware in your computer and make the necessary configuration changes whenever you change hardware or install NT itself.

Play and Play support will be included in Windows NT 5.0 Workstation, as will support for an interface modification called WebView. NT 5.0 will also extend DCOM, which enables OLE and ActiveX over local area networks and wide area networks.

CHAPTER 3

Getting Started in the Desktop

By Nelson King

Although you will spend far more time working with applications such as spreadsheets or word processing programs than you will in the Windows NT Desktop, the desktop is the place to start.

The desktop is also your personal window on computing. Over time you should customize it to help you do your work and also—this is important—to *enjoy* working with a computer. It's called a "desktop" because, it is the top of an important workspace in the same sense as the top of your desk. Just as you organize your desk, you can organize the main screen of your computer. You can also change its color, put pictures on it, and do many other things that make it *your* desktop.

33

Before we get into the details of customizing the desktop, we'll start with the basics. In the first part of this chapter, you will learn:

- How to start Windows NT
- How to locate things in the Desktop
- How to launch programs from the Desktop and the Start menu
- How to run several programs and switch between them
- How to quit Windows NT safely

Along the way and later in the chapter, we'll cover some advanced topics:

- Managing tasks in Windows NT
- Security issues on a network
- Customizing the Desktop

None of this presents any technical difficulty, but it's important to read and put into practice. You're urged to start Windows NT and try as many of the things covered in this chapter as you can. Don't be afraid of making mistakes. There is nothing you can do that will damage anything (in the physical sense), and in almost all cases you will be able to undo mistakes. We tend to learn best from our mistakes—or at least that's the common wisdom. With computers it's nice to have things go right the first time, and that's usually the case with Windows NT.

LOGGING ON TO WINDOWS NT

To get started with Windows NT, you must *log on*. Windows NT was designed to be a secure operating system, one that protects your computer and data. So it requires that you identify yourself and verify your identity with a password. That's why the first thing you will see after NT has finished loading (booting) is the request to press **Ctrl+Alt+Delete**.

This key combination is used to reboot a DOS computer, so it makes some people nervous. With Windows NT, however, it gets things rolling. (It can also be used to leave NT, but it's not the usual method.) You will be asked to enter your account name, password, and possibly a domain name. If this is your first time logging in to Windows NT, you may have been told what to enter (by a system administrator or someone similar); otherwise, you're free to make up the information. Before you make any entry, however, it's a good idea to think about it.

This information protects your security so that no one else can run your programs and look at your data. Use names and passwords that are not easy to deduce. Keep in mind that if you use uppercase and lowercase letters, you must enter them exactly the same way later (NT passwords are *case-sensitive*). The simplest way to make passwords difficult to steal is to make them rather long, at least eight characters. On the other hand, if you make them too long or complicated, you might not remember them. (As with standing at the front door of your home without a key, it's embarrassing to be locked out of your own computer.) Don't fall into the old habit of writing the password on a self-stick note. You may lose it, or someone who knows about this habit can check your desk for it.

NOTE   If your computer is on a company network and connected with many other computers, you may have been assigned or registered with an account name, password, and domain name. A *domain* is a group of workstations and servers. A domain name doesn't help you much, but it's necessary for Windows NT to keep track of who's who on large networks.

THE LAYOUT OF THE DESKTOP

Assuming that you remembered your password, greetings. You have arrived at the desktop (Figure 3.1). When you first arrive, there isn't much to see: a teal-blue expanse with some *icons* (picture buttons) lined up on the left side and a gray bar at the bottom with the word **Start** on the left and the time on the right.

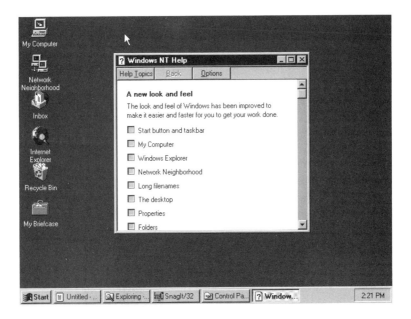

Figure 3.1 *Windows NT 4.0 Desktop.*

The open expanse of screen is the desktop window, number one among Windows' windows. The icons (created by Windows during installation) provide access to six important functions. We'll cover each one shortly. The gray bar at the bottom is the Start menu, a major new feature introduced with Windows 95 and carried over to Windows NT 4.0. That's it for the desktop; at this point, it looks pretty bare, but you'll be surprised how much information will be displayed in this simple *user interface*. As you work, the computer and its programs will change this desktop, send you messages, and give you many ways to control what's happening. In a sense, the desktop is an empty canvas waiting for your personal touch.

Desktop Objects

Everything you see on the desktop is called an *object* in the ordinary meaning of the word: A chair is an object, as is a car. However, in the world of computers and programming everything is an object, including windows, icons, menus, and even the desktop itself. This is not something you need to ponder, but you'll find the word *object* in all the official Windows documentation and in the literature of most other programs.

Using the Mouse on Objects

One important aspect of Windows User Interface objects is that they're *mouse active*. When you click on them or point to them with the mouse, something usually happens. *Clicking* means to put the mouse *cursor* (the small arrowhead you see while working in the desktop) on an object and click the left mouse button. This is called *selecting* an object. Try clicking on an object in the Desktop and see what happens.

Something similar happens when you use the right mouse button. Put the mouse cursor in the middle of the desktop (not on any other object) and click the right mouse button. You'll immediately see a *shortcut menu* like the one in Figure 3.2. As with any other menu (in or out of computing), you can make choices. In this case, to choose something you simply point to it with the cursor and click the left mouse button. The shortcut menu is a convention found in most (but not all) Windows 95 and Windows NT programs.

Figure 3.2 A shortcut menu.

Shortcut menus are said to be *context-sensitive*. The available options are the ones that are relevant to the location in NT where you are working. For example, if you call up the shortcut menu from in the desktop, you see only options that apply to the desktop.

To *double-click*, you put the cursor on an object and quickly click the left mouse button twice in succession. Double-clicking is the "launch" action; if the object (usually a program icon) is active, then a program or other process will be started. Try this with the **Recycle Bin** icon to see what happens.

Another thing to try with the mouse is *dragging.* Again using the Recycle Bin, point to it with the cursor and then click *and hold* the left mouse button. Without releasing the mouse button, you can drag the icon anywhere on the desktop. When you release the button, the icon will *drop*—stay where you put it. This technique—called *drag and drop*—is used often, and we'll visit it again when we discuss how to manage windows.

Icons in the Desktop

Most of the objects in the desktop are icons. They come in three kinds: applications, documents, and folders. The default Windows icons (see Figure 3.3), include *applications* (Inbox and Internet Explorer) and *folders* (My Computer, Network Neighborhood, Recycle Bin, and My Briefcase). You can find more information about these programs and folders in Chapter 6. The third kind, *document* icons, can be placed on the desktop from within applications; an example is a word processing document. The point of all the icons is quick access. Instead of going through a number of clicks and stops in a menu to open something, you just double-click on its icon.

Figure 3.3 The default icons.

Adding and Removing Icons from the Desktop

The technique we'll use for adding and removing icons from the desktop applies to a wide variety of situations within Windows NT and applications. Most of the time, Windows NT Explorer and the Recycle Bin are involved.

NOTE   As we go through the next steps, you'll probably notice that what you see in your monitor doesn't match the illustrations on these pages. That's because the software you've installed is different from what's on our computer. The listings in directories and the icons in folders and the desktops usually vary from computer to computer.

Start by double-clicking the **My Computer** icon in the desktop. This opens the My Computer window shown in Figure 3.4. My Computer is one of many windows that has its own name but looks and behaves like Windows Explorer.

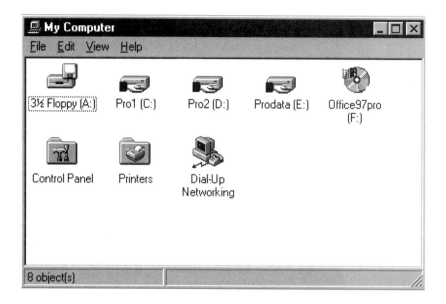

Figure 3.4 My Computer window.

Select any one of the icons in this window (**Dial-up Networking** is used as the example in Figure 3.5). Press down the **Ctrl** (control) key and use the mouse to drag the icon, as an image, to the desktop. If you had the right touch, a copy of the icon was created that says **Shortcut to Dial-up Networking**. That tells you the original icon represented a program or application. If you double-click this new desktop icon, Windows will launch the Dial-up Networking program. Because you've already been introduced to a shortcut menu, it might be confusing that we have another "shortcut" here. This time, *shortcut* refers to an icon or file reference that will start an application but isn't the application's real startup file. A shortcut contains a reference to the original program file.

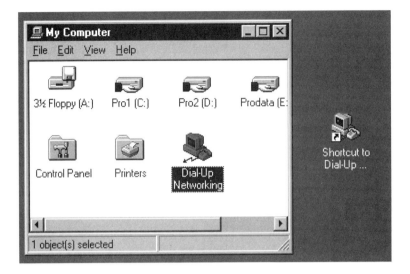

Figure 3.5 *Creating a program shortcut* .

Something similar happens when you select and drag a document file from the Explorer onto the desktop. To try this, open one of the disk drive icons in the My Computer window—for example, **C:**. If you have any folder in the drive, try to drag it to the desktop. Because you're not using the **Ctrl** key, the file or folder will be *moved* (and not just copied) to the desktop. But what does it mean when something is moved to the desktop? It means that the desktop, at least in these operations, is also part of the directory structure. In the Explorer, track down C:\WINNT\PROFILES\DEFAULT USER\DESKTOP, and you'll see that this directory probably contains some of the desktop icons.

This is one of many examples in Windows NT in which something that sounds like a distinct program or location is actually a folder in the directory structure of your primary (C:) disk. Printers, My Briefcase, My Computer, and Recycle Bin are other examples.

N O T E

To remove icons from the desktop, select and drag the icon to the nearest **Recycle Bin** icon, which may be on the desktop or in the Explorer. Alternatively, select the file and click the right mouse button to bring up the shortcut menu, where you can select the **Delete** option.

Arranging and Customizing the Desktop

As you begin to add icons to the desktop, you'll probably start to organize them. There's quite a bit of screen real estate (especially if you have 17-inch or larger monitor), but sooner or later things become crowded and messy. That's when you can turn to the desktop shortcut menu. Here, you can select **Line Up Icons**, which straightens the existing arrangement. Or you can choose one of the **Arrange Icons** options, which arrange the icons to fit a pattern (by name, type, size, or date). Otherwise, you can select **Auto Arrange** and let Windows organize the icons.

Also available from the desktop shortcut menu is **Properties**, which opens the Display Properties dialog box (actually part of the Control Panel). There are many options for decorating the desktop, and most people have fun doing it. The details are in Chapter 5 ("The Control Panel").

USING THE TASKBAR

The Taskbar, which also contains the Start menu, is one of the most important tools Windows NT gives you for managing your computer. Fortunately, it's also one of the easiest to use. As you launch programs from the Start menu, desktop, or anywhere else, they are automatically registered in the Taskbar (see Figure 3.6).

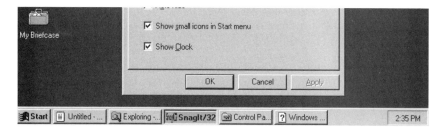

Figure 3.6 *The Windows NT Taskbar* .

Once you've opened a program, its icon and name appear as a *task button* in the Taskbar. When you close the program, its task button disappears. You can keep more than one program open at a time. Open a program and then *minimize* it. (In most Windows programs, click on the **Minimize** button in the upper-right corner.) This action *docks* the program to the Taskbar; the program is still running, and you can reopen it (*maximize* it) by clicking on the task button. You can open and minimize many programs and use the Taskbar to switch among them. The task buttons of the minimized programs appear gray in the Taskbar; the task button of the currently maximized program has a lighter background.

The Taskbar also is a kind of *status bar* (an element you'll see in many application programs) that contains information about your computer. In the beginning, this information includes only the clock, but other items will be added as you use programs.

Moving and Hiding the Taskbar

As useful as the Taskbar is, you may not want it at the bottom of the screen or visible all the time (using valuable screen space). You can move the Taskbar around, change its size, and make it disappear. To move the Taskbar, grab any part of it that isn't part of a task button and drag it north, south, east, or west to the edge of the screen. When you release the mouse button, the Taskbar will dock itself to the appropriate edge of the desktop (but not in the open desktop area).

You can grab the outside edge of the Taskbar (wait for the double-headed arrow icon to appear) and then pull the Taskbar in or out to size it. This helpful technique can be used to reveal more of the text in the task buttons.

If you want to have the Taskbar hide itself when not in use, click the right mouse button in any unoccupied space in the bar to bring up the Taskbar shortcut menu. Select **Properties** to display the Taskbar Properties dialog box shown in Figure 3.7.

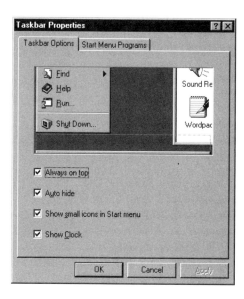

Figure 3.7 *Taskbar Properties dialog box.*

Click the **Auto Hide** check box to enable the option. The Taskbar will grace-fully retract itself to a thin gray line as soon as you click outside the bar. You can bring it back out by "bumping" the line (a quick touch) with the cursor. This option keeps the Taskbar out of your way and allows you to have a wider bar area without taking extra screen space.

Customizing the Taskbar

While we're in the Taskbar Properties dialog box (Figure 3.7), there are a couple of other options that you may prefer. Selecting **Always on Top** means that the Taskbar will always be on top of any windows in the screen. If you use **Auto Hide**, this option doesn't mean much because you see the Taskbar only when using it—and then it's automatically on top. The final option, **Show**

Clock, displays the system clock in the Taskbar. If you'd like a little more visible clock, there's the Clock program located in the **Programs**, **Accessories** option of the Start menu.

USING THE START MENU

Although there isn't much in the Start menu when you begin using your computer, it won't take long before it fills (see Figure 3.8). For most people, the Start menu is the focal point of using Windows NT because it's one of the easiest places to begin running programs.

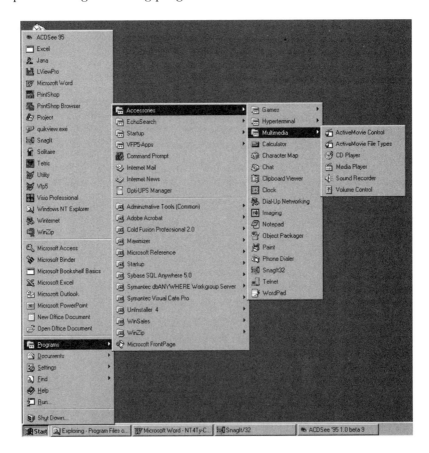

Figure 3.8 The Start menu expanded.

Most software that you install will automatically put an icon into the Start menu, sometimes referencing an entire directory folder as well as an individual program. Windows NT ... 0 does this when you first install it. It also breaks ... into permanent segments: At the bottom is the ... tton will cause the rest of the menu to pop up. As ... the menu is partitioned into sections of the ... ory: Administrator, All Users, and Default User. ... rmanent Windows NT options.

... to use Explorer to look at all the folders under ... where you'll find most of the icons for programs you ... computer. It's also where you'll move them when ... t menu and other directories. If you're familiar with ... nenu, you'll notice that it doesn't have this kind of ... have user profiles.

... series of program icons, which may have been ... ure. Running programs from the Start menu is ... clicking once on the icon or text. This action ... associated with the menu option or open an ... the case for the Programs menu.

... e **Programs** option expands away from the ... ne by selecting an option in the Programs ... kind of menu is a *cascading* menu, a nicely ... sing down programs two or three levels ... g, so most people move their favorite or ... desktop or into the main Start menu.

... n an unoccupied area of the Taskbar. You'll ... t the option **Properties**. Select that, and the ... ... appear. Select the **Start Menu Programs** tab

(Figure 3.9)

Figure 3.9 Taskbar Properties dialog box, **Start Menu Programs** tab.

The **Add** button starts the Create Shortcut Wizard, which will step you through to completion of a shortcut. The **Remove** button doesn't use a Wizard. Instead, it gives you a list of the current shortcuts in the Start menu. You can delete any shortcut by selecting and clicking **Remove**. The **Advanced** button starts a copy of Windows Explorer and logs it to the folder where the Start options are located.

As an exercise in using Windows Explorer, find the Start Menu folders for the Administrator, All Users, and Default Users profiles. These are located in the C:\WINNT\PROFILES directory. Most people like to use the All Users Start Menu folder to store the entries for their favorite programs. (The Administrator folders are available only if you log in as Administrator.) Find the program file you wish to move in the Programs folder (it could be in any of the three profiles) and drag it to the Start Menu folder. You could also copy it, leaving the original in the Programs folder.

Folders (directories) that contain other folders or contain shortcut icons occupy most of the Programs menu. Some programs do not have their own icon, and that can be misleading. In those cases, you'll need to identify a program either by name, or as a last resort, by its file type. Program files have a file extension (the part after the dot) of EXE, such as **EXCEL.EXE**.

Documents Menu

The **Documents** option in the Start menu opens a folder window (all these directory-style windows are related to Windows Explorer). In it you'll see a list of documents you have previously created or opened—a *history*. You can double-click the name of the document to start the program in which it was created and load the document. For example, if you see a file with a Microsoft Word icon, such as **MYLETTER.DOC**, double-clicking it will start Word and load this file. This approach is useful if you want to search for previously used documents, although it's quicker to launch documents that have been placed on the desktop.

To clear the Document menu, return to the **Start Menu Programs** tab of the Taskbar Properties dialog box. Click the **Documents Menu Clear** button (shown in Figure 3.9).

NOTE If you use Microsoft Office 97 with the Outlook personal information manager, you should note that most of the functionality of the Documents menu has been superseded by the Journal function in Outlook.

Settings Menu

The **Settings** option in the Start menu is yet another folder. It contains three entries: Control Panel (a folder), Printers (a folder), and Taskbar (a program). The Control Panel gives you access to some of the most important features of Windows NT, and Chapter 5 covers 26 common applets, or sophisticated dialog boxes used to control specific features in NT. The **Printers** option opens the Printers folder, where you'll see an icon and name for each of the printers that have been installed on your computer or are available to you over a network. Double-clicking these printer entries will display the Windows NT Print Manager dialog box (covered in Chapter 6). The **Taskbar** option opens the Taskbar dialog box, which has already been discussed.

Other Start Menu Options

Four more options round out the Start menu: **Find, Help, Run**, and **Shut Down. Help** is the topic in Chapter 4, and **Shut Down** is the last item in this chapter. Let's take a quick look at the **Run** option (see Figure 3.10). You can use this dialog box to run a program, much like double-clicking a program icon.

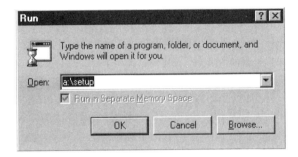

Figure 3.10 *The Run dialog box.*

There are only three situations in which the Run dialog box is needed:

- To install software. Typically you use the **Browse** button to locate a file called **SETUP.EXE** or **INSTALL.EXE** (you'll get instructions about this).
- To run a Windows or DOS program that isn't in the Start or Programs directory.
- To run a program that takes custom startup parameters. This option is mostly for programmers.

In some ways, **Run** is a throwback to the good/bad old days of DOS and is not used much anymore.

Customizing the Start Menu

A limited amount of customization is available for the Start menu. The major categories (partitions) are determined by Windows NT, and the same is true for the **Programs**, **Settings**, **Find**, **Help**, and **Run** options. You should try the right mouse button on the Start menu itself. The shortcut menu that appears gives you quick access to the Start menu folder (use **Open**) and to the All Users section of the WINNT directory (mentioned previously), where most of the program icons are located.

CONTROL WITH THE TASK MANAGER

Most of the time you'll handle tasks by switching between them, but occasionally it's necessary to have a better look at what's running and what's not—taking the pulse, so to speak. That's where the Windows NT Task Manager (Figure 3.11) comes in. It isn't the most sophisticated monitoring tool, but it has its uses.

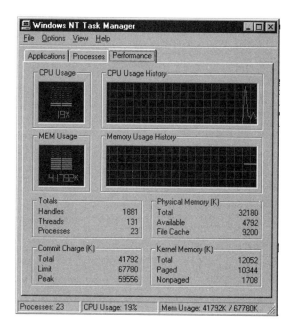

Figure 3.11 *The Task Manager dialog box.*

To see the Task Manager dialog box, click the right mouse button in an empty space in the Taskbar. When the Taskbar shortcut menu appears, select **Task Manager**. This dialog box has three tabs. The first one, **Applications**, shows which programs are active (in the Taskbar) and their current status. You can use this dialog box to select programs that are hung up (not running because of an error) and clear them from memory. The second tab, **Processes**, goes beyond the currently running Taskbar applications and shows you all the programming that's running in Windows NT. This screen is dangerous: You can end any process you see, often with unpredictable if not disastrous results. The final tab, **Performance**, gives you a graphic representation of how much processing (CPU) time and how much memory are being used. If you suspect that a program is hogging resources, checking this box can give you a better idea.

The **Performance** tab contains lots of fairly technical information, such as handles (open files), threads (subprograms), and so on. This information can be difficult to interpret even for experienced users.

N O T E

LOGGING OFF OR SHUTTING DOWN

At the end of a working session, it's tempting to press the computer's off button and walk away. Don't do it. Although Windows NT is very forgiving of sudden events, turning the computer off before NT has a chance to clean up and close programs can lead to data loss and occasionally even to damaged programs. It could be bad enough that you might not be able to restart the computer. The right thing to do is to log off.

The normal route for leaving NT goes through the Start menu, where you'll see the option **Shut Down**. Selecting this option gets you the Shut Down Windows dialog box (Figure 3.12). It has three pertinent options. **Shut down the computer** is the normal way to quit NT and turn off the power. **Restart the computer** is used primarily during software and hardware installation. **Close all programs and log on a different user** is used if you don't want to leave the computer entirely.

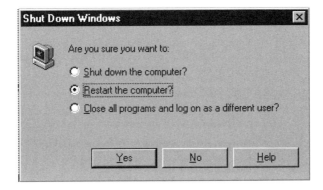

Figure 3.12 Shutting down.

SUMMARY

The user interface of Windows NT 4.0 is almost identical to that of Windows 95. There have been a few refinements, such as the handling of the Task Manager. Some of these improvements reflect NT's superior technical capabilities in the areas of controlling tasks, security, and protection against crashes. Most people need to become familiar with how to use the Desktop, but pushing into the obscure references—such as understanding the final page of the Task Manager—is purely elective. That's the nice thing about complex programs such as NT. They leave a lot of room for personal tastes and interests.

CHAPTER 4

The Help System

Windows NT's Help system is a great resource when you need to find out more about the operating system or about an application. Help has been improved and now includes a useful search feature. Help also contains links to Control Panel applications and other Help files. For example, if you are having problems setting up your modem, Help contains a link to the Modem Setup Wizard.

In this chapter you will learn about:

- Invoking Help
- Exploring the Help interface
- Customizing Help
- Copying Help information to other applications
- Printing Help topics

INVOKING HELP

The kind of help you need dictates how you invoke Help. To obtain descriptions of specific items in a dialog box, you can usually press **F1** or use the **What's This (?)** help button, which we'll discuss a little later. For information on a specific application, you invoke Help by using the Help menu in that application. To obtain general information on Windows NT, such as how to set up devices, you can invoke Help from the Start menu.

Using the Start Menu

One of the options listed in the Start menu is **Help** (see Figure 4.1).

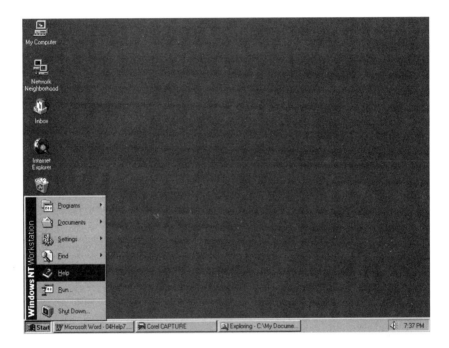

*Figure 4.1 The **Help** option on the Start menu.*

NOTE

Most applications regard the **F1** key as the Help key. In Windows NT system programs or if the Desktop is the current selection, pressing **F1** brings up Windows NT Help.

From within an Application

Most applications developed to run under Windows provide their own Help information. You can usually select Help from within the application by selecting the Help menu, as shown in Figure 4.2. You can also invoke Help by pressing **F1** while the application is the current selection.

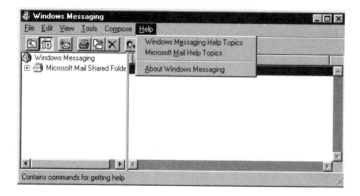

Figure 4.2 *The Help menu in Microsoft Messaging.*

In addition to the help that is accessible from the Help menu, most applications offer help in several other ways. Many dialog boxes offer context-sensitive Help, or help that is specific to the dialog box. This type of help often does not launch the full Windows Help application. It sometimes displays a small shadow dialog box rather than a separate window.

In many dialog boxes, you can access Help in several ways in addition to pressing **F1**. You can right-click a field, button, or other control and then pick **What's This** from the context menu, as shown in Figure 4.3. You can also click the question mark button in the corner of the title bar and then click any element in the dialog box to see information specific to that item, as shown in Figure 4.4.

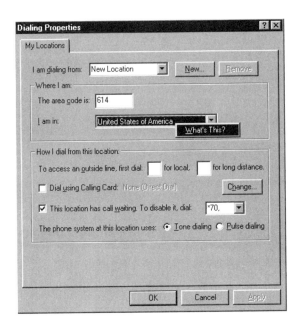

*Figure 4.3 **What's This*** *on the right-click context menu.*

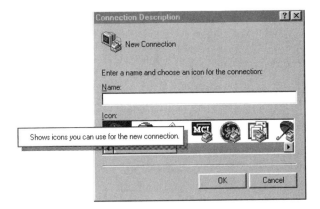

Figure 4.4 *Context-sensitive Help within a dialog box.*

EXPLORING HELP

In Windows NT 4.0, the look of the Help system has been revamped. Help dialog boxes designed for the latest versions of Windows (95 and NT 4.0) have three tabs: **Content**, **Index**, and **Find**. Older Help files have **Index** and **Find** but may not have the **Contents** tab. Some applications include a fourth tab, usually for an Answer Wizard. You enter questions in English, and the **Answer** tab finds Help topics that may answer your question. The Windows NT Help dialog box (invoked from the Start menu) is displayed in Figure 4.5, showing the three standard tabs. Each of these tabs is explained in more detail in the following sections.

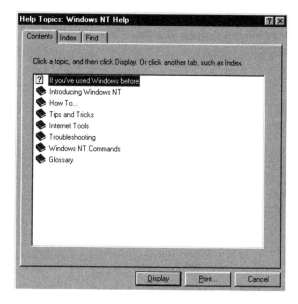

Figure 4.5 *Windows NT Help.*

The Contents Tab

The **Contents** tab uses a book metaphor to display Help information, as shown in Figure 4.5. Each major section, much like a chapter in a book, is displayed with a book icon to the left. To see the contents of a "book," double-click it; or you can select it and press **Enter**, the + key on the numeric keypad, or the **Display** button at the bottom of the dialog box. The book expands by displaying either sections or topics. *Sections* still have the book icon to the left but are indented slightly. *Topics* are displayed with a question mark icon to the left. To display a Help topic, double-click it or select it and press **Enter** or **Display**.

Figure 4.6 shows the **Contents** tab with several levels of the hierarchy of a chapter expanded.

Figure 4.6 Help Contents tab displaying a chapter expanded.

To close an open chapter, double click it; or select it and press **Enter** or press **–** on the numeric keypad.

Figure 4.7 shows a Help topic displayed. When you display a Help topic, a new window pops up with the text for that topic, and the previous dialog box disappears. You can return to the Help dialog box by pressing the **Help Topics** button at the top of this page. Later in this chapter, we'll go into more detail about the Help topic window.

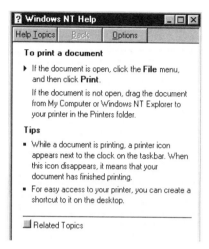

Figure 4.7 *A Help topic displayed.*

The Index Tab

The **Index** tab in the Help dialog box displays Help topics much like an index in a book, as shown in Figure 4.8.

Figure 4.8 *The Index tab in Help.*

You can home in on a topic by typing a keyword in the text box labeled **Type the first few letters of the word you're looking for**. As you type, the second text box automatically scrolls to the first keyword that matches the letters you've typed. Select a topic and then click **Display**, or simply double-click the matching topic or any other topic you want to display. If the item in the Index list matches only one topic, that topic is displayed and appears in a separate window like the one shown in Figure 4.7. If your Index entry matches more than one Help topic, you'll see another dialog box. This one shows you the list of Help topics that matched the item you selected, as shown in Figure 4.9.

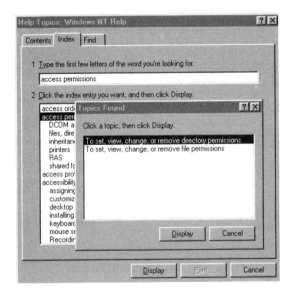

Figure 4.9 *Additional Index topics.*

You then select a topic from within this dialog box and press **Display** to open the Help topic window. The Help topic will display as in Figure 4.7.

The Find Tab

The **Find** tab, shown in Figure 4.10, is probably the most useful tab in the Help dialog box. It is also the tab that requires the most fine-tuning.

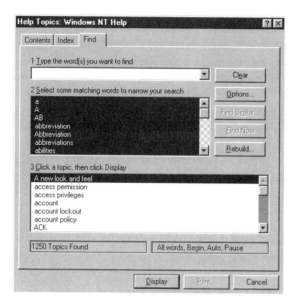

Figure 4.10 *The **Find** Tab in Help.*

The first time you access the **Find** tab for NT's Help dialog box or within any application, the Find Setup Wizard displays, as shown in Figure 4.11.

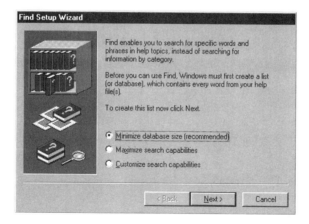

Figure 4.11 *The Find Setup Wizard.*

Generate the Word List

The three choices listed on the first page of the Find Setup Wizard enable you to control the size of the Find database or to customize the search capabilities. If you select **Minimize database size**, the Wizard creates a word list that contains the most important keywords to search for. If you select **Maximize search capabilities**, the Wizard generates a much more extensive search database. You may not want such a large search database file if your disk space is limited. If you decide to set up Find using either of these choices, select the option and then press the **Next** button. On the next screen, select **Finish**. After the Wizard creates the word list, you'll go back to the Find dialog box, where you can enter your search.

You can change the size of the word list database at any time by selecting the **Rebuild** button on the **Find** tab, shown in Figure 4.10. This action starts the Find Setup Wizard.

Customize Search Capabilities

The third option on the first page of the Find Setup Wizard enables you to customize Find's search capabilities. If you select **Customize search capabilities** and press **Next**, you'll see a series of dialog boxes that enable you to control exactly how Find behaves. The first page lists Help files to include in the search database, as shown in Figure 4.12.

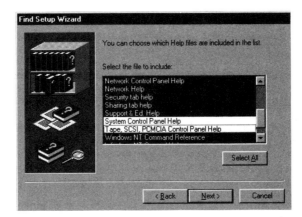

Figure 4.12 *Selecting Help files to include or exclude from searches.*

By default, all Help files are selected and included in the search database. You can deselect any topics that you feel you will never use in a search and then press **Next** to go to the next page in the Wizard.

The second custom search page in the Wizard, shown in Figure 4.13, asks you whether you want to include untitled topics in the search database. Untitled topics are usually those that appear in the **What's This** pop-up shadow boxes. They often duplicate information that is covered in more detail elsewhere, but sometimes they are the only source of information on a specific item. Make your choice and press **Next**.

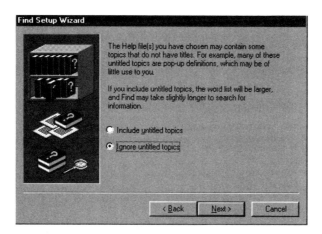

Figure 4.13 Including or excluding untitled search items.

The third custom search page in the Wizard, shown in Figure 4.14, enables you to specify whether you want to include phrase searching. Phrase searching increases the size of the generated database, but it enables you to search for specific combinations of words, such as **Task Manager**. It also includes all search items that match the root or roots of the word you enter. For example, if you enter **justify** in the search text box, Find matches items that start with **justifies** and **justifying**. Specify whether you want to enable phrase searching and then press **Next**.

Figure 4.14 *Enabling or disabling phrase searches.*

The fourth custom search page in the Wizard, shown in Figure 4.15, enables you to specify whether Find displays matching phrases as you type in your keywords. If you choose **Display matching phrases**, Find will show matching search items as you type each letter into the Find text box. Make your selection, and then press **Next**.

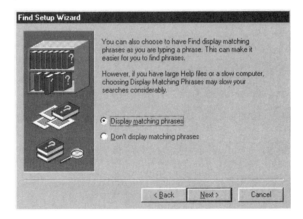

Figure 4.15 *Enabling or disabling dynamic phrase matching.*

The last page in the custom search series of dialog boxes, shown in Figure 4.16, asks you whether to enable or disable similarity searches. If you turn on similarity searches, the **Find Similar** button on the **Find** tab will become active. This button enables you to expand your search by looking for items that are similar but are not specific matches to your search keywords. If you are setting up search capabilities for a small application, it may not make sense to enable similarity searches. However, for large Help files, such as Windows NT Help, you probably want to enable similarity searches. Click the **Next** tab and then select **Finish** to set your custom search capabilities.

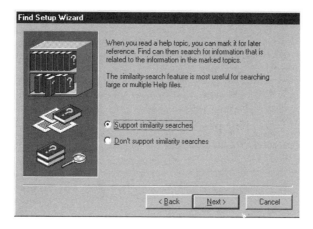

Figure 4.16 *Enabling or disabling similarity searches.*

Using the Find Tab

After running the Find Setup Wizard, you're ready to use the **Find** tab for searches. Simply type in the search keyword(s) in the text box labeled **Type the word(s) you want to find**, as shown in Figure 4.17.

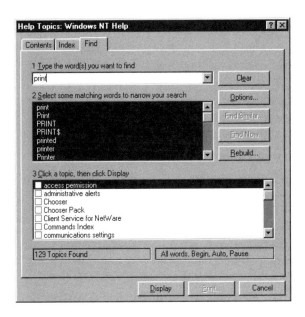

Figure 4.17 Entering Find keywords.

Matching words display in the box in the middle of the page, and all associated topics display in the topic list at the bottom of the page. You can deselect the items in the middle box to narrow your search. You choose topics by clicking the box to the left in the topic list at the bottom of the page. Then click **Display**, and Find displays the highlighted topic in a separate window. To return to the **Find** tab in Help and read other topics, press the **Help Topics** button at the top of the topic window.

Find Options

To change how Find searches using the keyword you enter, press the **Options** button. The Find Options dialog box, shown in Figure 4.18, displays.

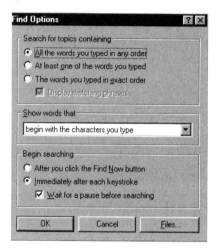

Figure 4.18 *The Find Options dialog box.*

The items in this dialog box work with the settings you make using the custom search capabilities in the Find Setup Wizard. If you have minimized the database or if you disabled some of the custom search capabilities, many of these options will not be activated.

HELP TOPICS

Microsoft has changed the way the Help topics are presented. Instead of explaining how things work, the Help topics tell you exactly how to perform specific tasks. For example, the Help topic in Figure 4.19 shows a Help topic that lists numbered steps for performing a task.

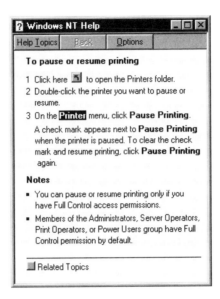

Figure 4.19 A Help topic showing steps for performing a task, a **Related Topics** button, and a shortcut.

Help topics also include links to glossary terms, buttons to jump to related topics, shortcuts to other applications or applets, and troubleshooters. A **Related Topic** button and a shortcut button are shown in Figure 4.19. Figure 4.20 shows a shortcut to the Install New Modem wizard, and Figure 4.21 displays a troubleshooter Help page.

Figure 4.20 A Help topic that includes a shortcut to a Wizard.

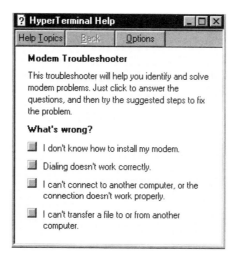

Figure 4.21 *A troubleshooter in Help.*

The Options and Context Menu

At any time you can right-click within a Help topic and pop up the Context menu, as shown in Figure 4.22. These same items are shown if you click the **Options** button at the top of the Help topic.

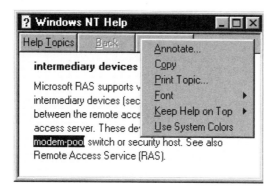

Figure 4.22 *The Options and Context menu.*

This menu enables you to do the following:

- Annotate the topic.
- Copy the text of the topic to the clipboard.
- Print the topic.
- Specify the Font size (**Small**, **Normal**, or **Large**) used to display the Help topic.
- Keep the Help topic window on top of other application windows.
- Use system colors (your current Windows colors) or keep the default Help colors.

These menu items are fairly simple and easy to use. The Annotation and Print topics are described in a little more detail in the following sections.

Annotations

If you are reading a Help topic and find that it is incorrect or incomplete or if you just want to add a comment, you can create a note and attach it to the topic. Select the **Options** button from the top of the page, or right-click within the page and select **Annotate**. The dialog box shown in Figure 4.23 displays. Type in your note or comment and then click the **Save** button.

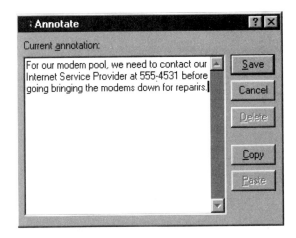

Figure 4.23 The Annotate dialog box.

After you've saved your annotation, a small paper clip icon displays to the left of the topic title, as shown in Figure 4.24. You can click this paper clip to view your annotation.

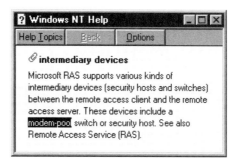

Figure 4.24 *A Help topic shFowing the paper clip icon.*

PRINTING HELP TOPICS

If you are reading a Help topic and recognize that you need a hard copy of the Help item, you can choose the **Print** item from the right-click context menu or option menu. The Print dialog box displays, as shown in Figure 4.25, enabling you to specify the printer and printer options before you send the job to the printer.

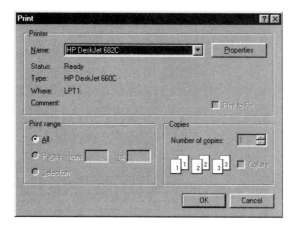

Figure 4.25 *The Print dialog box.*

PRINTING CONTENTS BOOKS

You can also print major chapters or sections in the **Contents** tab. Select the book you want to print and press the **Print** button at the bottom of the dialog box, as shown in Figure 4.26. All subsections and topics for the selected book are printed. After you select **Print**, you'll see a dialog box like the one shown in Figure 4.25.

Figure 4.26 *Printing a book in the **Contents** tab.*

SUMMARY

You can invoke Help from within Windows NT and other applications by selecting **Help** from the Start menu. The **Contents** and **Index** tabs help you search the database of topics. The **Find** tab lets you set up the search term database and control the behavior of Help using the Find Setup Wizard and Find Options. Help now includes procedure-based text that describes how to perform specific tasks. Help also includes links to glossary terms, buttons to jump to related topics, and shortcuts that invoke other applications or applets. Interactive troubleshooters help you isolate and fix problems with your system or attached devices.

Help lets you take notes and attach them to a specific topic. You can copy the text from within a Help topic to the clipboard, and that means you can paste it into any other Windows application. You also have limited control over the font size and colors used to display Help topic information.

CHAPTER 5

The Control Panel

By Nelson King

The Control Panel provides access to many things that you will use frequently early on and only occasionally, if ever, thereafter. The Control Panel settings for the NT operating system let you connect to various pieces of hardware, establish communications with other computers, and customize your working environment with sound, color, and fonts. In short, the Control Panel is where you go in Windows NT to configure your computer system.

There are several ways to open the Control Panel, but the one most commonly used is through the Start menu: Open the Start menu, select **Settings**, and select the **Control Panel** icon. (Alternatively, the Control Panel folder can be opened from NT Explorer.) It may take a few seconds for NT to find all the components. Then you'll see the opened Control Panel folder (shown in Figure 5.1), which usually displays an icon for each of the Control Panel dialog boxes.

Figure 5.1 *The Control Panel.*

The number of icons in the Control Panel varies depending on the hardware and software installed on your computer. There are usually between 25 and 30 icons, although 26 of them are considered basic for Windows NT (Table 5.1).

Table 5.1 Control Panel Dialog Boxes

DIALOG BOX	DESCRIPTION
Add/Remove Programs	You can uninstall some applications from here as well as install or remove any Windows NT programs.
MS-DOS Console	Use this dialog box to set colors, sizes, and other properties of the DOS window.
Date/Time	Set the date or time for your computer and select your time zone.

continued on next page

Dialog Box	Description
Devices	This dialog box is used to configure the various hardware and software devices in your computer. Don't experiment here. Use only if you have specific instructions.
Dial-Up Monitor	This dialog box is often kept on screen during a communications session (e.g., Internet).
Display	Almost everything to do with your monitor and the appearance of the desktop and windows is found here.
Fonts	Add or delete fonts from your system. There are also limited viewing capabilities.
Internet	One of the main places to configure your system for using the Internet.
Keyboard	Make adjustments to keyboard response.
Mail and Fax	Provides access to some of the configuration options for your internal mail and fax system.
Modems	Install and configure modems.
Mouse	Adjust the movement speed, cursor image, and other properties of your mouse.
Multimedia	Install and configure various multimedia aspects of your computer, including music, audio, video, and MIDI.
Network	Install and configure network protocols, hardware, and other options.
PC Card (PCMCIA)	This dialog box is not available unless you have a PCMCIA controller active in your computer (probably a portable). If the controller is present, this is where it can be configured.
Ports	Used to configure serial ports.
Printers	Primarily used as access to the Windows NT print server.
Regional Settings	Set the display and formats for numbers, currency, dates, and times to match the current locale.

continued on next page

DIALOG BOX	DESCRIPTION
SCSI Adapters	Used to install and configure SCSI devices such as CD-ROMs.
Server	The Server dialog box is the administrative center for your computer if it is acting as a server on a peer-to-peer network.
Services	Provides a list of all services available to the Windows NT system.
Sounds	Associate software events with sounds from **.WAV** files.
System	Provides information and settings options for many hardware-related services and devices.
Tape Devices	Used to install and configure tape backup devices.
Telephony	A number of telephone communications options are set in this dialog box.
UPS	Used to install and configure Uninterruptible Power Supply products.

N O T E

If you sometimes become confused about what is where in the Control Panel, don't worry, you're not alone. Microsoft has traditionally thrown everything and anything into this folder without giving us so much as a road map. In this chapter we'll do the best we can to help you identify what's what and what's where, but we hope that someday Microsoft will create a more helpful approach to accessing the vital and sometimes complex options in the Control Panel.

MODIFYING THE LOOK AND FEEL OF THE DESKTOP

Most of the options that change colors, sounds, fonts and the like are not required by NT. They're matters of taste, and you're free to customize your system as you see fit. For many people, this is the fun part of working with an operating system.

Add/Remove Programs

Over time you will have software that you want to remove. Perhaps a program has become obsolete or you don't use it any more. Whatever the reason, it's not a good idea to clutter your system with the files and entries of software that you don't use. It's a waste of disk space and other computer resources. Some of the software on your computer came with the ability to uninstall itself, and you may have noticed an **Uninstall** program icon. Many programs can also be uninstalled from the Windows NT Add/Remove applet (Figure 5.2).

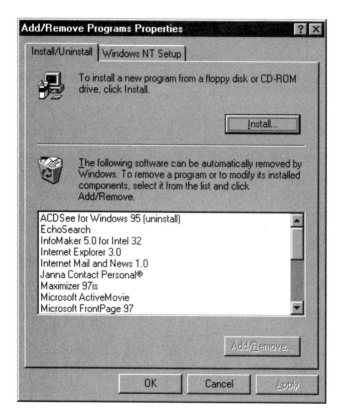

Figure 5.2 *Add/Remove Programs dialog box,* ***Install/Uninstall*** *tab.*

Once this dialog box is open, search in the list for the program you want to uninstall. Select it and click the **Add/Remove** button to begin. The uninstall routine from the software manufacturer will take over, and you'll need to follow those instructions.

You may wonder whether this facility makes commercial uninstallation software, such as Uninstaller and Remove-It, unnecessary. The answer is no. For one thing, not all Windows NT programs have their own uninstall routines. For those that have such routines, some don't register themselves with NT to be put into the Add/Remove list. For another thing, it isn't just applications that need removal from your disks. Internet software in particular is notorious for leaving dead files all over your system. Commercial uninstall programs take care of removing these miscellaneous files along with applications.

Programs can also be installed from the Add/Remove dialog box. This is rarely used, because most programs either begin installation automatically or have specific instructions on how to proceed. However, the second tab of the Add/Remove dialog box (Figure 5.3), labeled **Windows NT Setup**, is definitely the place to install or remove additional NT software.

Figure 5.3 Add/Remove Programs dialog box, **Windows NT Setup** tab.

It helps to have your Windows NT 4.0 CD-ROM already in the drive before you select any of the additional components from the list.

Date/Time

As you're probably aware, your computer has its own clock. It's used in all kinds of programs and in many situations, not the least of which is putting a date and time stamp on every file you create or change. The Date/Time dialog box is used to set the date and time (Figure 5.4) and to tell NT what your time zone is (Figure 5.5).

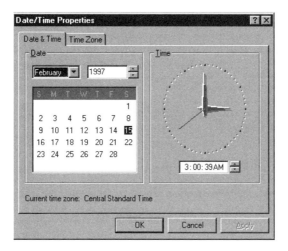

Figure 5.4 Date/Time Properties dialog box, **Date & Time** tab.

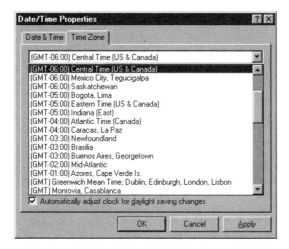

Figure 5.5 Date/Time Properties dialog box, **Time Zone** tab.

For date and time, you can enter the information directly by typing or use the mouse to click on dates and drag the hour or minute hand around the clock. The time zone selection is nothing more than picking your zone from the list. Note that you can also click the **Automatically adjust clock for daylight saving changes** check box in this tab.

Display

The Display dialog box covers the operating-system level of customization for almost everything you see in your monitor (except fonts). This includes the way your monitor is configured, the look of the Windows desktop, and the colors of the windows themselves. This dialog box was designed to invite user experimentation. You could make a hobby out of designing wallpaper (the screen variety) and constructing color sets for Windows. Even if you don't have that much time, the Display dialog box is worth a visit now and again to give your computer an occasional face-lift. On a more serious side, the Settings options are vital for the proper configuration of your monitor. You probably made a trip to this tab soon after you got your computer.

Background Tab

"Background" in this context means the background of the Windows NT desktop—that's what you look at when you dock all other windows in the Taskbar. By default, the desktop is a solid blue-green (dark cyan) with a few program icons (e.g., **Internet Explorer** and **Recycle Bin**). If you find this color or lack of pattern a bore, you need to pay a visit to the **Background** tab (Figure 5.6) of the Display dialog box.

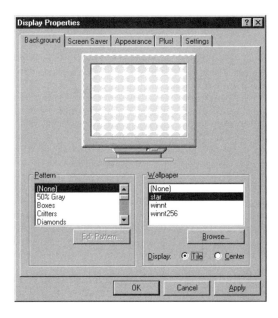

*Figure 5.6 Display dialog box, **Background** tab.*

The simplest changes you can make are to the pattern in the **Pattern** list box. Try several—they're immediately displayed in the monitor image—or use the **Apply** button to see what they look like on the desktop. If you don't like any of the patterns, use the **Edit Pattern** button to access a dialog box where you can create your own pattern.

When you select **Wallpaper**, you're taking an image (which must be a bitmap image) and plastering it all over the desktop. Choosing **Wallpaper** overrides any pattern or color selected for the desktop. The **Wallpaper** list box probably has only two wallpapers listed unless you chose to install **Wallpaper** when you installed NT. You can add your own—any image file with a **.BMP** extension is fair game—by putting the file into the C:\WINNT folder or using the **Browse** option to open a bitmap file in another directory. If you choose **Tile** for display, the image will be copied over and over until it completely fills the desktop. Alternatively, you can pick **Center** and a single image will be centered in the screen.

You can install additional Wallpaper files from the NT CD by running the Add/Remove Programs applet, selecting the *Windows NT* setup tab, and selecting the Accessories. If you click the Details button, you'll see the **Wallpaper** option listed.

N O T E

If you would like to use a bitmap image for wallpaper and have it cover the entire screen, use the **Stretch desktop wallpaper to fit the screen** option in the **Plus!** tab (If you have a **Plus!** tab). Not all images take kindly to being blown up to large sizes, so pick something with the highest initial resolution (image quality) possible.

T I P

Wallpaper, screen savers, sounds, and a number of other items are wonderful ways of customizing a computer. They also chew up a fair amount of memory. This is no problem if you have lots of RAM, but if you're running with a bare minimum—say, 16 MB—all these extras may add up to a big chunk of RAM that would be better used for programs.

WARNING

Screen Saver Tab

In the olden days, about 10 years ago, most people had monochrome monitors. If you left the monitor on all the time, or even through the working day, you would eventually get "burn in," in which an image would be permanently etched into the phosphors of the screen. Some people say this even happened to color monitors. Monitors can be quite expensive and many people fear that leaving the monitor to display the same image can seriously shorten its useful life. Some monitors can shut off automatically, but many don't. Therefore, Microsoft includes screen savers to help extend the life of the monitor. Over the years, screen savers have become a bit of an art form, and many of them are beautiful. Windows NT comes with a fairly good selection of these images (usually animated), such as the one you see in Figure 5.7.

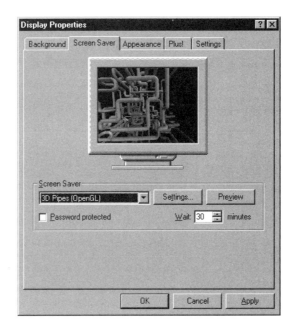

Figure 5.7 *Display dialog box,* ***Screen Saver*** *tab.*

Select the screen saver image in the drop-down list (images display in the little monitor), click **Settings** to see which display options are available, and use **Preview** to see what the image will look like in the full screen. You can also set how long NT will wait after the last keystroke or mouse movement before it turns on the screen saver. Don't set this too short, or you'll find your work being interrupted. You can also set a password so that people can't get into your computer while you're away (and the screen saver is running). This is a good security practice, but woe to you if you forget your password!

Appearance Tab

If there's one tab in the Display dialog box that tempts people into hours of fiddling, it's **Appearance** (Figure 5.8). In this case, appearance means the ability to change the color of almost every screen and window element in Windows NT. You can choose from one of 27 color schemes provided by Microsoft (in the **Scheme** list box) or create your own scheme and save it for posterity.

Figure 5.8 *Display dialog box,* **Appearance** *tab.*

To create your own color scheme, use the **Item** list box to select each screen element in turn. These are called *objects* in Microsoft's terminology (e.g., **Desktop**, **Active Window Title**, **3-D Objects**). Depending on the object, you'll be able to change the size, color, font, font size, font color, and font style. Only those screen elements that have text enable the **Font** options: **Icons**, **Menu**, **Active Title Bar**, **Inactive Title Bar**, **Message Box**, **Palette Title**, and **ToolTip**.

Because the color combinations are nearly infinite, it can take a while to go through all the elements and create a pleasing color scheme. Be sure to save your work as a color scheme with the **Save As** button.

Plus! Tab

The **Plus!** options, shown in Figure 5.9, are a bit of a grab bag. At the top you can substitute icon images for many of the familiar Windows NT desktop icons and toolbar buttons. For example, you may not think much of the Recycle Bin image, so you replace it with a flaming trash can. When you click the **Change Icon** button, you'll be asked to locate the new icon. All you do is to select the right icon image—they have either a **.BMP** or **.ICO** file extension—and specify the directory in which it is located. If you regret your choice of icon, you can always use the **Default Icon** button to go back to the original Windows icon.

Figure 5.9 *Display dialog box,* **Plus!** *tab.*

The visual settings portion of the **Plus!** tab cover some visual effects that are easier to see than to describe. The first, **Use large icons**, changes the size of all toolbar and desktop icons. **Show window contents while dragging** does just what it says, although the advantages are dubious. **Smooth edges of screen fonts** will remove the "jaggies," the step-like edges seen on large characters. This has little effect except on fonts larger than 48 points. **Show icons using all possible colors** is relevant only if you have a high-capacity color adapter (set at millions of colors) and the icons themselves contain pictures or other high-resolution graphics. Most don't, so this, too, is of dubious value. **Stretch desktop wallpaper to fit the screen** also does what it says (see the note in the "Background" section).

Settings Tab

The **Settings** tab of the Display Properties dialog box (Figure 5.10) is where software controls meet the hardware of your monitor and graphics adapter. This is serious business, in part because the settings of your monitor are vital for readability (and your eyesight) and in part because the jargon surrounding the hardware options can be difficult to understand. If you click the **Display Type** button, the dialog box that appears should show you information about your current graphics adapter. If you've installed a new adapter, this is one place where you can see whether it's correctly registered with NT.

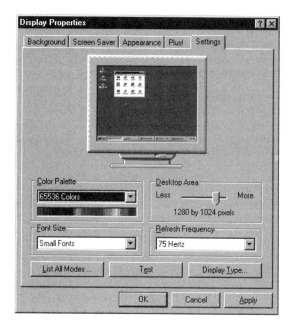

Figure 5.10 *Display dialog box,* **Settings** *tab.*

The three key components in this window are labeled **Color Palette**, **Desktop Area**, and **Refresh Frequency**. They are all a function of the capacity of your graphics adapter. The more colors that can be displayed, the more realistic the image. The higher the resolution, the sharper the image. The faster the refresh frequency (how often your monitor repaints an image), the better it is for your eyes.

The settings for each of the three components depend on the relationship between your graphics card, which produces the signal carrying all three elements, and your monitor, which creates the image you see. At the bottom end—say, 16 colors, 480x640 pixel resolution (desktop area), and 60-Hertz refresh in a 14" monitor—you have coarse pictures, grainy text, and unrealistic color. At the high end you might have "true color" (16 million), 1280x1024 pixels, 80-Hertz refresh, and a huge 21" monitor. The images at this level are extremely "lifelike." Most computer systems fall in the middle range—for example, 65,536 colors, 1024x768 pixels, 75-Hertz, and a 15" or 17" display. The options you see in this dialog box will be determined by what your current hardware is capable of producing.

It's possible that you may have already made some changes to these settings when you first got your computer, and you certainly did if you bought a new graphics adapter. You don't make changes here often, but they're important. Most adapters and monitors will let you try a number of different settings that are combinations of the three elements. You need to be guided by the specifications of the graphics board and monitor. They'll tell you what is possible and what is pleasing to your eyes. To a certain extent, this is also a matter of the kind of programs you use most often. Graphics programs and software development are very demanding of screen size and capacity. Other applications, such as accounting or word processing, may require much less.

To see all the possible settings for your graphics card and monitor, click the **List All Modes** button. When you've decided on a new configuration, it's mandatory to use the **Test** button to see whether it works. Some configurations can damage your monitor or graphics card, so NT won't let you change the display settings without first testing them. If everything checks out, you can use the **Apply** button to have NT make changes immediately. In some cases you may need to restart NT to have the changes take effect.

Screen resolution, font size, and the size of screen elements all play a role in the readability of the Windows screen. If you need to make adjustments because of your eyesight, here are the most relevant Display dialog box options: **Settings** tab: **Desktop Area** (pixel size) and **Font Size** (large or small fonts). **Plus!** tab: **Use large icons. Appearance** tab: text elements **Font, Size, Color,** and **Style.**

Fonts

The Fonts dialog box provides access to the font files you have on your system and can assist you in adding fonts so that Windows NT will recognize them. You'll notice in Figure 5.11 that this dialog box is actually a variation of Windows Explorer with only font files displayed. NT assumes that all your working fonts are in the same directory, C:\WINNT\FONTS.

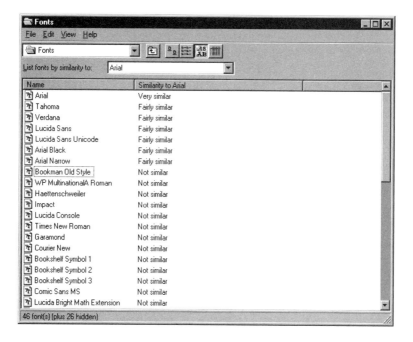

Figure 5.11 Fonts dialog box.

Although most of the options in this window are standard for the Explorer, we'll describe the few that are specific to fonts:

- **File**, **Install New Font**. Use this option when you want to add a new font to your system, especially if you're copying it from a floppy disk or from a network.

- **View**, **List Fonts By Similarity**. Fonts come in families or type groups that NT will recognize and use to arrange the font file display.

- **View**, **Hide Variations**. Many fonts come with variations such as bold, italic, small, and so on. This option will hide the variation files to simplify the display.

Perhaps the most important option is to simply double-click on any font entry in the window. This action will display a description of the font (with considerable detail) and show samples at several font sizes, as illustrated in Figure 5.12. This is a good way to see how an individual font appears, but it's not very helpful in comparing one font to another.

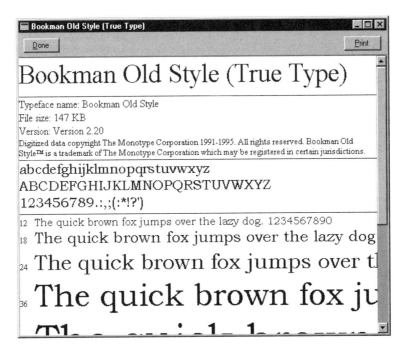

Figure 5.12 Font information display.

The Fonts dialog box is one of the least sophisticated in the Control Panel. If you're interested in fonts for fun or profit, you might check out the wide variety of commercial and shareware font management programs.

Keyboard

The Keyboard and Mouse dialog boxes don't see much action, but you might visit them occasionally if you feel that response speeds are not optimal. For the keyboard, there are two speed settings (as shown in Figure 5.13):

- **Repeat delay**. Grabbing this slider and moving it from **Long** to **Short** changes the interval between the time you depress and hold down a key and the time it starts to repeat.

- **Repeat rate**. The repeat rate is how often a character (or whatever the key represents) will be repeated while you continue to hold the key down (this is called *standing on* a key). The default setting is usually sufficient, although people who do a lot of word processing and like to repeat keys such as the arrow keys to move around in a document. You can test your settings in the text box about midway in the dialog box.

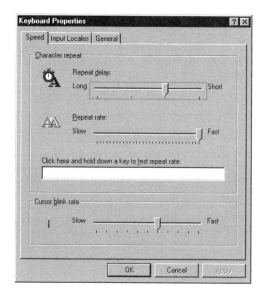

Figure 5.13 Keyboard Properties dialog box.

The other setting in the first page of this dialog box is the **Cursor blink rate**. That's the blinking line (or other shape of the editing cursor) when you edit text or work in a graphics program. It blinks so that it's easier to find, but some people prefer that it doesn't blink while others like it to zip along as if on a caffeine high.

There are two other pages in the Keyboard Properties dialog box. **Input Locales** is used to change the keyboard layout for international use. Each layout provides character sets and keyboard representation for a language. You can also use it to switch between keyboard layouts if you do computing in more than one language. The **General** tab is the place to go if you ever change the type of keyboard. Because a new keyboard type (in the hardware sense) hasn't been developed in the last 10 years, you probably won't be using this option.

Mouse

This Mouse Properties dialog box might make using the mouse seem complicated. Most of the options will be set once, if at all, and never visited again. Still, you need to know that the options are here and what they can do. The **Buttons** tab (Figure 5.14) has two options. The one at the top defaults to a right-handed mouse, but southpaws can (finally) switch to the other orientation. The second option, **Double-click speed**, uses another slider. Grab the control and move to **Slow** or **Fast** to set how quickly the mouse responds to a double-click. For most people the default speed (medium) is perfect, but you might need to change it if you're really quick or slow on the trigger. You can test the speed in the **Test area** to the right.

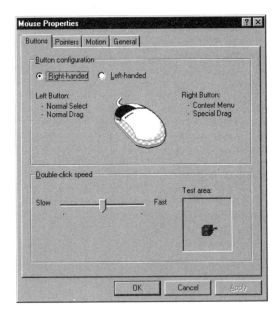

*Figure 5.14 Mouse dialog box, **Buttons** tab.*

The second tab, **Pointers** (shown in Figure 5.15), is used to replace the standard Windows pointers (cursor shapes) with those of your own choosing. You can use any file that has a **.CUR** or **.ANI** (animated cursor) extension. Some people are particularly fond of animated cursors, and this is the place to install one. Just select the pointer you want to replace and use the **Browse** button to locate the replacement file. If you replace many of the standard pointers, use the **Scheme** and **Save As** option to save a pointer scheme.

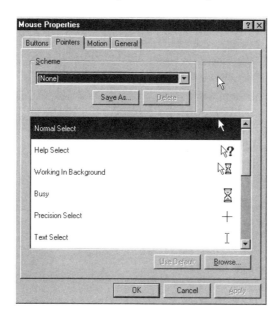

Figure 5.15 *Mouse dialog box,* **Pointers** *tab.*

The **Motion** tab has two options: **Pointer speed** lets you set how fast the pointer will move around the screen. Some people like it slow so that they can follow it, and others like it very fast so that they don't have to wait for it to arrive where they're pointing. The default speed is good enough for most people. One button you may consider selecting, is the **Snap to default** option. When this option is checked, the mouse cursor will automatically be placed on the default button of a dialog box.

As with the Keyboard Properties dialog box, there is a **General** tab where you can indicate a change in mouse hardware. Because of the many types of pointing devices (including mice, glide pads, pointer sticks, trackballs, and pens), you may need to use this if you deep-six the standard mouse.

Multimedia

The Multimedia dialog box is the access point for configuring the hardware and software components that produce sound, play video, make music, or run the CD-ROM drive. This assumes that you have the required hardware installed in your computer. You'll need a sound card, speakers, microphone, CD-ROM, and video-capable graphics board, and these elements are becoming part of the usual multimedia package for NT computers. You'll visit some of the tabs in this dialog box only when installing new equipment with instructions from a manufacturer. We'll describe here the tabs that have options you might want to change for personal reasons.

The **Audio** tab, shown in Figure 5.16, gives you considerable control over the volume and quality of sound for both recording and playback. At the top are the playback options, essentially for controlling the output volume. Most PC computers must add a sound card and connect to some kind of speakers to play music or make other kinds of sounds. If you have a sound card, its name will appear in the **Preferred device** box. If you have more than one, it can be selected here. Setting the check box for **Show volume control on the taskbar** is usually a good idea.

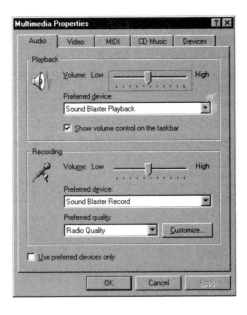

*Figure 5.16 Multimedia dialog box, **Audio** tab.*

The **Recording** area applies only if you have a microphone attached to your sound card. You can set the volume, select a preferred recording device, and set the preferred audio quality. This last option can be important for two reasons: The higher the quality, the better the recorded sound—and the more disk space it will require. There are three choices: **CD Quality** (large disk space, 44k sampling rate), **Radio Quality** (best general setting, 22k sampling rate), and **Telephone Quality** (kind of tinny but uses much less disk space, 11k sampling rate).

The **Video** tab doesn't do much except allow you to pick the size of the video frame in your monitor. This is largely a function of your computer's CPU speed and the amount of memory you have on your video card. The faster your computer can display an image, and the more memory you have on your video card, the larger an image you can display smoothly.

The **MIDI** tab (which stands for Musical Instrument Digital Interface) is used to configure MIDI instruments for your computer. If you have any (usually with a sound board), they will already be registered here. MIDI is a wonderful way to make music and a fascinating topic in its own right.

The **CD Music** tab is used to tell Windows NT which drive the CD-ROM is on (usually D:, E:, or F:). It also sets the output volume for headphones attached to the CD-ROM (not the headphone port on the sound card).

Finally, the **Devices** tab gives you a listing of all the multimedia-related devices in your computer. This list is used when you're configuring new hardware or changing the operational parameters of an existing piece of hardware or software. It's not a good idea to change anything here without consulting the related manuals.

Regional Settings

Microsoft changed the name of the International Settings dialog box to Regional Settings Properties in Windows 95 (and now in Windows NT 4.0) to emphasize that many of the settings are not bound to a particular country or language. Still, this set of six tabbed pages (Figure 5.17) is where you go to configure your computer for operation in a particular area of the world—often for a specific country and language. Table 5.2 summarizes the options for each tab.

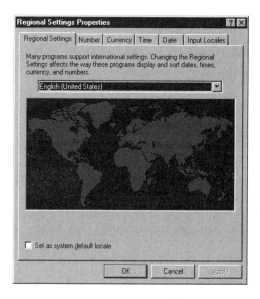

Figure 5.17 *Regional Settings.*

Table 5.2 Regional Settings Options

TAB	ITEM PRESENTED	HOW DISPLAYED	DEFAULT
Number	Decimal symbol	Decimal point symbol	.
	Number of digits after decimal	Default number of decimal places	2
	Digit grouping symbol	Marking divisions (by thousands, etc.)	,
	Number of digits in group	Number of digits in a division group (e.g., 000,000)	3
	Negative sign symbol	The sign used for negative numbers	–
	Negative number format	The format of a negative number.	–1.1
	Display leading zeros	Show how leading zeros are displayed	0.
	Measurement system	Local measurement system from list	U.S.

continued on next page

TAB	ITEM PRESENTED	HOW DISPLAYED	DEFAULT
	List separator	The symbol used to separate list items	,
Currency	Currency symbol	The local currency symbol (from list)	$
	Positive currency format	Currency formats for positive numbers	$1.1
	Negative currency format	Currency formats for negative numbers	($1.1)
	Decimal symbol	Decimal symbol for currency	.
	Number of digits after decimal	Number of digits after decimal for currency	2
	Digit grouping symbol	The symbol used to group currency digits	,
	Number of digits in group	Number of digits in a division group	3
Time	Time style	The format for time display (from list)	:mm:ss:tt :
	Time separator	The standard separator for time values	
	AM symbol	The symbol for AM.	AM
	PM symbol	The symbol for PM.	PM
Date	Calendar type	Options change with locale selection	Gregor-ian
	Short date style	Short date (no long year) style	M/d/yy
	Date separator	Separator between date groups	/
	Long date style	Long date (full year) style	Dddd, mmm, yyyy
Input Locales	Region and keyboard layout		

N O T E   Most, but not all, programs rely on these Windows NT settings for handling international values. If you're traveling and need to make these changes often, be sure you are using software that can be easily configured from this dialog box and does not require you to configure the changes separately.

Sounds

Some people love to have computers make sounds; other people hate it. The Sounds dialog box, shown in Figure 5.18, is where you can turn the sounds on or off and reconfigure them to suit your own taste. This dialog box is simple to use, but you must first know where your sounds are stored. In the Windows operating system the sounds are recorded as wave files, which have the extension **.WAV**. (There are many other kinds of sound files, but they won't work here.) In most systems, the default sound files are located in C:\WINNT\MEDIA. If you want additional sounds, it's easiest to copy the **.WAV** files to this directory.

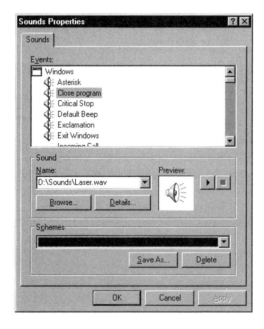

Figure 5.18 Sounds dialog box.

Once you have your sound files in place, go to this dialog box to associate a file with particular events. *Events* is the word used to describe various points of activity in the operation of software—for example, opening a program, closing a program, and the appearance of error messages. In the **Events** list of the dialog box, you can see that there are quite a few events (some software adds even more). Each one of these events can be matched with a **.WAV** file to make a sound when the event occurs.

To match an event with a sound, first select the event from the **Events** list; then go to the **Name** box and enter the **.WAV** file name and path. Or use the **Browse** button to locate the file. If you're not sure that the sound is what you want, use the **Preview** button (to the right of the speaker icon) to listen to it. To get more information about the sound and its file, click the **Details** button.

It can take a while to experiment with sound and event combinations, so when you've gone to the trouble to customize your system, it's highly recommended that you save it using the **Schemes** text box. Give your scheme a name and use **Save As** to save it as a file.

CONFIGURING FOR COMMUNICATIONS

There are two kinds of communications within a Windows NT 4.0 system: telephone and network. Configuring either of these systems can be a major task, for the most part beyond the scope of an introductory book like this. This section will give you a quick tour through the Control Panel dialog boxes involved with networking and telephones (they overlap on some points). Because the features and options that are accessed through these dialog boxes are somewhat jumbled, we've tried to order the sections by how they're related to one another.

Modems

The usual place to start for telephone communications is with a modem. Once you've made a purchase, you typically go through the manufacturer's installation routine. This installation process usually informs Windows NT that a new modem is available—assuming that Auto detect worked—and you may not need to visit the Modem dialog box in the Control Panel.

On the other hand, you may need to use the Modem dialog box to install your modem or make adjustments. In addition to selecting the modem from the list (there may be more than one), the business end of this dialog box is reached through the **Properties** button. Which options are available depends on the modem you've installed. In the **General** tab, you can set the volume of the modem speaker (if it has one) and set a default transfer rate (baud rate). This setting is often set much higher than the rated speed of a modem because it will be "negotiated" when two modems connect.

The **Connection** tab handles communications basics such as **Data bits** (usually 8), **Parity** (usually none), and **Stop bits** (usually 1). Three options control when the phone should connect or hang up. The default settings here as well as in the **Advanced** features are usually sufficient. The **Address** tab is used if you have distinctive phone ring service—something that the modem must recognize for you to get a connection. The **Forwarding** tab serves a similar purpose. It tells the modem to ignore the signals from call forwarding so that the connection is not broken.

Telephony

If you're just becoming familiar with the words *computer telephony*, some of the options and configurations in the Control Panel will seem confusing. This isn't helped by the redundancy of the telephony-related options in Windows NT. Double-clicking the **Telephony** icon in the Control Panel brings up the Dialing Properties dialog box (Figure 5.19), which has some of the important telephone communications settings.

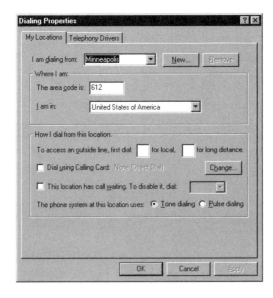

Figure 5.19 *Dialing Properties dialog box.*

A nice feature of Windows 95 and Windows NT is the ability to maintain several telephone locations, such as home, office, on the road, and at the cabin. In the **I am dialing from** box, you select or enter a location (use the **New** button and enter a name of your choice), and Windows will save the other settings under this name. In the **Where I am** area, you should make an entry for **The area code is** and select a country in the **I am in** list. In the next section, enter any that apply: local and long distance dialing access, use of a calling card, call waiting (note that call forwarding is in the Modems dialog box), and whether you are using tone or pulse dialing.

The **Telephony Drivers** tab is rarely used. The two options—TAPI kernel-mode service provider and Unimodem service provider—are industry standards. Most of the software you're likely to encounter will use one of them automatically.

Dial-Up Monitor

The Dial-Up Monitor can be used to watch the status of your telephone connection(s); in fact, it's of most use when more than one connection is active. The top tab, **Status**, tracks a number of technical values. Of more relevance to most people is the **Hang Up** button, which is sometimes the only way you can break a connection. The **Summary** tab displays each of the active modems, and the **Preferences** tab has a number of options to specify how Windows should show the modem status and make sounds for various parts of a connection. If you're one of those people who like to read the MR, TR, HS, DH, CD, TX, and RX lights but you have an internal modem, you can use the **Show status lights** options to see them in your monitor.

Internet

Hooking up with the Internet is a big deal, of course, and it's taken for granted that you'll be connecting with the grand Net. Many people make their Internet connection by installing software (a modem is a prerequisite)—for example, using one of the jillion disks sent out by America Online. In such cases, most of the setup is accomplished automatically. Otherwise, as is likely if you're connecting with an ISP (Internet service provider), you'll need to do some of the installation directly. Some of the installation is accomplished when you configure a modem and set the telephony options. Another big part of it is done in the Network dialog box (establishing TCP/IP as a network protocol) and finally in the Internet dialog box. If you use a Web browser, either Netscape is or

Microsoft is, it will also have options for you to set. This path can be tortuous, and we hope that someday soon Microsoft will straighten it out.

For its part, the Internet Properties dialog box of the Control Panel (see Figure 5.20) covers most of the options relating to the full Internet (not just the World Wide Web) including the Usenet, Gopher, FTP, and other services. We'll review the options in the six tabs of this dialog box to explain what they are and suggest why you would use them.

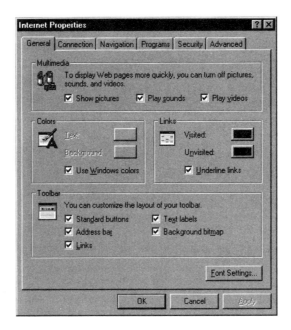

Figure 5.20 *Internet Properties dialog box.*

General Tab

The Multimedia options let you choose whether to show the pictures, play the sounds, and play videos to be found at Web sites. Each of these can be very demanding of the resources of your computer and can take a long time to download over the Internet. Some people will turn off one or more of these options to speed up their Internet connection. Of course, you may also lose some of the fun, particularly for Web sites.

If you uncheck the **Use Windows colors** option in the **Colors** area, you'll need to define your own foreground and background colors. This is strictly a matter of personal taste.

One of the greatest features of the Web is the ability to jump from place to place through hyperlinks (or *links* for short). However, because you may take many jumps, it's more convenient to be able to tell at a glance whether you've visited a link before. The color options in a **Link** area highlight the visited and unvisited links. The default colors, maroon and blue, are not very striking but they do the job.

In the **Toolbar** area, you can change the properties of the Internet toolbar (which appears in various applications) by checking or unchecking the options.

The **Font Settings** button presents options that used primarily to change the appearance of the browser and other Internet displays based on a locale or linguistic region.

Connection Tab

The options in this tab apply only if you are connecting to the Internet (or an intranet) through a proxy server. (A *proxy* server is a device to protect a Local Area Network from outside intrusion, particularly from the Internet.) Most of the settings here are quite technical and are usually from a set of instructions, often by a systems administrator.

Navigation Tab

In the **Customize** section you indicate the default Internet location of your browser when you first connect. By default, this is the start page of Microsoft's Web site (how convenient). If you're not happy with this arrangement, you can type in the address (URL) of any other site, e.g., *www.netscape.com.*

Many people don't realize that Web browsers store a large number of files in both an image cache and a history directory. The history directory lets you go back in time to see which sites you visited. From time to time, the number of entries should be cut down. As you specify in the **History** area, this weeding is done every so many days. You can also clear the History folder completely or view its contents.

Programs Tab

In general, this tab deals with the programs that run in conjunction with your browser.

The **Mail and News** options let you set the default mail handler and news reader (from the lists provided).

The **Viewers** dialog box, which is usually displayed from NT Explorer, lets you associate file extensions from the Web (e.g. HTML, WAV, GIF, and JPEG) with specific software on your computer. Normally this is done automatically when you install the software.

Note the sneaky check box at the bottom. If you don't have Microsoft Internet Explorer as your default browser, checking this box will, as *Star Trek* captains say, "make it so."

Security Tab

This tab and the **Advanced** tab are becoming increasingly important for your use of the Internet. As many stories in print and on TV have pointed out, there are problems with security on the Internet and the Web in particular. The options in this tab turn on or off certain protection features.

Microsoft, in conjunction with many other Web site providers, has devised a rating to let you filter what the Internet browser will see. Sites that do not fit the criteria you set in the **Content Advisor** area will not be visible in your browser.

Certification, which you can specify in the **Certificates** area, is one of the schemes used to verify that connection to a site, downloading of software, or purchasing of goods or services is legitimate. Once you join this program, your Internet browser will converse with each site to verify whether it is certified.

Not all Web content is passive—that is, waiting for you to read it. Some content will actively download to your system, set up shop, and provide a service. This is not always desirable, so if you have an aversion to the risk involved you can use the options under **Active Content** to turn on or off various kinds of active content, such as Java applets and ActiveX controls. If you use the **Safety Level** button, you'll also be able select whether your protection level is high, medium, or none.

Advanced Tab

A number of operations in a browser can leave your computer system open to attack by viruses or other unpleasant programming. The **Warnings** section lets you choose to have the browser warn you before one of these potentially disruptive events occurs. The flip side is that each warning slows your progress while surfing.

NOTE You'll notice the reference to "cookies" in this section. Cookies are pieces of code left on your computer by Web sites so that the next time you return, the site can learn more about you and have a reference to what you did before. Many people find this objectionable.

Browsers store thousands of files from the Internet (most of them picture images). From time to time, these files must be cleared or at least reduced in number. You can perform that housekeeping in the **Temporary Internet files** section.

The final set of options covers a wide range. **Show friendly URLs** displays site addresses that are active, and **Highlight links when clicked** makes them easier to see. **Use smooth scrolling** is almost mandatory for the Web, where you must often scroll to see the bottom part of Web pages. **Use style sheets** lets you view the style sheets that are used to create many Web pages. **Enable Java JIT compiler**: Java applets run much faster if run through the Just In Time (JIT) compiler provided by your browser. **Enable Java logging** lets Java programs create a record on your computer. The **Cryptography Settings** button gives you access to encryption options for Web pages and other documents.

NOTE The Internet applet is also discussed in Chapter 11.

Mail and Fax

Exactly what you see after clicking the **Mail and Fax** (or **Mail**) icon depends on what software has been installed on your computer. In many Windows NT installations, you'll see a dialog box with a series of tabs for Microsoft Messaging or Exchange. For others, it will be something that was installed with Office 97 and Outlook. For still others, it may be related to Lotus Notes or Novell's GroupWise. Given the variety and the technical nature of configuring a mail system, we've left this dialog box to the instructions you may have received with your computer or when the mail system was installed.

FAX support was not included on the original CD-ROMS for Windows NT. However, FAX support is included in the NT Service Pack #1, or separately by downloading the FAX application on the Web at *www.microsoft.com.*

NOTE

Network

Installing even a simple network on Windows NT is a task for someone with considerable experience with Windows and preferably also with networking. Chapter 16 provides an introduction to the topic and also explains how the Network dialog box is used.

Server

The Server dialog box is a modest window that is used to monitor the status of your computer when it is acting as a server in a peer-to-peer network. The details of this dialog box are covered in Chapter 16.

HARD-CORE HARDWARE CONFIGURATION

Most of the options grouped into hardware configuration are aimed at system administrators and NT specialists. Non-experts usually arrive at these options when following the directions for installing something. It's useful to know what these dialog boxes can do—even if it means knowing enough to keep hands off.

Devices

Device is the word Windows NT uses to describe both hardware and software processes. The Device dialog box is used to examine the devices installed on a computer system and to set when and how they are to be run. Normally this configuration is done automatically during the installation of NT or by other software. You should make changes here only when you have got specific instructions or know exactly what the effect will be.

MS-DOS Console

If you run MS-DOS programs under Windows NT, the MS-DOS Console dialog box allows you to customize the screen size, fonts, colors, and other minor options of the DOS window. The options work much as they do in the Display dialog box. Chapter 9 describes this dialog box in more detail.

PC Card

If you have a PC card (formerly called a PCMCIA card) in your system, the PC Card dialog box will be available to do installation and configuration. What you can do will depend on the type of card (modem, network, or memory) and the particular driver that goes with it.

Ports

Although you have both parallel and serial ports on your computer, this dialog box is only for configuring the serial ports. There isn't much to it. Most of the configuration is performed by using the **Settings** and **Advanced** buttons. They display small dialog boxes that have options to set the port number, base address, IRQ number, and other aspects of a communications or serial port.

Printers

For configuring individual printers, this is the least convenient place to go (**Start** menu, **Settings**, **Printers** is quicker). However, Windows NT doesn't just connect to a printer; it can handle many printers through its Print Server capacity, and that's what you can configure only through the Printers dialog box of the Control Panel.

When the Printers dialog box is open (again, it's really just a form of NT Explorer), you'll find **Server Properties** in the File menu. Clicking this will display the Printer Server Properties dialog box. Here you can review and configure the printer ports (**Ports** tab), set the standard paper forms and sizes (**Forms** tab), and check some print spooler options (**Advanced** tab).

System

It would be nice if the System dialog box were really the central point for inspecting system options and setting for both hardware and software. It does some of this, but its range is limited. The first tab, **General**, provides some unproductive background information about your computer. The second tab, **Performance**, has an option to set the relative CPU time assigned to foreground programs (the one currently active on the screen) and background programs (those running off the screen). By default, the foreground is given maximum priority, and that is where it should be unless you're running a large number of critical programs in the background. The **Virtual Memory** options are critical to Windows NT, but you shouldn't change the default configuration unless otherwise instructed, such as by an error message that tells you to increase the size of the Registry.

The **Environment** tab presents two lists of system variables that contain paths to software and other system-level information. System administrators who are using one machine with several hardware configurations use the **Hardware Profiles** tab. It can create and save hardware profiles that are used to automatically change the settings of the computer. Arguably, the **User Profiles** tab belongs with the Network dialog box, because this is where a system administrator can create a profile (a stored record of settings) for each user. This feature is useful only when more than one user works with the same computer or a user roams between different computers.

The **Startup/Shutdown** tab covers what Windows NT should do when it starts and when an error forces it to shut down (stop). You may recall seeing a number of messages when you reboot or turn on your computer. The **System Startup** options let you choose which set of messages to use and how long they will be displayed. The **Recovery** options are for programmers and system administrators who want to track what happens when the operating system is forced to shut down.

Services

The Services dialog box contains a harmless-looking list of software or hardware *services* (procedures and processes) that are integral to the operation of Windows NT 4.0. If you're not sure of what you're doing, making changes of any kind in this display can cause bad things to happen to your system. Programs will stop running, and your computer might not even boot. Sorry to be so blunt, but it would take a chapter to explain all the things that go on in Services and why you need to be careful.

SCSI Adapters

Like the PC Card dialog box, the SCSI Adapters dialog box won't be accessible unless you have some kind of SCSI (pronounced "skuzzy") device in your computer. With CD-ROM drives becoming standard, your CD-ROM drive may well be attached to a SCSI adapter. If that's the case, the name of your CD-ROM will show up in this dialog box and you can set some of the operating parameters. As usual, this is not something you should attempt without specific instructions for installation from the manufacturer of the device.

Tape Devices

Like the PC Card and SCSI Adapter dialog boxes, Tape Devices becomes active when a device (in this case, tape backup) is present in the system. When you purchase a tape backup machine, it will usually come with instructions for installation. Most of the work will be done automatically, including configuring this portion of Windows NT. In a few cases you may need to open this dialog box and use the **Detect** (devices) or **Add** (drivers) button to do manual installation.

UPS

Most of the uninterruptible power supply (UPS) devices you can purchase come with their own installation software, and you won't need to use this Control Panel dialog box. In fact, most UPS devices bypass the Windows configuration entirely and have their own system for managing power.

SUMMARY

The Windows NT 4.0 Control Panel covers a vast range of functions, options, and features. It would be an unusual user who didn't need (or want) to change something about the configuration of his or her computer and software. The Control Panel is usually the first place to go for system configuration changes..

CHAPTER 6

File Management Tools

As a Windows NT user, you often need to manage files and folders. (Folders are also known as *directories*.) Windows NT has several powerful file and folder management tools to make these important tasks easy. These new tools replace the File Manager of previous versions of Windows and Windows NT. With these new tools, you can easily perform file management jobs, such as moving or copying files, using pull-down and cascading menus and keyboard shortcuts. The same tools can perform exotic tasks such as connecting to remote network drives and formatting disks. One new tool, the Recycle Bin, can be used to restore any file that you have deleted but have not removed from the Recycle Bin. All in all, these new tools are a powerful, friendly addition to the new user interface.

In this chapter you will learn about:

- File and disk tools
  - Using My Computer
  - Using Network Neighborhood
  - Using Recycle Bin
  - Using NT Explorer

- Working with files and folders
  - Creating and deleting files and folders
  - Viewing files and folders
  - Copying and moving files
  - Finding a file or a folder

- Working with floppies and hard drives
  - Viewing the disks attached to your computer
  - Viewing the contents of a disk
  - Formatting a disk
  - Checking a disk for errors

FILE AND DISK TOOLS

You can quickly find important facts about your computer and files and folders by using Windows NT's file and disk tools. Whereas previous versions of NT came with one basic file management tool, called File Manager, the new interface in Windows NT 4.0 Workstation includes four separate tools, each with a distinct purpose but all closely related. Three of these tools are displayed as icons on the desktop by default. The fourth tool, NT Explorer, is not on the desktop by default, but you can easily add it with a shortcut icon. Explorer is also accessible by right-clicking any of the other three tools.

The icons for the four tools are illustrated in Figure 6.1.

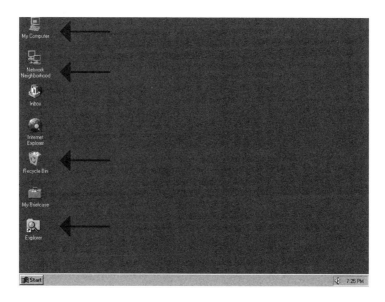

Figure 6.1 *The desktop showing the four file management tools highlighted.*

The four file management tools illustrated in Figure 6.1 are as follows:

- **My Computer**. This tool resembles Finder, the MacOS file management tool. In Finder and My Computer, folders and files are displayed as large icons by default. My Computer is provided for people who didn't like the File Manager in previous versions of NT and Windows and for Mac users who are using NT Workstation for the first time. It contains icons for folders, drives, the Recycle Bin, Control Panel, and the Printers folder.

- **Network Neighborhood**. Similar to My Computer, except that by default the Network Neighborhood focuses on other computers on your network and not on the files and folders on your computer. If you aren't on a network, you may never use this tool. If you are on a network, this tool can be fairly useful.

- **Recycle Bin**. The trash can icon means that the Recycle Bin is where your files go when you delete them using My Computer, Explorer, or

Network Neighborhood. The files are not deleted from your hard drive until you "take out the trash" by emptying the Recycle Bin. If you find that you need a file again after you have deleted it, you can open the Recycle Bin, find the file, and restore it. You might want to keep an eye on the size of the Recycle Bin. If you don't empty it regularly, it can end up taking up a lot of disk space.

- **Explorer**. The most versatile file management tool—but also the most complicated—Explorer is the tool that is most like the File Manager tool included in previous versions of Windows NT and Windows. It displays folders in a hierarchy tree in a pane on the left, and files and folders in a pane on the right. It can be used to access network resources, format drives, and access the Control Panel, Printers folder, and Dial-Up Networking (if you have it installed). The **Explorer** icon is not usually included on the desktop, but you can easily create a shortcut for it.

The following sections look at each of these tools in more detail. After that, you'll learn how to use these tools to perform specific tasks, such as copying files.

Using My Computer

The **My Computer** icon appears in the upper-left-hand corner of the desktop, as shown in Figure 6.2.

*Figure 6.2 The **My Computer** icon in the upper-left-hand corner of the desktop.*

Your Computer's Properties

In addition to being a file management tool, My Computer enables you to access the System Properties dialog box without first opening the Control Panel. We'll look at this feature of My Computer before we open the My Computer window. To access System Properties from My Computer, right-click on the **My Computer** icon and then select the **Properties** option, as shown in Figure 6.3.

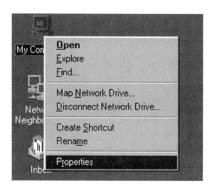

Figure 6.3 *The right-click context menu for My Computer.*

The System Properties dialog box shown in Figure 6.4 appears. The **General** tab displays the version of NT, the company or person to whom it is registered, the model of the PC processor installed, and how much memory the computer has. The other tabs in this dialog box are described in detail in Chapter 5, which covers the Control Panel applets.

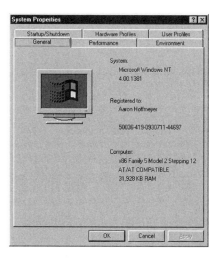

Figure 6.4 *The System Properties dialog box is accessible from My Computer.*

This dialog box is also accessed in the Control Panel by double-clicking the **System** icon.

NOTE

Opening My Computer

You use My Computer to find information about the drives and external devices connected to your computer. Double-click the **My Computer** icon to open a window that displays the computer's storage devices, Printers folder, Control Panel, and other applications, such as Dial-Up Networking (if it is installed), as shown in Figure 6.5.

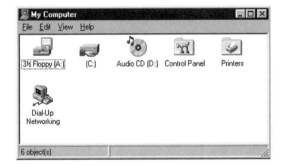

Figure 6.5 *The My Computer window.*

Navigating Drives and Folders with My Computer

To see what's on a particular drive, such as the C:\ drive, double-click its icon. A new window with folder icons and files will appear, as shown in Figure 6.6.

Figure 6.6 *A window showing the contents of the C:\ drive.*

When you double-click on a folder, you'll see the files contained in it, as shown in Figure 6.7.

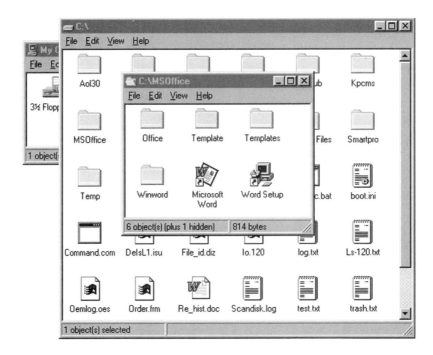

Figure 6.7 *Multiple My Computer windows with the one most recently opened showing the contents of a folder.*

Every time you open a drive or a new folder, a new window appears on your screen. This is the default behavior of My Computer. As you navigate through multiple folders, you probably will want to go back to a folder previously opened. To do this, either select it on the screen, switch to it using the Taskbar or **Alt+Tab**, or close the other windows until you find it again.

You might find that navigating among various windows gets confusing after a while, especially when your screen is filled with windows. (It also requires additional memory every time you open a window.) You can change the default behavior so that My Computer does not open a new window every time you open a folder but instead updates the current window to display the contents of the drive or folder you open. In the My Computer window illustrated in Figure 6.5, select the View menu and choose **Options**. The dialog box shown in Figure 6.8 displays.

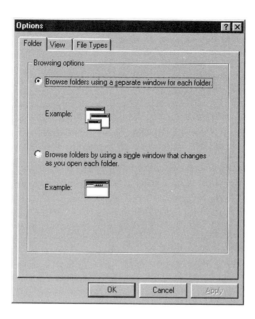

Figure 6.8 *The My Computer Options dialog box.*

The **Folder** tab of this dialog box enables you to change the default behavior so that a single window changes as you open each folder or drive.

Menu Selection Options for My Computer

The My Computer menu selections are common across all the file management tools within Windows NT. The menu is shown in several of the figures you have already seen in this chapter. The four menus are File, Edit, View, and Help.

- **File**. The File menu lists options that are standard for most Windows NT windows: **Close**, which closes the window, **Properties**, **Rename**, **Delete**, and **Create Shortcut**. Only **Close** is active when nothing is selected. When you select one or several objects within the My Computer window, you will see additional options on the File menu, such as **Open**, **Explore**, and **Find**. You might also see some File menu options that are unique to the item you have selected in the window. For example, if you select the Printers folder, you will see two new File menu options: **Capture Printer Port** and **End Capture**.

- **Edit**. The Edit menu enables you to cut, copy, paste, and make selections within the My Computer window.

- **View**. The View menu enables you to display a Toolbar at the top of the My Computer window and a Status Bar at the bottom of the window. The View menu also enables you to change how icons are displayed and to arrange them within the window. The View menu's **Options** item lets you change the behavior of My Computer when you open a file or folder. Figure 6.9 shows a My Computer window with the Status Bar and Toolbar turned on and with the Detail icons displayed. It's still the same My Computer window, but the View options have been changed.

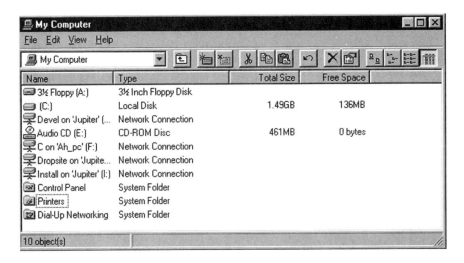

Figure 6.9 *The My Computer window with the Detail icon view and with the Toolbar and Status Bar turned on.*

- **Help**. The Help menu enables you to obtain Windows NT help and to view the About window, which tells you the current version of Windows NT.

Other My Computer Right-Click Context Menu Options

As you can see in Figure 6.10, there are several other options on the right-click context menu for My Computer. We've looked at the Properties item, and now we'll look at the other options.

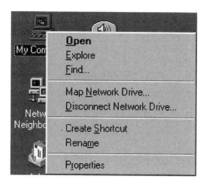

Figure 6.10 *The right-click context menu for My Computer.*

Depending on the software configuration of your system, you may not see all the options shown, such as the two options about network drives. The options are as follows:

- **Open**. Selecting this option is effectively the same as double-clicking the **My Computer** icon. It opens the My Computer window.

- **Explore**. This option opens Microsoft Explorer, which was briefly described earlier and will be described in more detail later in this chapter.

- **Find**. This selection opens the Find tool, which is the same tool that appears when you select **Find** from the Start menu. The difference is that when you select it from the right-click context menu for My Computer, it opens with the default starting point for your search at My Computer. From the Start menu, **Find** opens with the C:\ drive as the starting point. The difference between the two starting points is that My Computer includes all your drives and network drives in its search. In both cases you can change the starting point, so both options are equally useful.

- **Map Network Drive** and **Disconnect Network Drive**. These options apply only to those with access to a network running Windows NT. Both options open similar dialog boxes. One enables you to connect to or mount shared network drives, and the other enables you to disconnect from one, several, or all network drives.

- **Create Shortcut**. This option creates a shortcut copy of My Computer, which isn't very useful. There's really no need to have multiple copies of an icon on the desktop. You could drag the shortcut to the Start menu and drop it there or drop it in any folder, but the **My Computer** icon on the desktop is usually adequate.

* **Rename**. This option enables you to change the name of the My Computer icon. When you select this option, "My Computer" is highlighted. Type in a new name and then press **Enter**. The name you enter does not affect the name you gave your computer for networking purposes. It simply changes the text that appears below the My Computer icon.

Using Network Neighborhood

When your computer is part of a network, a Network Neighborhood icon will be present on the desktop. Network Neighborhood allows you access to other drives that are part of the network. This feature is handy, because files and folders that you want to obtain will often be stored on a network drive.

Double-clicking on the **Network Neighborhood** icon will open a window that shows icons representing parts of your *workgroup*, or *domain*—those computers and devices that your computer is connected to. This window also contains an icon called **Entire Network**, which can depict all other machines on the network that aren't part of your workgroup (Figure 6.11). If you aren't part of a workgroup or if your machine is the only computer in the workgroup that is logged on, you won't see other computers.

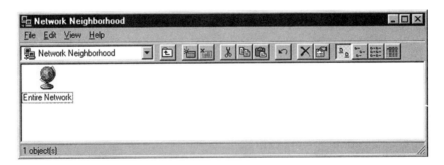

Figure 6.11 The Network Neighborhood window.

To look at the computers on your network, double-click the **Entire Network** icon. To look at the contents of a computer, double-click its icon (Figure 6.12).

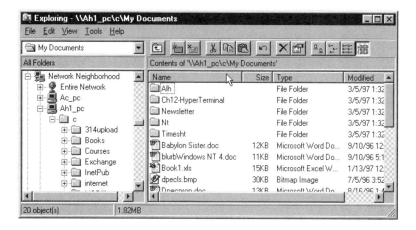

Figure 6.12 *Browsing a computer on your network.*

Finding particular files is easier if you know which computer to search. Windows NT 4.0 has a Find tool to simplify this task. To use this feature, right-click **Network Neighborhood** and select **Find Computer** from the menu. Type in the name of the computer you're searching for and then click **Find Now**; or press **Enter** to start the search.

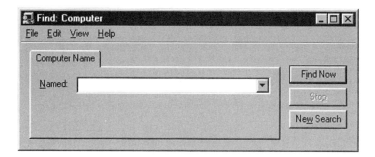

Figure 6.13 *Searching for a computer on your network.*

You can identify the name of your computer by right-clicking **Network Neighborhood** and then selecting **Properties** from the menu. Selecting **Identification** displays this data. Note that if you are part of a domain, the system administrator will tell you the domain name and the name to use for your computer.

Using the Recycle Bin

In earlier versions of Windows and Windows NT, recovering deleted files was difficult. A third party utility program, such as Norton's Desktop, had to be installed. Windows NT 4.0 includes the Recycle Bin, which stores deleted files or folders. With Windows NT 4.0, erased files and folders are no longer automatically deleted. Instead, they are sent to the Recycle Bin, which stores them for a set period.

Recovering a Deleted File

If you unintentionally erase a file, you can recover it by opening the Recycle Bin and using its features (Figure 6.14). To see a listing of all the documents you've erased, double-click the **Recycle Bin** icon. Right-click on any file in the Recycle Bin. A menu will appear. The menu selections let you send a file back to its original location (**Restore**); make it accessible to other documents by copying it to the Clipboard (**Cut**); or remove it from the Recycle Bin permanently (**Delete**). The right-click context menu selections are also included on the File menu.

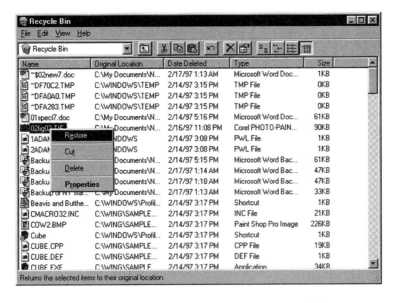

Figure 6.14 *Restoring a "deleted" file from the Recycle Bin.*

Viewing the Recycle Bin Properties

Right-click the **Recycle Bin** icon and then choose **Properties**. The Recycle Bin Properties dialog box displays, as shown in Figure 6.15. The **Global** tab allows you to set how much hard-disk capacity the Recycle Bin will consume. (Files that haven't been deleted from the Recycle Bin take up useful disk space.) Selecting **Do not move files to the Recycle Bin. Remove files immediately on delete** will bypass the Recycle Bin altogether.

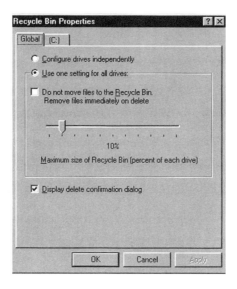

Figure 6.15 *The Recycle Bin Properties dialog box.*

Any time you clear out the Recycle Bin, a dialog box opens and asks you whether you really want to delete the files, as shown in Figure 6.16. You may find this message an unnecessary irritation. To skip seeing this dialog box, uncheck the selection in the Recycle Bin Properties window that reads **Display delete confirmation dialog**.

Figure 6.16 *The Confirm File Delete dialog box.*

Using NT Explorer

Windows NT Explorer is an important and versatile tool that enables you to create folders, view folders and files, and move and copy files or folders.

Normally, you open NT Explorer by clicking the **Start** button and then choosing **Programs** and then **Windows NT Explorer**. You can also open Explorer at any time by right-clicking on the **My Computer** icon or any folder or drive displayed in a My Computer window and selecting **Explore** from the context menu. Some people use Explorer often, so they create a shortcut icon for it on the desktop.

The Explorer window, when opened, displays a window with right and left panes (Figure 6.17). The left pane contains an ordered listing of all folders on the current disk. The right pane, which is known as the *content window*, shows everything within the selected folder, whether the contents are files, programs, or other folders.

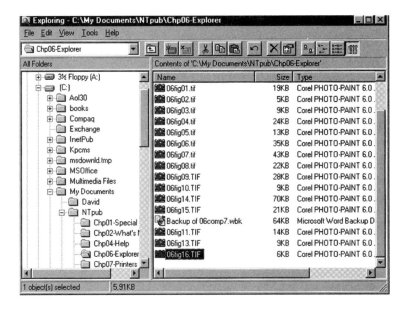

Figure 6.17 *The Explorer window showing files in Detail view.*

In the left pane, choose the folder whose contents you wish to see. Note that there are plus (+) and minus (-) signs beside folder symbols. Click on these to extend (+) or collapse (-) the folder's contents.

Only folders with subfolders have a (+) or (-) sign beside them.

N O T E

View a folder and its contents by clicking on the folder in the left pane. Explorer will then display all the folder's files in the content window in the right pane. To make viewing easier, these windows can be easily resized. Move the cursor carefully over the dividing line between the windows until the arrow becomes a double-sided arrow. Then drag the arrow to the right or left to resize the windows, as shown in Figure 6.18.

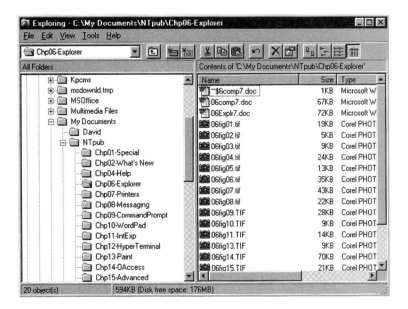

Figure 6.18 *Changing the size of the panes in the Explorer window.*

Explorer lets you arrange how to view the items in the content window to suit your preferences (Figure 6.19). Do this, for example, by opening the View menu, selecting the **Arrange Icons** option, and then selecting to have files listed by file name, by file type, by file size (smallest to largest), or by date (beginning with the most recently updated file). You can also change how the files are sorted by clicking on the **Name**, **Size**, **Type**, and **Date** boxes at the top of the right pane.

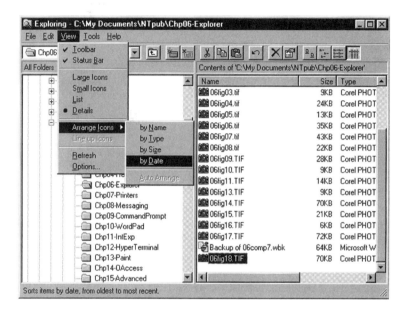

Figure 6.19 *Rearranging files in the Explorer window using the View menu.*

You can change how icons are displayed in the Explorer window using the Toolbar icons. First, make sure that the Toolbar is displayed (select **View**, **Toolbar**). You can choose four views for the files and folders in the right pane.There is an icon for each view on the Toolbar and a listing on the View menu. The four views are **Large Icons**, **Small Icons**, **List**, and **Details**. When you click one of these icons, the view changes in the right pane, as shown in Figure 6.20.

To open a file or folder shown in the right pane of the Explorer window, simply double-click its icon in the content window.

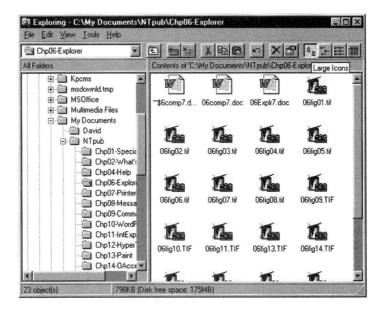

Figure 6.20 The **Large Icon** *view in the Explorer window.*

WORKING WITH FILES AND FOLDERS

This section explains how to perform file management tasks using either My Computer or NT Explorer. Most actions are the same from within either tool. To simplify the explanations, Explorer is used in the examples.

Creating and Deleting Files and Folders

To create a new folder using Explorer, first move to the disk or folder where you want the new folder. Make sure that no file or folder in that location is selected. If a file or folder is selected, you can deselect it by clicking in an empty area in a My Computer or Explorer window. Next, click on the File pull-down menu; select the **New** option and then **Folder** from the cascading menu, as shown in Figure 6.21. You could also right-click in an open area and select **New, Folder** from the right-click context menu.

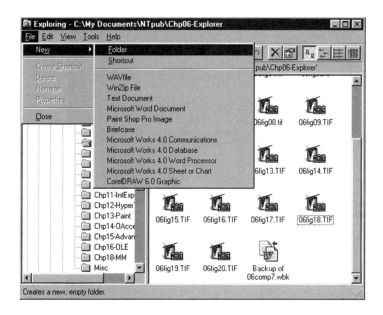

Figure 6.21 *Creating a new folder.*

You'll see a new folder icon appear where you chose to create it, as shown in Figure 6.22.

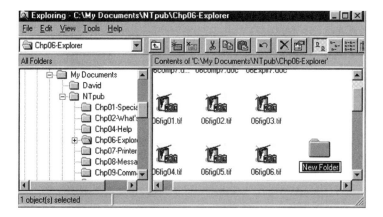

Figure 6.22 *The new folder.*

By default, the new folder is named New Folder. To rename the folder, start typing at once. As you type, you replace the "New Folder" tag. Press **Enter** after typing the new folder name.

Windows NT also allows you to create new folders on the desktop without opening Explorer or My Computer. To do this, place the cursor on a blank area of the desktop and click the right mouse button. Choose **New**, **Folder** from the menu that appears. A new folder will appear on the Desktop, as shown in Figure 6.23.

Figure 6.23 *A new folder on the Desktop.*

You can change the default name of the folder by typing the new name while the current name is highlighted. You can also change the name by right-clicking on the folder and selecting **Rename** from the context menu, as shown in Figure 6.24. This highlights the folder name again, enabling you to enter a new name.

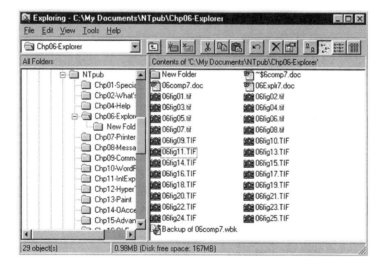

Figure 6.24 *Renaming a folder.*

Or if you click slowly twice (slower than a double-click) on the folder name, you can highlight it and then type in the new name.

To delete a file or folder, select it, press the right mouse button, and then choose **Delete** from the menu. Or you can simply press **Delete** on the keyboard after you have selected the file or folder. Immediately thereafter, the system prompts you to confirm that you want to send the selected file(s) or folder(s) to the Recycle Bin, as shown in Figure 6.25. Click **Yes** to send the file to the Recycle Bin.

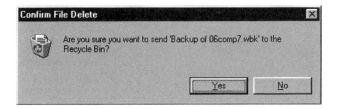

Figure 6.25 *The Confirm File Delete dialog box.*

 Windows NT does not automatically delete files and folders. Rather, it sends them to the Recycle Bin, where you can recover them if you choose to. When you empty the Recycle Bin, the file is deleted from your hard disk. See the section "Using the Recycle Bin" for more details.

N O T E

Viewing Files and Folders

The View pull-down menu and the right-click context menu can be used with NT Explorer, My Computer, Network Neighborhood, and the Recycle Bin to arrange the way files and folders look in the content window. The size of icons representing files and folders can be changed; files can be listed by chosen categories, such as type; or files can be listed by size, among other options. These tools let you group similar files, and NT enables you to perform these functions intuitively. This section discusses some of these options.

The appearance of file icons can be changed so that the icons are large by choosing **Large Icons** from the View menu or by clicking the **Large Icon** button on the Toolbar. This was illustrated in Figure 6.20 and other figures.

Folders with numerous icons might be easier to view if they appeared smaller. To do this, choose **Small Icons** from the View menu, or select the **Small icons** button on the Toolbar. The files and folders will now appear as in Figure 6.26.

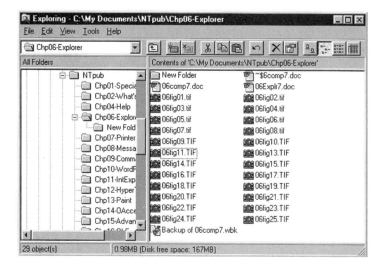

Figure 6.26 *Small Icon view in the Explorer.*

A summary list of the files in a folder can be obtained by selecting **List** from the View menu or the **List** button on the Toolbar. More information on files in the list will be shown by selecting the **Details** button or the **Details** item on the View menu: the file name, type, size, and date of last file modification will be noted in the window, as shown in Figure 6.27.

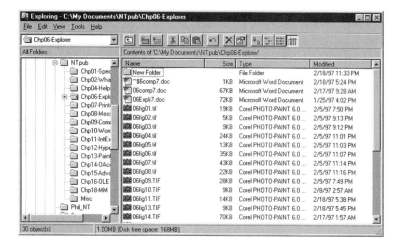

Figure 6.27 *The Detail view in Explorer.*

Whether you show files as icons or in a list, you can rearrange them by selecting **Arrange Icons** from the View menu or the right-click context menu. Icons will then be automatically rearranged in the manner of your choice: alphabetically, by name; by file type; by size; or by date (with the most recently updated ones at the top of the list). In Detail view, you can also rearrange the files by selecting the column bars (at the top of the right pane) labeled **Name**, **Size**, **Type**, and **Modified**. When you click one of these bars once, the files are arranged by sorting the list using the contents of that column as the primary item to sort in ascending order. If you click the bar again, the files are sorted in descending order.

NT Explorer also lets you choose which file types you want to see. Open the folder you want to see. From the View menu, select **Options** and then the **View** tab, as shown in Figure 6.28.

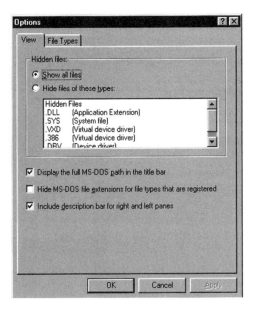

Figure 6.28 *The Explorer View Options dialog box.*

Check **Show all files** to see files with any extension. You can exclude files of specified extensions by selecting the extensions from the list box and selecting **Hide files of these types**. (File extensions are three-character identifiers that show which application was used to create the file. For example, all documents created with Word will have a **.DOC** extension.)

While using NT Explorer, you might want to switch to an application such as Excel to create a new file. But when you return to NT Explorer, you won't see this new file unless you update the view: Open the View menu and choose **Refresh**.

Copying and Moving Files and Folders

Any computer user will routinely copy and move files. You can copy and move files several ways using My Computer, Explorer, and Network Neighborhood. This section discusses the most common techniques.

The Drag Method

First, select the files or folders you want to copy or move, as shown in Figure 6.29.

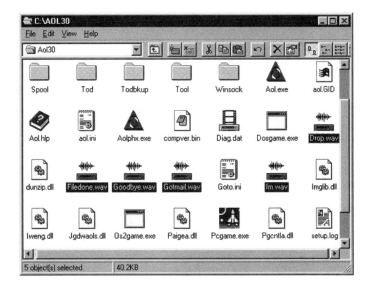

Figure 6.29 *Selecting individual files to copy in My Computer.*

To select a range of files or folders, click the first one; then press the **Shift** key and select the final one in the range by clicking on it. All files or folders between and including the items you clicked will be selected.

To select all items in the current open folder or drive, choose the Edit menu and then click **Select All**; or simply press **Ctrl+A**.

You can select one or more files or folders by holding down the **Ctrl** key and selecting the files to copy individually.

Another way to choose objects for moving or copying is to use the cursor to draw a rectangle around the set of files or folders to be copied or moved. Do this by starting with the cursor above and slightly to the left of the file or folder you want to copy or move. Then press the left mouse button and, keeping it depressed, drag the cursor until you have formed a rectangle around the rest of the files or folders you wish to select, and release the mouse. All files and folders so selected should be highlighted.

You can then copy the selected items by holding down on the **Ctrl** key and dragging the items to the destination drive or folder in another My Computer window or the left pane of an Explorer window, as shown in Figure 6.30.

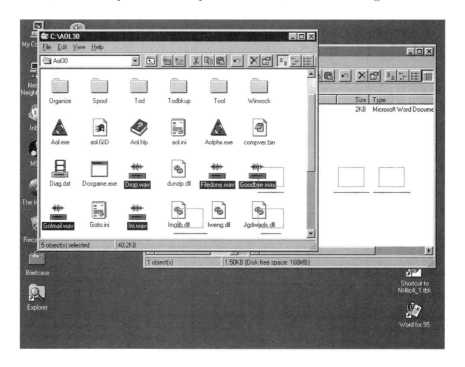

Figure 6.30 *Copy files from a My Computer window to an Explorer window.*

You move files or folders by dragging the selected files or folders to the destination drive, folder, or the desktop without holding down the **Ctrl** key. The original files in folders will then no longer be seen in the source location.

NOTE

Using the dragging method, you can copy or move files from My Computer, Explorer, Network Neighborhood, or the desktop to another My Computer, Explorer, or Network Neighborhood window or the desktop. One of the disadvantages of this method is that you usually have to open two windows: one for the source drive or folder and another one for the destination (unless the source or destination is the desktop).

If you inadvertently moved files when you intend to copy them, select **Undo Move** from the Edit menu or the source location. Or you can click the **Undo** icon from the Explorer's toolbar. You could also copy the files back to the original source location. **Undo** works for copying and moving no matter what method you used to copy or move the files or folders.

Menu, Keyboard, and Toolbar Methods

Using the menu method, select the files or folders you want to copy or move. Then open the Edit menu in the source window. If you are copying the files, select **Copy**. If you are moving the files, select **Cut**; the selected files or folders will appear as "ghost" images. Using **Copy** or **Cut** places the files on the Clipboard. Now you can move to a destination folder or drive using the same window as the source. When you get to the destination location, select **Edit, Paste**. The files or folders will be copied from the Clipboard to the current location. If you chose **Cut** in the source location, the original files will be deleted.

A variation of this method uses the right-click context menu instead of the Edit menu. There is no Edit menu on the desktop, so if the source or destination is the desktop, you can use the right-click context menu. The right-click menu lists the **Cut**, **Copy**, and **Paste** options for any valid source or destination.

Another variation uses the keyboard shortcuts for **Cut**, **Copy**, and **Paste**. **Ctrl-X** is cut, **Ctrl-C** is copy, and **Ctrl-V** is paste. You might find that using the keyboard shortcuts is the quickest method for copying or moving files, because these simple keystrokes are quicker than using either the Edit menu or the right-click context menu.

A final variation of this method uses the **Cut**, **Copy**, and **Paste** icons on the Toolbar.

Right-Drag Method

Probably the most interesting way to copy or move files or folders is to right-drag the items. You select items as described earlier. After you've selected the last item, click and hold the right mouse button on one of the selected files or folders. Now drag the items to the destination, continuing to hold down the right mouse button. At the destination, release the mouse button. A context menu pops up. Choose **Move Here**, **Copy Here**, or **Create Shortcut(s) Here**, as shown in Figure 6.31.

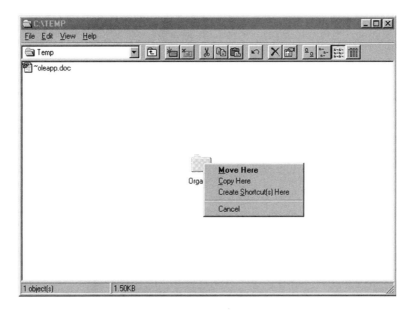

Figure 6.31 *Using the right-drag method to copy or move files.*

The Find, Save, and Open Dialog Boxes

You learned about the Find dialog box (accessed by selecting **Find** on the Start menu) in Chapter 3. If you've skipped ahead in this book or if you've used NT, Windows 95, or even previous versions of Windows, you might also be familiar with the Save, Save As, and Open dialog boxes. These dialog boxes allow you to perform some limited file management tasks, such as copying and cutting files or folders. You can't paste into them, so they can't be destinations, but they can be source locations any time you want to copy or move files.

WORKING WITH FLOPPIES AND HARD DRIVES

Every computer relies on different types of disks for storing and using data. The two main types of disks are floppy disks and hard disks. Floppy disks are typically 3.5 inches square and are small enough to be easily carried and stored. However, they store a limited amount of data, usually 1.44 MB. Hard disks are much larger and much more expensive than floppy disks and are permanently installed within computers. Their storage capacities are hundreds or thousands of times greater than that of floppy disks. Hard disks are essential to modern computers; floppy disks allow for easy exchange of data between computers. Other types of drives, such as CD-ROM drives, tape backup machines, and special ZIP drives—which resemble floppies but can store many times more information—are also used in or with many computers.

Viewing the Disks Attached to Your Computer

Computer arrangements vary, but a typical computer running Windows NT 4.0 Workstation has a 1.44-MB floppy drive (usually denoted A:); at least one hard drive (typically called C:); and a CD-ROM drive (typically called D:, E:, or F:). There may also be a removable media drive and drives mounted from the network. Recall that you can access all devices attached to your computer using any of the file management tools.

When you double-click the **My Computer** icon, a window appears with icons showing all the disks accessible to your computer. A different icon is used to show each different type of drive or remote hookup, as shown in Figure 6.32. Explorer shows the same disks in the hierarchical view in the left pane of the window.

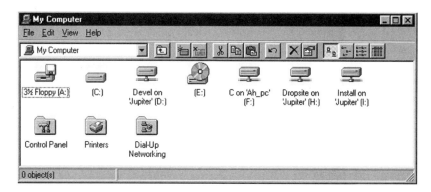

Figure 6.32 Viewing drives using My Computer.

Some disks, such as a removable disk drive or network drives, may be marked by a red **X**. If you see this sign, it means that the drive is not currently available. If it is a network drive, the computer on the network housing this drive may not be turned on. The different icons, such as the floppy disk icon, will look the same whether or not a disk is present in the drive.

N O T E

An error message displays if you click on one of these icons when no disk is present.

N O T E

Viewing the Contents of a Drive

You'll need to know what's on a disk or drive before you can work with it. Right-click on the disk if you need more information about it. (We'll select the network drive D: in the system for illustration purposes.) Then select **Explore** from the menu that appears (Figure 6.33).

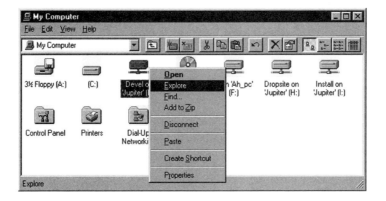

Figure 6.33 Right-clicking a drive in My Computer.

The Explorer window opens, listing all the disks in the left window pane as shown in Figure 6.34.

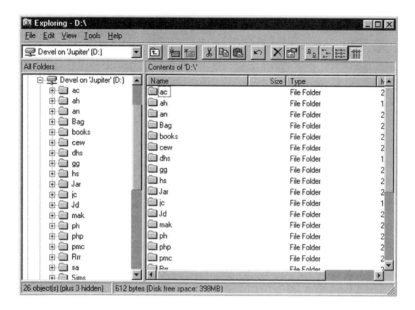

Figure 6.34 *The Explorer window showing the contents of the previously selected drive.*

The components of the disk you chose are displayed in the content window on the right. Folders are shown by a yellow folder icon. Figure 6.34 shows only folders. Opening the **ah** folder and then switching to **Large Icon** view results in the window displayed in Figure 6.35.

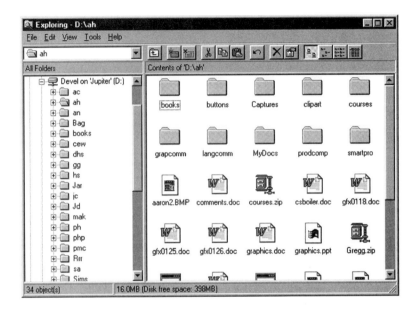

Figure 6.35 *Contents of a folder showing additional folders and files.*

Files are shown either by the file's unique icon or by a generic file icon. If you double-click on a file icon, you open that file. This means that if the file has an associated application, the associated application starts and loads the selected file. For example, double-clicking the icon for a Microsoft Word document launches Microsoft Word with the document loaded.

Formatting a Disk

Before you can save data to a disk, it must be formatted. Almost all computers now ship with their hard drives preformatted, and most floppy disks are also preformatted. Still, you will probably find that you need to format a disk at some point. You might have found a deal on some used, degaussed floppy disks that can be used only if they are formatted again. Formatting hard disks is also possible but is generally not advisable unless you know what you are doing, because it can render a hard disk unusable. We'll walk you through formatting a 3.5-inch floppy disk.

NOTE

If you want to format a hard disk, you can choose between two file systems: FAT (File Allocation Table) and NTFS (New Technology File System). For example, you might have purchased a new 3.8-GB hard drive because your old drive didn't have enough space. Knowing the benefits of NTFS over FAT, you want to format this new drive using NTFS. To do this, you must have Administrator rights and privileges in NT. You also should partition the drive using the Disk Administration tool before the disk can be formatted. Because you can also format the drive from within the Disk Administration tool, it is unlikely that you will ever use the **Format** command in My Computer.

NOTE

You can't format a hard drive that contains the files for Windows NT using My Computer. So if Windows NT is installed on your C: drive, you can't format the C: drive.

To format a floppy, first double-click **My Computer** or open Explorer. In the resulting window, right-click the **A:** drive (if that is your floppy drive). The right-click context menu appears. Choose **Format**, as shown in Figure 6.36.

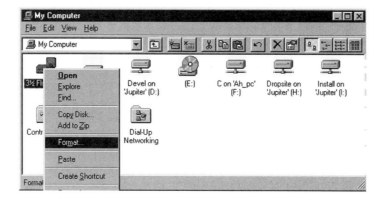

Figure 6.36 Formatting a floppy disk.

The Format dialog box appears, as shown in Figure 6.37.

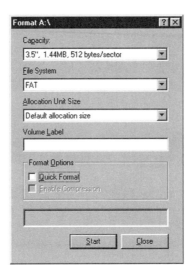

Figure 6.37 *The Format dialog box.*

Choose the capacity you want. You'll choose the highest capacity possible unless you will be using the disk in a drive that doesn't support that capacity. If you are formatting a hard drive, you'll be able to choose a file system other than FAT. However, for floppies, FAT is the only choice. Choose the allocation size, enter a disk label if you want to, and specify whether you want to use quick format. Quick format can be used if the floppy was formatted previously and was not degaussed. Effectively, it rebuilds the file index at the beginning of the disk and deletes any files that may have been on the disk. It does not scan the disk for bad sectors. Although quick format is much faster than regular format mode, you should use this mode only if you are sure there are no bad sectors on the disk.

When you've made your formatting choices, click **Start**. You'll receive a message warning that all data on the disk will be erased, as shown in Figure 6.38.

Click **OK** to proceed. The progress of formatting displays as a graph at the bottom of the dialog box. When the disk is formatted, a pop-up dialog box notifies you.

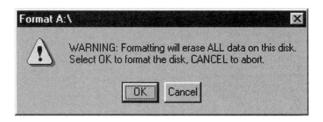

Figure 6.38 *The Format warning.*

Checking a Disk for Errors

You might at some time encounter disk errors. If things are behaving strangely or if you can't access some file or program, you might have disk errors. Fortunately, NT can detect and correct errors on hard and floppy disks. In this section, we'll check a floppy disk for errors.

Open My Computer or Explorer and right-click the disk you want to check for errors. The right-click context menu appears. Choose **Properties**, as shown in Figure 6.39.

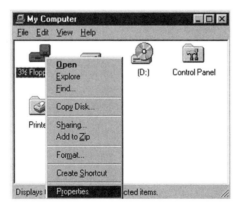

Figure 6.39 *Accessing the Disk Properties dialog box.*

This action brings up the Disk Properties dialog box, which contains three tabs. By default, the **General** tab is displayed, as shown in Figure 6.40.

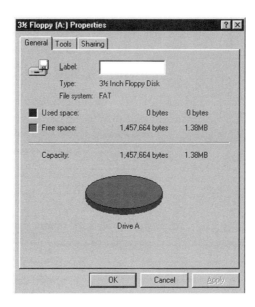

Figure 6.40 *The **General** tab of the Disk Properties dialog box.*

To check the disk for errors, select the **Tools** tab. The Tools page displays, as shown in Figure 6.41.

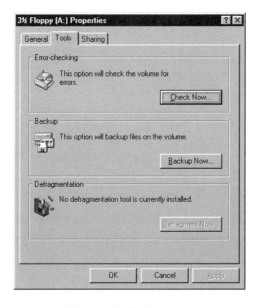

Figure 6.41 *The **Tools** tab.*

Click the **Check Now** button at the top of the page. You'll see another dialog box that allows you to specify whether you want to automatically fix file system errors or scan for and attempt to fix bad sectors, as shown in Figure 6.42. After you've made your selections, click **Start**. Error checking progress is shown in the graph at the bottom of the dialog box.

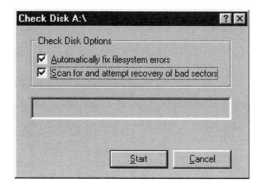

Figure 6.42 *The Check Disk dialog box.*

The automatic repair option will not run if the disk contains any open files.

N O T E

You can also check for errors on a hard drive using the Disk Administrator tool. It can't be used to check floppy disks for errors.

N O T E

SUMMARY

Windows NT 4.0 Workstation provides a wealth of new file management tools: My Computer, the Network Neighborhood, and Explorer. My Computer was designed for people who didn't like the File Manager tool from previous versions of Windows, for users who migrated from the Mac world to the PC workstation running Windows NT, and for first-time computer users. It has an intuitive interface and is not as complicated as Explorer. Network Neighborhood is like My Computer except that by default it looks at the network your computer is attached to. If you aren't on a network, you'll probably never use this tool. Explorer is for people who liked the File Manager tool from previous versions of Windows and Windows NT. It is the most versatile tool of the three but also the most complicated.

The Recycle Bin is a temporary holding bin for files that you want to delete. The files are not completely deleted from your hard drive until you empty the Recycle Bin, so if you find later that you need a file that you recently deleted, you can find the file in the Recycle Bin and restore it. You'll want to empty your Recycle Bin regularly, just as you take out the trash at home, because after a while it can take up a lot of disk space. You can also limit the percentage of disk space you'll allow the Recycle Bin to use. When you exceed that percentage, the oldest files are automatically removed permanently from your disk. In other words, if you forget to take out the trash, NT will take out your oldest trash for you.

You can use these tools to create folders, to delete folders and files, and navigate through disks and folders. You can copy and move files and folders using several methods. Finally, NT's file management tools let you format disks and check disks for errors.

CHAPTER 7

Printing

You use the Printers folder to set up printers and manage printer activity. Here, you can connect to printers either locally or remotely, and you can set up your printer as a shareable resource for others to use. You can stop, pause, or resume print jobs in progress. You can find a printer on the network that is not too busy to process your job quickly. The Printers folder also lets you pool printers; when you submit a job to the pool, the first available printer takes the job. You can also set properties, such as hours of availability or access permissions, for your printers.

In this chapter you will learn about:

- The Printers folder interface
- Setting up a printer
- Changing printer and document properties
- Printer security
- Managing the print queue

149

THE PRINTERS FOLDER AND PRINTERS WINDOW

Printing in Windows NT starts with the Printers folder. You can access the Printers folder in a variety of ways.

- From the Start menu, select **Settings**, **Printers**.
- From the Control Panel, select the **Printers** folder.
- In the Explorer window's left pane, select the **Printers** icon.
- In My Computer, select the **Printers** folder from the Desktop.

Selecting the **Printers** Folder opens the Printers window (Figure 7.1), which is a form of the Explorer window. The main features of the Printers folder are shown in detail in Figure 7.2.

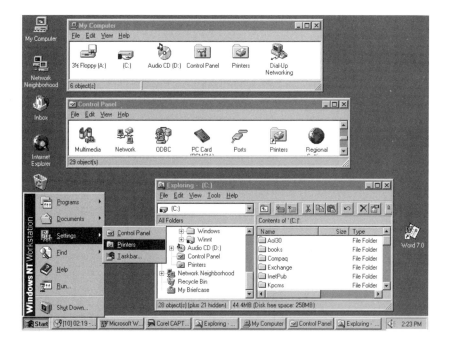

Figure 7.1 *Accessing the Printers folder.*

Figure 7.2 The Printers window.

The Printers window has four main areas:

- **Menu Bar**. Menu options are listed here.
- **Toolbar**. This bar provides a number of standard Explorer commands for easy access (see Table 7.1).
- **Printer area**. This area lists the available installed printers and contains the icon for adding printers.
- **Status Bar**. This area at the bottom of the window displays messages related to the object in the window.

Table 7.1 Printers Toolbar Commands

TOOLBAR ICON	DESCRIPTION
	Go to a different folder; Move up one level
	Cut, Copy, and Paste
	Undo rename
	Delete; Properties
	Display details about a document

SETTING UP A PRINTER

For Windows NT to know about the existence of a printer, you must formally add it. If your printer is connected physically to one of the ports on your computer, such as LPT1, you can add your printer by following these steps:

1. From within the Printer window, double-click the **Add Printer** icon to invoke the Add Printer Wizard, as shown in Figure 7.3.

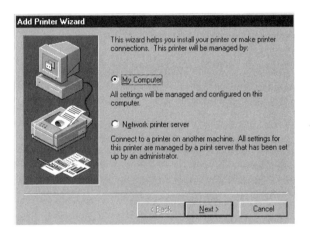

Figure 7.3 *The Add Printer Wizard.*

2. Select **My Computer** if the printer is attached locally. (If the printer is on the network, select **Network printer server**. The Wizard does not set up the printer at this point but enables you to connect to an existing shared printer on the network.) After you select **My Computer** and click **Next**, the next screen of the Add Printer Wizard appears, as shown in Figure 7.4.

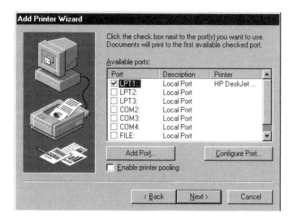

Figure 7.4 *Selecting the printer port.*

3. Select the check box next to the port to which your printer is attached. For most computers, the port is LPT1. Click **Next** to display the next screen, shown in Figure 7.5.

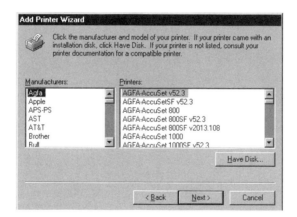

Figure 7.5 *Choosing the manufacturer and model of your printer.*

4. Choose the manufacturer and model of your printer. If your printer does not appear on this list, check the documentation that comes with your printer, or check with Microsoft. Often, you can load a printer driver from a disk supplied by your printer's manufacturer or obtain one from Microsoft or the manufacturer on the Internet. If you have a disk or CD-ROM that contains the driver for your printer, click the **Have Disk** button and specify where the disk or CD-ROM is located. Your manufacturer or Microsoft might tell you that a similar printer driver that is included on the Windows NT CD-ROM will work for your printer. When you have selected the driver you want, click **Next** to display the next screen of the Add Printer Wizard. If you have previously defined a printer that uses the driver you are installing for the current printer, you will see Figure 7.6, and then Figure 7.7. Otherwise, you will see the screen shown in Figure 7.7.

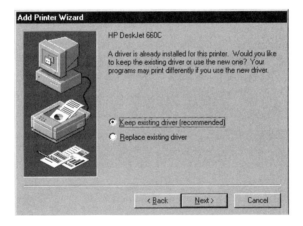

Figure 7.6 *Keeping or replacing an existing printer driver.*

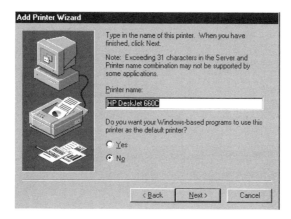

Figure 7.7 *Name the printer.*

5. In the screen shown in Figure 7.7, type the name of your printer in the **Printer name** box. If you want to use this printer as your default, click **Yes** at the bottom of the screen. Click **Next**, and the screen shown in Figure 7.8 displays.

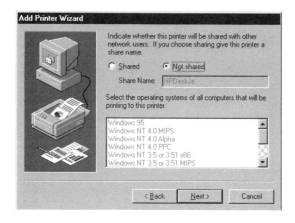

Figure 7.8 *Specify whether the printer will be shared.*

6. If the printer will be shared, select **Shared**, enter **Share Name**, and specify the other operating system that will access this printer. For example, if you know that other systems in your network run Windows NT 4.0 on DEC Alpha computers, you would select **Windows NT 4.0 Alpha** from the list. Depending on your choice, you might be prompted to insert a disk or CD-ROM to load the additional drivers. Click **Next** to go to the next screen, shown in Figure 7.9.

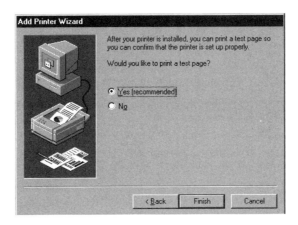

Figure 7.9 *Print a test page and finish setting up the printer.*

7. You should specify that you want to print a test page at this point; then click **Finish**. The test page will start printing (as long as everything works), and the new printer will appear on your Printers folder window, as shown in Figure 7.10.

Figure 7.10 *Your new printer.*

Changing Printer Properties

You have options in the Printers folder to change any of your printer settings. Select a printer and then select the **Properties** option from the File menu, the **Properties** button on the Toolbar, or **Properties** from the right-click context menu. You will see the dialog box pictured in Figure 7.11.

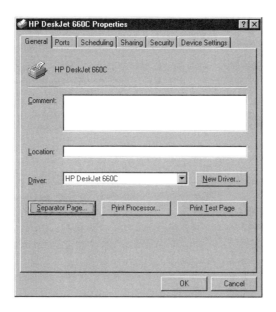

Figure 7.11 *The Printer Properties dialog box.*

Among other things, the Printer Properties dialog box enables you to change any of the settings you made when you set the printer up using the Add Printer Wizard.

The General Tab

The first tab, or page, displayed on the Printer Properties dialog box contains the **General** settings. You can add comments about your printer, such as whether the printer is available only during certain times. You can also specify a location for the printer, choose a different installed printer driver, and change the print processor or define a separator page. The file extension for the separator page file is **.sep**. Several separator files are provided with Windows NT, as shown in Table 7.2. You can edit the listed files that are editable, and you can save your own versions of the separator files. To define a separator file, click on the **Separator Page** button. You can specify the separator file you want to use or use the **Browse** button in the Separator dialog box to search for it. The default location for the files is in the System32 folder in your Windows NT folder.

Table 7.2 Separator Files Provided with Windows NT

FILE	EDITABLE?	TYPE OF LANGUAGE	FUNCTION
sysprint.sep	Yes	PostScript	Prints a page before each document, switches printing to PostScript printing
pcl.sep	Yes	PCL	Prints a page before each document, switches printing to PCL printing
pscript.sep	Yes	PostScript	Switches printing to PostScript printing

The **General** page also enables you to print a test page. If you have defined a separator page, it will not appear before the test page.

The Ports Tab

The **Ports** page in the Properties dialog box, shown in Figure 7.12, enables you to change port settings.

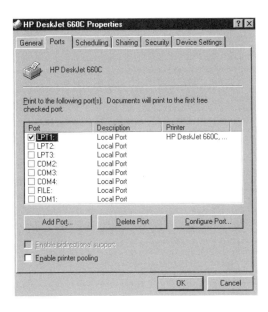

*Figure 7.12 The **Ports** page of the Printer Properties dialog box.*

Here, you can add, delete, or reconfigure a port. You can also select a different port for the printer output. For example, if you want to print PostScript output to a file that you can send to someone who has a PostScript printer, you can define a PostScript printer and send the output to the File port listed in the dialog box. If you send output to a file, users will be prompted for the file name when they send a print job to the "printer."

In this dialog box you can also specify whether the printer should use bidirectional support, and you can set up a printer pool. A *printer pool* is a collection of printers that all behave like a single printer. When you send jobs to the printer pool, the first available printer takes up the job and prints it. If you define a printer pool, you must also define multiple ports for the printer.

To ensure consistent results, all the printers in the pool should be identical (or nearly identical).

N O T E

The Scheduling Tab

The **Scheduling** page of the Printer Properties dialog box, shown in Figure 7.13, enables you to control scheduling and specify how the printer spools and prints jobs.

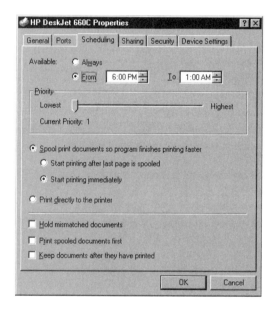

Figure 7.13 *The **Scheduling** page of the Printer Properties dialog box.*

At the top of this page are options to define the availability of the printer. This enables you to define a printer definition for sending large print jobs to a printer that prints jobs only at night. You can also use this page to set the priority of your printer from 1 (the lowest) to 99 (the highest). Because you can have multiple printer names and descriptions for the same printer, this option allows you to define a different priority for each description. For instance, if you want jobs from the marketing department to have a higher priority than development jobs, you can assign two names to the same printer. Then you tell the marketing folks to use the higher-priority printer name, and the development folks to use the lower-priority printer.

The other options on this page control how documents are queued and spooled. If you select one of these options and press the **F1** key, you'll see a detailed description of the option.

The Sharing Tab

The **Sharing** page of the Printer Properties dialog box, shown in Figure 7.14, enables you to share or stop sharing a printer. Shared printers can be used by other users on your network. Printers that are not shared can be used only by the computer they are attached to. There are many reasons you might want to change this property. Suppose a department printer is down for repair, and some critical jobs need to be printed. A supervisor might have a personal printer that is not shared but changes the definition so that others can print these critical jobs.

Figure 7.14 *The **Sharing** page of the Printer Properties dialog box.*

The Security Tab

The **Security** tab of the Printer Properties dialog box, shown in Figure 7.15, enables you to change security settings.

Figure 7.15 The **Security** page of the Printer Properties dialog box.

The button at the top of the page enables you to set printer permissions. If you click on the **Permissions** button, you'll see the dialog box pictured in Figure 7.16. In this dialog box, you set permissions for groups or individual users. The groups and their permissions are listed.

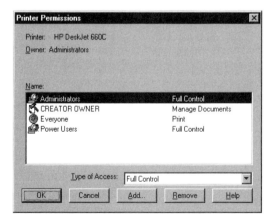

Figure 7.16 The Printer Permissions dialog box.

Controlling permissions for a printer is like limiting access to a file. You need to be the owner of the printer or be part of the Administrators group to change permissions. Four types of permissions are available for printers:

1. **No Access**. The assigned group members or users cannot use the printer.

2. **Print**. Group members or users are able to print.

3. **Manage Documents**. Users can control settings for documents and pause, resume, and delete documents from the queue. Permission for printing documents is not specified here.

4. **Full Control**. Users have full ability to change all settings for documents and complete control over the queue and submission of documents for printing.

Select a group and select a corresponding access under the **Type of Access** list box. To add a group, click the **Add** button. You will see another dialog box like the one shown in Figure 7.17.

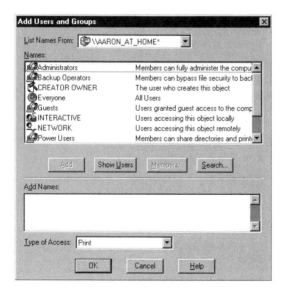

Figure 7.17 *Adding users or groups.*

Select the group you want to add as well as the type of access for that group. Once you're finished, click **OK**.

Two other options are included on the **Security** page: **Auditing** and **Ownership**. If you are an administrator, you can turn on auditing and then specify the printer actions you wish to audit. For example, you can specify that every time a print job fails, an event is generated for the Event Viewer. If you click the **Auditing** button, you will see the dialog box shown in Figure 7.18.

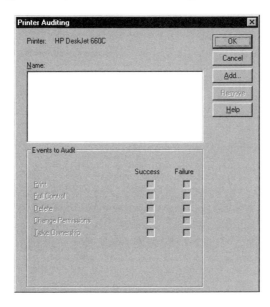

Figure 7.18 *The Printer Auditing dialog box.*

By default, no groups or users are listed, so none of the audit selections is available. You first need to add a group or user name to the list by clicking the **Add** button and choosing a group or user in the Add Users or Groups dialog box. After you select a group or user and click **OK**, this dialog box changes to enable audits, as shown in Figure 7.19.

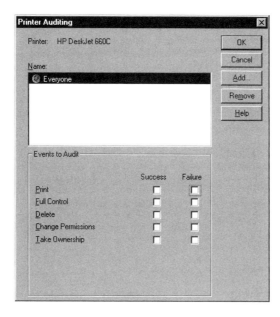

Figure 7.19 The Printer Auditing dialog box enabling audits.

Now you can specify audits, such as having an event generated for the Event Viewer whenever a print job fails or when someone successfully deletes a print job.

The final option on the **Security** page of the Printer Properties dialog box enables you to take ownership of a printer, such as when an employee leaves and someone else takes control of a printer. When you click the **Ownership** button, the Owner dialog box displays (see Figure 7.20).

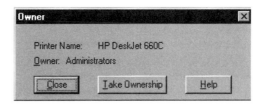

Figure 7.20 The Owner dialog box.

If you have the authority to take ownership of the printer, you can select **Take Ownership** and assume control of the printer.

The Device Settings Tab

The **Device Settings** page of the Printer Properties dialog box varies depending on your printer and the printer drivers NT is using to drive that printer. A fairly typical example of the dialog box is shown in Figure 7.21. The top half of the page lists options for the printer, and the bottom half lists possible settings for the option selected in the top half of the page.

Figure 7.21 The **Device Settings** page of the Printer Properties dialog box.

Changing Document Properties

To set default document properties, double-click the printer to open its printer window, as shown in Figure 7.22.

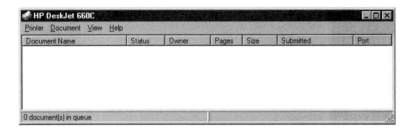

Figure 7.22 *The Printer window.*

In the Printer menu, choose **Document Defaults**. The [printername] Default Document Properties dialog box displays, as shown in Figure 7.23.

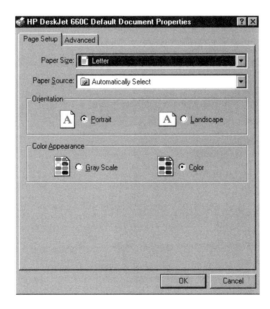

Figure 7.23 *The [printername] Default Document Properties dialog box.*

This dialog box has two tabbed pages. The **Page Setup** page enables you to set defaults for the paper size, source, the number of copies, printer orientation, color appearance, and several other options, all of them dependent on the printer drivers. The **Advanced** page enables you to set defaults for the preceding items as well as for certain printing characteristics that are also dependent on the printer and printer drivers. The **Advanced** page resembles the **Device Settings** tab of the Printer Properties dialog box.

Changing Document Properties at Print Time

You can change document defaults from within most Windows applications. Usually, there is a choice on the File menu such as **Printer Setup** or an **Options** or **Properties** button in the Print dialog box. When you select one of these options, you will see the dialog box pictured in Figure 7.23. However, the changes you make will be temporary, affecting only this document or print job.

Changing Document Properties for Queued Print Jobs

You can also change document settings for print jobs that have been sent to the printer, as long as they have not started to print. As shown in Figure 7.24, you can view the print job within the Printer window, which is opened by double-clicking the **printer** icon or by selecting the small **printer** icon on the Taskbar (next to the clock) that appears when you send a job to the printer.

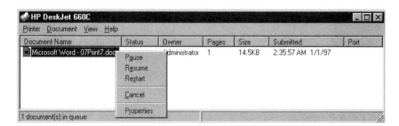

Figure 7.24 *Viewing a print job in the [printer] window.*

If you select the job and right-click, you will see the context menu shown in Figure 7.24. You could also select the Document menu, which lists the same choices. If you select **Properties**, you will see the dialog box pictured in Figure 7.25.

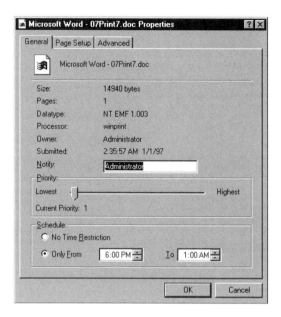

Figure 7.25 Changing properties for a print job.

Using this dialog box, you can change the priority of the print job, the time restrictions, or any of the **Page Setup** or **Advanced** options for the printer. Again, any changes you make apply only to the selected print job.

MANAGING THE PRINT QUEUE

After you've set up printing and the printers are working properly, you will rarely want to change any printer settings. However, you can still exercise some control over the printing process. You can view print jobs as they are spooled and printed. You can change job priorities and even reschedule spooled jobs. You can also manage remote printers and security.

Viewing Jobs in Progress

If you have connected to a printer, you can view its Printer window, as shown in Figure 7.26. You see the jobs in progress, their status, the owners of the jobs, the number of pages, the size of the jobs, the time jobs were submitted, and the ports or files to which the jobs were sent.

Figure 7.26 Viewing jobs in progress on a printer.

Changing Printing Order

If a very long job is queued before a short one, you may want to change the order. For some printers, you select the document by highlighting it and then click and drag it to the preferred place in the queue.

To alter the print queue, you must have the appropriate access privilege.

N O T E

Pausing, Resuming, and Restarting the Print Queue

You can interrupt printing of all jobs by clicking on **Printer, Pause Printing**. This selection is a toggle, so if you deselect it, printing resumes. You can pause printing for an individual job by highlighting it and selecting **Document**, **Pause** or right-click and select **Pause** from the context menu. You can resume printing by selecting **Document**, **Resume** or right-clicking and selecting **Resume**. If you want your document to begin printing again from the beginning, for example—perhaps paper got jammed in the printer—select the **Restart** option in the Document menu, or right-click and select **Restart**, as shown in Figure 7.27.

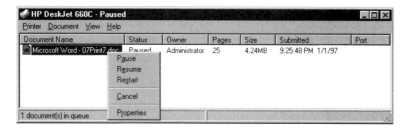

Figure 7.27 *The Printer right-click context menu.*

Deleting Entries in the Queue

If you want to get rid of entries in the queue, highlight them and click the **Del** key on the keyboard, or choose **Cancel** from the Document menu or right-click context menu. If you want to purge all entries in the queue, select the **Purge Print Documents** option in the Printer menu.

SUMMARY

With the Printers folder, it is possible to set up printers to be used locally or to be shared across the network. The Add Printer Wizard walks you through the process of setting up a printer or connecting to a shared network printer. You can change any of the printer settings after you have set up the printer by selecting the printer from within the Printers window and choosing **Properties** from the right-click context menu or selecting **File**, **Properties**. The Properties dialog box enables you to change a variety of settings specific to the printer definition.

You can set a pool of printers that act as one printer resource. You can define multiple printer definitions for the same printer. Combined with your ability to define access to your printer by different groups, this option allows you to have the same printer used by different groups at different times or at different priorities.

You can use the features in the windows for each printer to view the status of print jobs in progress. You can use information on the printer resources on the network to decide where you want to submit your document for printing. If you have authority to do so, you can also change the queue to allow short documents to print before long ones. And you can pause and resume the print queue or individual jobs in the queue.

CHAPTER 8

Messaging (E-mail)

One of the great features of Windows NT is integrated networking: the capability to access information and provide information to other computers and users. Applications that feature connectivity are becoming readily available. One example, *groupware*, helps increase the efficiency and output of a group of users. Lotus Notes is a pioneering application in this field, and applications such as schedulers and organizers also fall into this category.

Messaging applications are used to communicate with members of a group. Electronic mail, in its various forms and flavors, is a ubiquitous application in this category. Windows NT Workstation has an application called Microsoft Messaging that you can use to send electronic mail to your colleagues on Windows NT systems. With appropriate software, you can communicate with other mail systems, too.

NOTE

Microsoft has included electronic mail software in Windows for years. Microsoft Mail, introduced with Windows for Workgroups, was also included in the first versions of Windows NT. Microsoft Exchange Inbox was included in Windows 95. Microsoft Messaging is included with Windows NT Workstation 4.0, and Microsoft Exchange is included with Windows NT Server 4.0. Microsoft Office 97 introduces a new e-mail and scheduling program called Outlook. Internet Explorer has its own e-mail tool: Internet Mail and News. Which program should you use? If you are running Windows NT Workstation 4.0 as part of a network at work, that decision has been made for you and everyone else in your company. If that decision was to use Microsoft Messaging or Microsoft Exchange, this chapter applies to you. If you are running Windows NT Workstation 4.0 at home, you will probably choose to use the included e-mail package: Microsoft Messaging, which is also called Microsoft Exchange Inbox.

Microsoft Exchange Inbox and Microsoft Messaging are nearly identical, all-in-one e-mail programs. The name was changed to Microsoft Messaging for Windows NT Workstation 4.0 to avoid confusion with Microsoft Exchange for Windows NT Server 4.0. Microsoft Exchange is a big, expensive, complicated e-mail system designed for large companies. It includes the server version of the software that runs on the network as well as client versions that run on the clients. The client software for Microsoft Exchange looks almost exactly like Microsoft Messaging except that it includes several additional features. Windows Messaging, however, does not work as a client to Microsoft Exchange. You must install the Exchange Client software on the workstation to interface with Microsoft Exchange on the server. If your company includes many PCs running Microsoft Exchange Inbox, you can use Microsoft Messaging on the workstations to interface with Microsoft Mail running on the servers.

This chapter explains how to set up Microsoft Messaging as a client on a workstation that connects to Microsoft Mail on the server. If you are running Microsoft Exchange, your system administrators will handle the setup, but using the Exchange client software works as it is described in this chapter.

In this chapter you will learn about the following topics:

- How Messaging works
- Setting up Messaging

- Creating a Profile
- Using Messaging
- Using folders
- Attaching files and objects
- Using message templates
- Customizing Messaging
- Working offline

HOW MESSAGING WORKS

Messaging uses a *store and forward* technique. All mail messages are forwarded from a user's workstation to a centralized postoffice called a *workgroup postoffice* or WGPO. In Windows NT, the WGPO is a shared directory on a Windows NT computer. You access this postoffice to retrieve messages.

Let's say John sends a message to four people: Eric, Sara, Sandhya, and Mike. John's message is created first on his local computer. The message is then forwarded to the WGPO, which is shared by all these users. When Sara logs in to her Messaging account, she finds the waiting message from the WGPO. Each user runs a client application that retrieves mail from the WGPO. A *client* application is one that runs on a user's computer and interacts with a remote *server* computer. There is only one copy of each mail message in the WGPO, making it space-efficient. Whether John sends a message to one person or 10, only one copy of it is stored on the WPGO. If Sandhya wants to reply to John's message, she can compose a reply on her client application and then send it to John. The message travels from her local machine to the WGPO, where John can retrieve it. Once the reply message is retrieved by John, it is instantly deleted from the WGPO.

SETTING UP MESSAGING

Those who want to communicate with one another in Windows NT Messaging must belong to the same postoffice. A person who sets up a postoffice is called a workgroup postoffice administrator.

NOTE

The WGPO must be set up on a computer that is on at all times so that users can send messages at any time. It is recommended that a system administrator set up the postoffice and that this person use a system administrator account. The postoffice is set up using the Microsoft Postoffice applet in the Control Panel. After the administrator sets up the workgroup postoffice, this person can add users and create shared folders that all users can access. It is assumed that the postoffice will be created on a server, so we won't cover the procedures for creating a workgroup postoffice, adding users, and creating shared folders. A computer running Windows NT Workstation 4.0 can be used as the server and workgroup postoffice for Microsoft Mail. The Control Panel applet uses a wizard to create the postoffice, and the setup is fairly straightforward. In the first screen in the wizard, select whether you are creating a new workgroup postoffice or administering an existing postoffice. If you are adding users, specify that you want to administer an existing postoffice (see Figure 8.1).

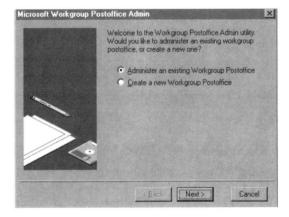

Figure 8.1 *The Microsoft Postoffice wizard.*

Creating a Profile

Windows Messaging maintains all the data on your information services, personal folders, and personal address book in a profile whose settings are stored in the system registry. Before you can use Messaging for e-mail, you must have a profile.

The first time you run Messaging by double-clicking the **Inbox** icon, the Windows Messaging Setup wizard runs, creating a profile for you automatically. Before you start the wizard, collect the information about your Microsoft Mail, Internet News, Netscape Transport, and any other services you want to use.

For Microsoft Mail, you need to know the following:

- Network path of your Microsoft Mail postoffice
- Name of your Mail account and password

Your e-mail administrator should be able to provide this information if you don't know it.

For Internet Mail, you need to know the following:

- IP address or name of the server to which you will connect for Internet Mail
- Your e-mail address in the format *user@domain*
- Your e-mail account name and password

For other services, the information required is usually the same as for Internet Mail.

After you've collected all this information, you are ready to create your profile. Follow these steps:

1. Double-click the **Inbox** icon on the desktop to start the Messaging Setup wizard. (It also runs when you add a new profile using the Mail and Fax applet on the Control Panel.) In the first dialog box, make sure that **Use the following information services** is selected. If you don't plan to use some of the services listed, deselect the check box next to those services. After you've made your selections, choose **Next** to continue (see Figure 8.2).

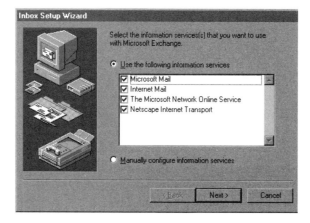

Figure 8.2 The Messaging Setup wizard initial screen.

N O T E

If you do not plan to use Microsoft Mail, Internet Mail, or any of the other services listed in this dialog box but wish to use some other service, select **Manually configure information services**. If you select this option, it is essentially the same setup as if you were adding services using the Mail applet in the Control Panel.

2. In the next dialog box, specify the name of this new profile and click **Next** (see Figure 8.3).

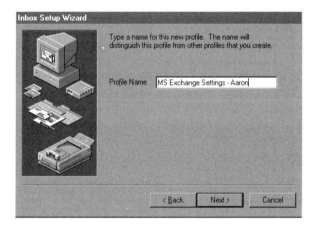

Figure 8.3 *Name the profile.*

3. In the next dialog box (which is the first for Microsoft Mail, if you chose that service), enter the path and location of your workgroup postoffice. Then click **Next** (see Figure 8.4).

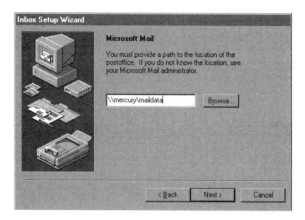

Figure 8.4 *Specify the path to the Microsoft Mail server.*

4. Select your name from the list of users. If you are not connected to your mail server when you create this profile, specify the mailbox name and password for your e-mail account on your Microsoft Mail server (see Figure 8.5). Click **Next** to continue.

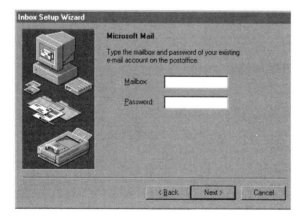

Figure 8.5 *Specify the mailbox account name and password for your account.*

5. In the first dialog box for Internet Mail, specify the service you use to access Internet Mail by selecting it from the list (see Figure 8.6). If you access Internet Mail through a local Internet Service Provider (ISP), it should provide you with the information necessary to set up Internet Mail in the Messaging profile. If your Internet Mail service provider is not listed, click the **New** button to set it up. If you are accessing Internet Mail through a local server on your network, your system administrator should be able to tell you whether you need to do anything to access that Internet Mail. Often, the server or postoffice will be set up to receive and send Internet Mail and you need not include the Internet Mail service as part of your profile.

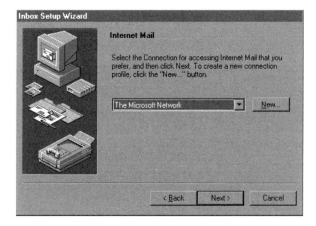

Figure 8.6 *Specify the service to use for Internet Mail.*

6. Under Internet Mail, enter the name or IP address (such as 240.97.144.15) for your Internet Mail server (see Figure 8.7). Click **Next**.

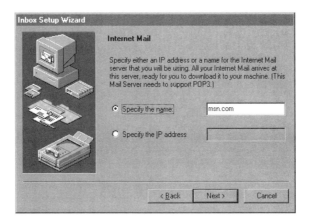

Figure 8.7 *Enter the name or IP address of your Internet Mail server.*

7. Specify whether you want to manually connect to your Internet Mail server by selecting **Off-line**, or select **Automatic** to have Messaging connect and transfer your Internet Mail at regular intervals (see Figure 8.8). Click **Next**.

Figure 8.8 *Specify how your Internet mail is delivered.*

8. Enter your e-mail address and your name as you wish them to appear in Internet e-mail messages (see Figure 8.9). Click **Next**.

Figure 8.9 Enter your e-mail address and name.

9. In the last Internet Mail dialog box, enter your mailbox account name and password (see Figure 8.10). Click **Next**.

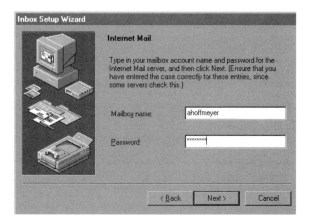

Figure 8.10 Enter your account name and password for Internet Mail.

10. Steps similar to those described for setting up Internet Mail are repeated for each service you want to use for e-mail. After you have completed filling out the profile information for all services, you are

prompted to enter the path and name of your personal address book (see Figure 8.11). Do not use the default name of the folder unless you are sure you are the only person who will be using Windows Messaging on this machine. Click **Next**.

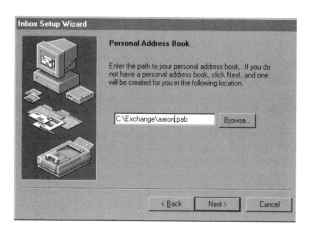

Figure 8.11 Enter the path and name of your personal address book.

11. Enter the name and location of your Personal Mail folder (see Figure 8.12). Once again, do not accept the default name unless you know you are the only person who will be using messaging on this machine.

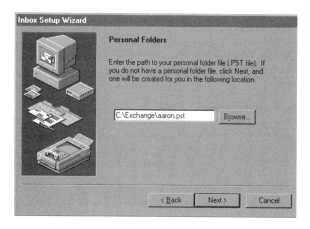

Figure 8.12 Enter the name and location of your Personal Mail folder.

12. Finally you will see a screen showing you which services you have set up (see Figure 8.13). Click **Finish** to complete the setup.

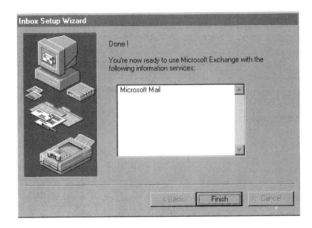

Figure 8.13 *Finish the setup.*

At this point you should be ready to start using Windows Messaging to send and receive e-mail. If you find that Messaging does not work, it is probably because some information you provided in your profile is not set up properly. You can change your profile using the Mail applet in the Control Panel.

USING MESSAGING

The rest of this chapter deals with the day-to-day process of using mail for communication.

Signing In to Messaging

If you've created a profile, you're ready to sign in. Click the **Inbox** icon on the desktop. Depending on how you have Messaging set up, you may be prompted for a password immediately. This is true if you are on a network and you are connected to your network mail server. However, if you are using Messaging at home, you won't see a sign-in dialog box until you try to connect to your mail server or provider. In this case, Messaging starts and you see the dialog box pictured in Figure 8.14. If you are prompted for an account name and password at this point, enter them and click **OK** or **Connect**.

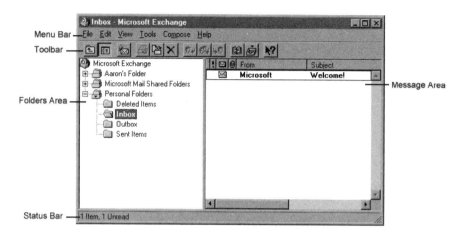

Figure 8.14 *The Messaging window.*

The Messaging Interface

After signing in to Messaging, you will see the window shown in Figure 8.14. This window is called the Messaging Viewer. It contains a Menu bar, a Toolbar, Folders and Message areas, and a Status Bar. The Toolbar contains the buttons for the most common operations you perform. You can create a message, reply to a message, forward a message, and manage folders (personalized collections of messages). You will see a number of folders listed (in Explorer format) in the Folders area. Among the default folders are Inbox, Outbox, Deleted Items, and Sent Items. If you are connected to a network or service that provides shared folders, you will also see the Shared folder, which will contain additional folders. The Inbox folder is used to view and manage all the incoming mail you have received. The Outbox is used whenever you work offline (when you are not connected to a mail server or provider) and you create messages ready to be sent. When you next log on to the network or service, the messages in your Outbox are sent automatically to their destinations.

COMPOSING AND SENDING MESSAGES

You can compose a message by clicking on the **New Message** button in the Toolbar (as illustrated in Figure 8.15), by selecting **New Message** from the Compose menu, or by pressing **Ctrl-n**.

Figure 8.15 *The **New Message** button.*

You will see a New Message window, as shown in Figure 8.16. There are three steps to the process of using the New Message screen: forming an address list, composing the message, and sending the message.

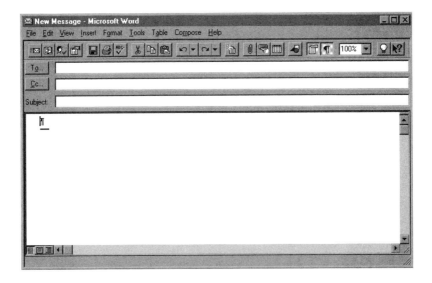

Figure 8.16 *Using the New Message window.*

Forming an Address List

To form an address list, you could type in names in either the To: the Cc: list box, but you might not know the exact spelling of a person's name. You also might not know whether the recipient is a member of your postoffice group. There's an easier way to retrieve the names: the Address Book. Click on the **Address Book** button, select **Tools**, **Address Book**, or press **Ctrl-Shift-b**.

Figure 8.17 The **Address Book** *button.*

You will see the Address Book dialog box, shown in Figure 8.18, which displays a list of names of people in your postoffice address list. You first should make sure that you select the correct address list at the top of the screen.

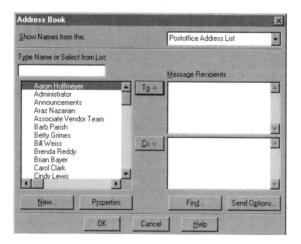

Figure 8.18 The Address Book dialog box.

After you have selected the correct address list, you can select from the names in the scrolling list area by highlighting the names with your mouse. To make multiple selections, click the first and last entries while pressing the **Shift** key.

You can select discontinuous names by clicking the first name and then clicking each subsequent one with the **Ctrl** key depressed. Add the selected names to the To: part of your message or the Cc: part of your message by clicking on the appropriate button after you have selected the names for each list. At the right side of the dialog box are two list areas displaying the names you've selected for the To: and Cc: fields.

Custom Entries

You can add names to the address book by selecting the **New** button near the bottom of the dialog box. You will see a dialog box like the one shown in Figure 8.19.

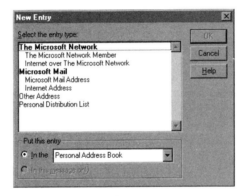

Figure 8.19 *The New Entry dialog box.*

Select the type of listing by specifying the type of entry to add and then click **OK**. For example, to send e-mail to a person's Internet address using your Microsoft Mail server (which must be connected to an Internet gateway), you would select the **Internet Address** type under Microsoft Mail. The resulting dialog box differs depending on the type of entry you specified.

The dialog box for the Internet Address for Microsoft Mail is shown in Figure 8.20.

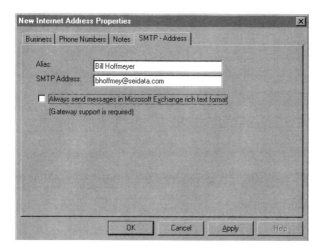

Figure 8.20 Adding a Microsoft Mail Internet address to your address book.

Here, you should the name and e-mail address of the person you're sending mail to. The details of the syntax depend on the specific gateway with which you are interfacing. Click **Apply** to create the entry, and **OK** to exit the dialog box.

Defining a Personal Distribution List

You can create your own personal distribution list as a shortcut for addressing people. Say you have 10 people in a development group. Rather than address each person with a mail message, you can put an entry for each of them into a personal distribution list. When you enter the list name in the To: field, all the individuals in that group will be addressed automatically.

To create a personal distribution list, select **File, New Entry**, or select the **New Entry** button in the Address Book. The dialog box shown in Figure 8.19 displays. **Select Personal Distribution List** as the entry type. The dialog box shown in Figure 8.21 displays.

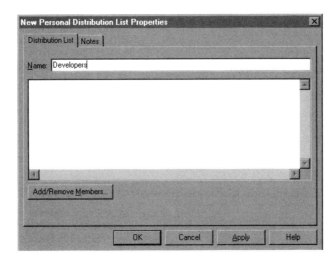

Figure 8.21 *The New Personal Distribution List Properties window.*

Enter the name (**Developers**, for example) in the Name field. To add members to this list, click the **Add/Remove Members** button. You will then see another dialog box, as shown in Figure 8.22.

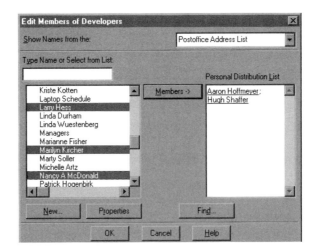

Figure 8.22 *Adding members to the personal distribution list.*

From the scrolling list at the left, select the members to add and press the **Members** button to add them to your personal list on the right. You can change the address list from which you choose members by selecting the list box at the top of the dialog box. After you've added the names of the members in this personal distribution list, click **OK**. The members are added to the list in the Personal Distribution List window (Figure 8.21). Click **OK** to save the list.

Thereafter, to send mail to all the members in this list, simply include the name of the list in the To: field of your message.

Checking Names

At any time, you can click the **Check Names** button (or **Compose, Check Names** or simply **Alt-k**) to verify that all the names you have entered are valid Address Book entries. You will be warned about any names that are not found in any of the various address lists.

Creating Message Text

Now you are ready to create a message (see Figure 8.23). The first step is to add a Subject: entry that tells the recipients what your message is about. This optional entry will be displayed in the list of messages in recipient's Inboxes. Then click your cursor on the body area of the New Message window and start typing. If your message recipient receives mail using a mail reader that supports rich text format, you can include special fonts, add color to your message, and even include pictures.

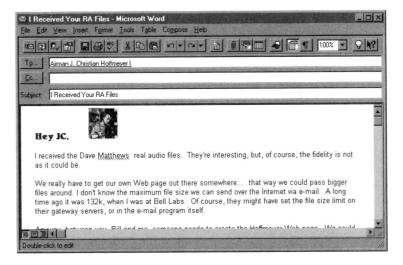

Figure 8.23 Creating a message.

Using Message Templates

Message templates are standard form letters that you can compose and save. If you need to do a weekly status report, you can create and save a template for it, including the format, subject, and addressees. Then you can tweak the template each week and spend the time you save on more important things.

To create a message template, create a generic form of the message you will be sending regularly. Then save the message using **File, Save As**, making sure you give it a name that you will remember. To send a message using a message template, select the template file using **File, Open**. Modify the message and send it.

Including Other Text Files

Your messages can include other text files—file created, for example, in the WordPad editor. (You will see more about WordPad in Chapter 11). Any ASCII file, which is a plain vanilla text-file format, can be placed in your mail message. You use the Insert menu's **File** option to insert a file.

Embedding Other Files or Objects

Messaging supports the object linking and embedding standard OLE2 so you can place other types of documents into your mail messages. For instance, you can include a file from Word, Excel, or Paint in your message. The files will be represented as icons; when the receiver opens the file, he or she will see the document.

You can also include objects by using the Clipboard. In another application, such as Paint or Word, copy the object you want to include using **Edit, Copy** or **Ctrl-c.** Then return to the New Message window and include the object using **Ctrl-v** or **Edit, Paste** or **Paste Special**. **Paste Special** gives you more control over how the object is included in your message. Figure 8.23 includes an embedded JPEG picture.

Attaching Other Files

Not only can you embed files from OLE-compliant servers—that is, from programs that support object linking and embedding—but you can also attach files. Attaching a file keeps the file separate but sends it along with the mail message. Imagine an envelope with a note, a floppy disk with an **.exe** file, or a floppy disk with a **.doc** file. Your note is like the mail message, and the floppies are like the attached files. The floppies can be removed from the envelope and put to use separately. This is how attached files work. You can attach any kind of file you choose, including program files, batch files, and document files. Once recipients get the message, they can detach the files. The Messaging system automatically compresses the file when a message is saved, so sending attached messages is efficient and does not hog network resources.

You attach files by clicking the **Insert File** button in the New Message window or by selecting **Insert, File**. You will then see the dialog box shown in Figure 8.24.

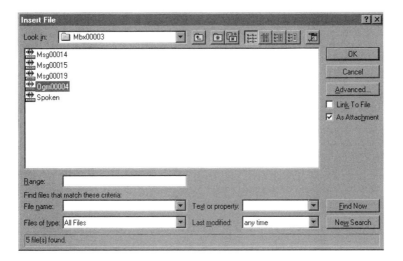

Figure 8.24 The Insert File dialog box.

Pick one or more attachments using the Insert File dialog box. Be sure to select the **As Attachment** check box at the right of the dialog box. After you finish making your selection, click **OK**.

You will notice, as shown in Figure 8.25, that when you apply attachments to your mail message, you see icons of the files you've attached. NT recognizes file types and will represent them with their appropriate icons. For files that are unknown to Windows NT, you will see a generic icon.

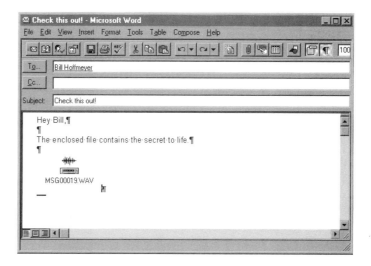

Figure 8.25 *A mail message with an attached object.*

Setting Send Options

Before sending your message, you can set options such as return receipt, a priority level for the message, or message sensitivity (Private, Personal, Confidential and so on). You set these options by selecting the **Properties** item on the File menu or by selecting the **Properties** button on the Toolbar. The dialog box shown in Figure 8.26 displays, enabling you to specify properties for this message. The options you specify apply only to this message.

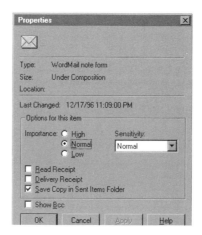

Figure 8.26 *The message Properties dialog box.*

Spell-Check the Document

If you are running the 32-bit version of Word or Microsoft Works or running another word processing program with a 32-bit spell-check utility, you can spell check your message before you send it. Choose **Tools, Spelling** or press **F7**. To change the way the spell checker works on your system, choose **Tools, Options** and switch to the **Spelling** tab, where you can set options and determine which words are ignored by the spell-checker.

Sending the Message

We have now composed a message, included an attachment in it, and even spell-checked it. To send it, just click the **Send** button in the New Message window (or select **File, Send** or simply press **Alt-s**). If you are connected to your mail server, your mail message is copied to the Outbox, where it is sent on its way. (Actually, it is delivered at the interval specified in the **Check for New Mail** setting or when you use **Deliver Now** or **Remote Mail** on the Tools menu.)

If you aren't connected to your mail server, the message is stored in the Outbox folder. The next time you connect to your mail server or service provider, you can send the message by selecting **Tools, Deliver Now** (and a service name if you have multiple mail services) or **Tools, Remote Mail**.

READING MESSAGES

You read messages in the Inbox (or any other folder) by double-clicking the message, by selecting the message and choosing **File, Open**, or by highlighting the message and pressing **Enter**. Figure 8.27 shows a typical message window.

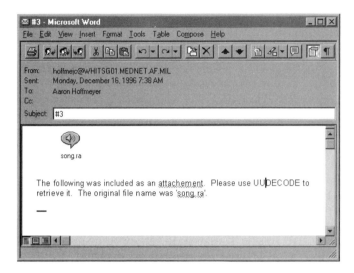

Figure 8.27 *Reading a message.*

If the message contains an attachment, as this one does, you can open the attachment with the associated application by double-clicking the attachment's icon. To save the attachment, select **File, Save As**. In the Save As dialog box, select the **Save these Attachments only** item, as shown in Figure 8.28.

Figure 8.28 *Saving an attached file.*

REPLYING TO A MESSAGE

To reply to a message, you must first have the message highlighted in a folder. Figure 8.27 shows a message being read. Notice that the Toolbar has a few more buttons available: **Reply to Sender**, **Reply to All**, and **Forward** (see Figure 8.29).

*Figure 8.29 The **Reply to Sender**, **Reply to All**, and **Forward** buttons.*

The **Reply to Sender** button sends a reply to the sender. The **Reply to All** button sends a reply to the sender as well as the other parties that were addressed in the sender's mail message. If you click the **Reply to Sender** button, a dialog box will open, as shown in Figure 8.30.

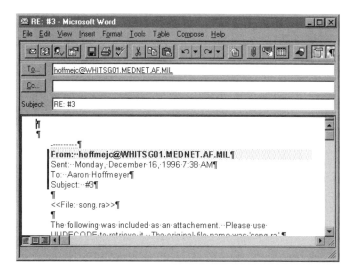

Figure 8.30 Composing a reply.

The body of text from the sender is included in the reply text. You can delete or edit the original message text if you want to. Compose a reply the same way you compose a message from scratch. When you are finished, press the **Send** button. The Subject field, which you can also change, shows the same subject that the sender sent with the RE: prepended to show that this is a reply message.

FORWARDING A MESSAGE

Forwarding a message is similar to replying to a message. When you are reading a message or have a message highlighted, click the **Forward** button. You will then see a dialog box that is identical to the Reply dialog box and the one in which you compose a new message.

DELETING MESSAGES

To delete messages, first select them using the mouse and the **Shift** or **Ctrl** key. To delete the messages highlighted, do one of the following:

- Click the **Delete** button.
- Select **Edit**, **Delete**.
- Right-click with the mouse and choose **Delete** from the context menu.
- Press the **Delete** key on the keyboard.

Any of these actions erases the selected files from your current folder.

N O T E

Deleted files are moved to the Deleted Items folder. This arrangement gives you a safety net if you delete a message and discover later that you need it. To save disk space, you should clean out this folder by deleting messages periodically.

FINDING MESSAGES

Suppose you have hundreds of messages stored in more than 20 folders. For a year, your administrators and power users have been sending updates on viruses. Now you have a program that is acting strangely, and you want to find the virus messages. You can use the Find utility to search for them. Select **Tools, Find**, or simply press **Ctrl-Shift-f**. As shown in Figure 8.31, you will see the Find dialog box.

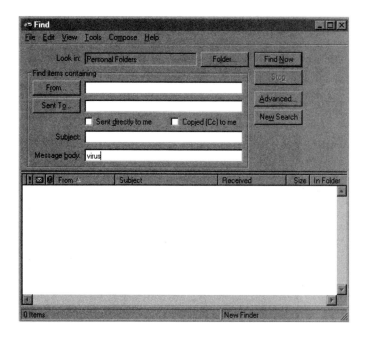

Figure 8.31 *Finding a message.*

The Find dialog box accepts a variety of information to help in the search. You can enter the name(s) of the person(s) who might have sent the message or the people they sent the message to. You can enter parts of the Subject field or parts of the body of text. In the example shown, Windows NT will search for all messages that contain the word *virus* in the message box. Click the **Find Now** button to begin the search. To halt the search at any time, click **Stop**. Any matches will appear in the Find box as they are made (see Figure 8.32). You can double-click on any message to read it.

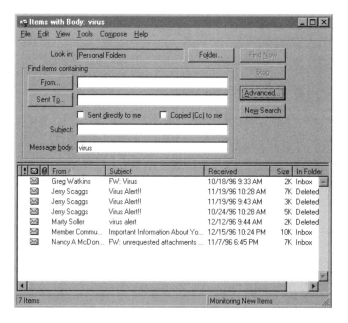

Figure 8.32 *Result of find.*

PRINTING MESSAGES

You can print an individual message or a group of messages from within Messaging. To print a group of messages, select them using the mouse and **Shift** or **Ctrl** key. Then do one of the following:

- Click the **Print** button on the Toolbar.
- Choose **File**, **Print**.
- Press **Ctrl-p**.

In the standard Print dialog box, specify the printer, number of copies, and other printer options. To send the print job to the printer, click **OK**.

USING FOLDERS

The left side of the Exchange Inbox or Messaging window lists the folders you can use in working with the messages.

Private Folders

To help you organize your messages, you can add your own personal folders to those listed. You can, for example, create folders for each project you are working on. Then you can move messages from your Inbox folder to these folders and minimize clutter in your Inbox.

Inbox itself is a personal folder. When the **Inbox** folder is open, the Inbox folder icon appears to be open. Other standard personal folders are Sent Items, Deleted Items, and Outbox.

N O T E

Shared Folders

In the Folder list you might see a Shared folder. Shared folders—those you share with your colleagues—are stored in the postoffice and can be accessed by anyone belonging to your postoffice group. Personal folders reside on your local hard disk and are accessible only by you.

Making a New Folder

To make a new folder, first make sure that **Personal Folders** is selected; then choose the **New Folder** option from the File menu in Messaging. You will see the dialog box shown in Figure 8.33.

Figure 8.33 The New Folder dialog box.

Type the name of your folder in the dialog box and click **OK.** The folder appears under the Personal Folders list, as shown in Figure 8.34.

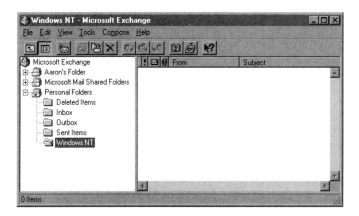

Figure 8.34 Your new folder.

Putting Messages into a Folder

All messages will initially come into your Inbox. You can move messages to different folders and delete messages from folders. The first step in moving messages is to select the ones you want to move. To select a block of contiguous messages, click on the first message and then click on the last message while pressing the **Shift** key. If the messages are not next to each other, click on the first one and click on the next ones while pressing the **Ctrl** key.

Next, click on the **Move Item** button in the Messaging toolbar; or right-click and select **Move** in the context menu. The Move dialog box appears, as shown in Figure 8.35. The list box shows the folders you've created. Select the appropriate folder and click **OK.** If you need to create a folder at this point, you can click the **New** button. Click **OK** when you are finished.

Figure 8.35 *Moving messages to another folder.*

You can select and drag messages to a folder instead of going through the menus. Just drop the messages over the folder and they will move there.

N O T E

WORKING OFFLINE

Suppose your mail server is down or you're working remotely and want to reduce the time you spend on your service provider to minimize charges. You can compose mail messages offline to send later. You load the Outbox with a stack of composed mail messages and then connect to your mail server. The messages will be mailed in the order in which you placed them in the Outbox.

CUSTOMIZING MESSAGING OPTIONS

If you intend to become a guru of Windows Messaging, you need to know how to use the Options dialog box to customize your messaging settings. Some of the most important features of Messaging are controlled using this dialog box, which includes seven tabbed pages. To access the Options dialog box, select **Tools, Options**. The dialog box appears, as shown in Figure 8.36.

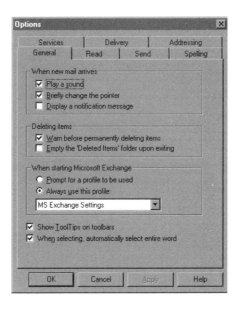

Figure 8.36 *The Options dialog box.*

This dialog box lets you change most of the default Messaging behavior. The **Help** button provides fairly detailed descriptions of the controls on each of the tabbed pages.

SUMMARY

Windows Messaging is a versatile communications program that enables you to send and receive messages using a variety of mail services. It is closely related to Microsoft Exchange Inbox, which is used in Windows 95 and Microsoft Exchange client, which is used if your company purchases Microsoft Exchange for your mail server.

To use Messaging, you must connect to an existing workgroup postoffice or create a new one, along with a user account for your machine; or you can connect to a mail service such as an Internet Service Provider. A messaging profile is created (using a wizard) when you start messaging for the first time on a machine or when you create a new profile. The wizard enables you to specify what postoffice or services you will use for e-mail, and how they will be used.

You can simplify the process of sending mail by using message templates and by creating personal distribution lists.

You can include a variety of fonts, colors, and objects in your messages, including pictures and sound files. However, if you are sending Internet mail, be aware that recipients' mail systems may not support the bells and whistles you've included.

You can use folders to manage message storage. The Inbox folder is the first point of entry for new mail. The Outbox folder is used to store any messages that need to go out. If you are connected to your mail server, outgoing mail is stored in the Outbox until the next delivery interval unless you select **Tools**, **Deliver Now**. If you are not connected to the network—such as when you are working remotely or there are problems with the network—the Outbox holds all messages you create until you connect to your network server mail server, or service provider.

CHAPTER 9

Command Prompt (MS-DOS)

Some users prefer the command-line environment of MS-DOS to the graphical user interface of Windows NT, especially for certain tasks. Windows NT supports the MS-DOS command-line environment in the Command Prompt program. Even though the icon for the Command Prompt shows an MS-DOS symbol, the utility accepts commands for Windows NT, Windows 3.1, and POSIX, in addition to the commands for MS-DOS version 6.x. The Command Prompt also supports network connections, letting you use network resources.

The Command Prompt is useful for transferring information from one operating-system environment to another, either by cutting and pasting, by redirection, or by piping. Redirection and piping are ways to transfer the output of one program to another program or file. You can also write and run batch programs from the Command Prompt environment.

In this chapter you will learn about:

- Getting started with the Command Prompt
- Configuring your Command Prompt window
- Running programs and batch files
- Using the command set and help
- Transferring information between protected subsystems (copying and pasting)
- Command history

GETTING STARTED

You start Command Prompt by clicking the **Start** button on the Taskbar and selecting **Programs**, **Command Prompt**. You will get a Command Prompt window, as shown in Figure 9.1.

Figure 9.1 *The Command Prompt window.*

You can exit Command Prompt by closing the window: Double-click on the Control Menu box (the MS-DOS icon in the upper-left corner) or the **x** in the upper-right corner. You can also type **Exit** as a command, and your Command Prompt session will be terminated.

Trouble-shooting

If you ever open a program in the Command Prompt window and the title of the window changes to **Frozen**, close the Command Prompt window by clicking the window's **Close** button. The Windows NT Security dialog box appears. Choose the **Task List** button and select the application's name from the list of Active Tasks in the Windows NT Task Manager (Figure 9.2). Choose the **End Task** button to close the application, in which case you'll lose any unsaved data. Choose the **Close** button to return to the open window and application.

Figure 9.2 *Closing an application using the Task Manager.*

CUSTOMIZING THE COMMAND PROMPT WINDOW

You can customize several aspects of the Command Prompt. You can change fonts and colors, and you can choose the default size of your Command Prompt window: full-size or window. To change any of the various properties of the current Command Prompt window, click the **Control** menu in the corner of the window and select **Properties**, as shown in Figure 9.3.

Any changes made this way apply only to the current Command Prompt window.

N O T E

Figure 9.3 *The Control menu Properties selection.*

The Command Prompt Properties dialog box displays, as shown in Figure 9.4.

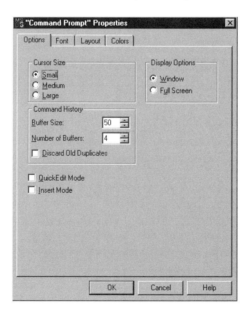

Figure 9.4 *The Command Prompt Properties dialog box.*

The dialog box has four tabbed pages that enable you to change general settings, the font selection, the screen size and position, and the screen colors.

Changing Options

The **Options** tab of the Command Prompt Properties dialog box (shown in Figure 9.4) enables you to change the cursor size, command history buffer size, edit mode, and window display mode.

Changing Fonts

You can change the font displayed in the Command Prompt window using the **Font** page of the Command Prompt Properties dialog box, shown in Figure 9.5.

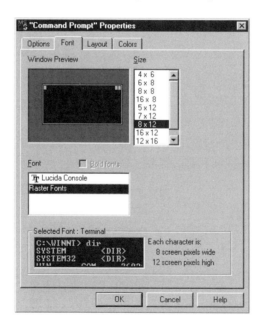

Figure 9.5 *The Font page of the Command Prompt Properties dialog box.*

The **Font** page has a list box of different font sizes. Scroll down to the size you want and select it; then watch the effect of your selection in the Terminal window. Once you are satisfied, click **OK**.

Changing Screen Layout

You can change the window size and position or the screen buffer size using the **Layout** page of the Command Prompt Properties dialog box, shown in Figure 9.6.

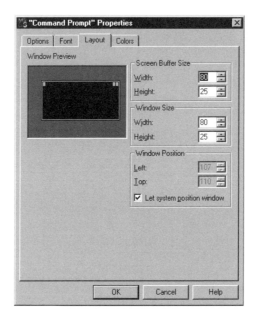

Figure 9.6 *The Layout page of the Command Prompt Properties dialog box.*

If the window size is smaller than the screen buffer size, scroll bars appear in the window. You can't resize a Command Prompt window to be larger than the current buffer size.

Changing Colors

The **Colors** page of the Command Prompt dialog box, shown in Figure 9.7, enables you to select the screen's text and background colors as well as the colors of the popup text and background.

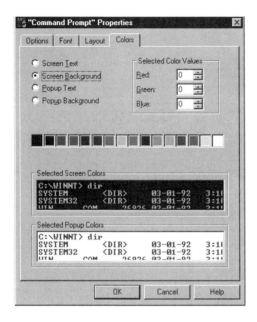

Figure 9.7 *The Colors page of the Command Prompt Properties dialog box.*

With your mouse, choose the radio buttons one at a time and select the desired color from the palette of colors. A dark black square will define your color choice, and the two windows below the colors will dynamically display the effect of your choices. You can also create custom colors by setting the **Red**, **Green**, and **Blue** values for a selected color in the **Selected Color Values** area of the page. If you decide to keep the new color configuration for the current Windows NT session, click **OK**; otherwise, choose **Cancel**.

Customizing All Command Prompt Windows

In addition to changing properties for the current Command Prompt window, you can make changes that apply to all future Command Prompt windows. You can modify the same settings for all future windows that you can for the current one, although the procedure is a little different. Instead of selecting the **Properties** item on the current window's Control menu, you select the

MS-DOS Console icon in the Control Panel. This action displays a dialog box that looks exactly the same as the current Command Prompt dialog box. Make your changes as described on the previous pages, and then click **OK** to make the changes apply to all future Command Prompt windows.

RUNNING PROGRAMS AND BATCH FILES

The Command Prompt gives you a virtual MS-DOS machine that can also call any of the other subsystems in NT. You can therefore run any program that you normally would run under MS-DOS or from within Windows NT's graphical user interface.

To run almost any program in Windows NT, you simply enter the name of the program. You can use the **cd** command (for "change directory") to move to the directory or folder where the program is located, or you can enter the path along with the program name and run it from a different directory. When you run a program this way, the current Command Prompt window is not available for use until you exit the program. If you want to start a program and retain the ability to use the Command Prompt window, precede the program name with the word **start**. The program starts and then NT takes control of the program and allows you to use the same Command Prompt window to issue additional commands or run additional programs.

To switch the Command Prompt application from full-screen to a window display or vice versa, use the **Alt-Enter** key combination.

N O T E

Batch files are programs that contain legal Command Prompt commands. These files are like transcripts of what you type during a Command Prompt session. When you start a batch file, each command in the file is run in turn. You can automate many activities this way. Suppose you want to execute 100 commands. You can create a batch file with 100 lines, each one having a different file-name argument or command; then you can start the batch file and go have a doughnut while it's processing. Or, if you wanted to, you could let the batch file process while you work with another Windows NT application in another window. Batch files can also perform conditional processing. *Conditional processing* uses statements such as **IF...THEN** to control which parts of a batch file get executed. Any MS-DOS batch file can be run in Windows NT. In addition, you can use the full Windows NT command set.

Breaking a Program's Execution

If you want to abort a program that is currently executing, type **Ctrl-C**, or **Ctrl-Break**. This can be done only for a command that is initiated without the **start** qualifier. To kill a program initiated with **start**, use the Task Manager. Press **Ctrl-Alt-Del** to display the Security dialog box. Select the **Task Manager** button. Select the **Applications** tab, as shown in Figure 9.2. Select the program to kill from the list and check the **End Task** button.

Pausing Output and Resuming

You can pause the output of a program in the Command Prompt by pressing **Ctrl-S** or the **Pause** key. If your program is spewing out data faster than you can see it, use **Ctrl-S** to pause the output. To resume the output, press any key except **Pause**. You can pause and restart the output as many times as you want.

OVERVIEW OF AVAILABLE COMMANDS

The best source of the available command set is found within the Command Prompt window itself. You can get a list of all commands from the Command Prompt by typing **help**. For help on a specific command, type **help** and the command name. For help on network commands, type **net help**. To list help for a network command, type **net help** *command*. To list syntax for a specific command, type *command* /?.

Windows NT commands are divided roughly into five types:

- Native commands
- Subsystem commands
- Configuration commands
- Utility commands
- Command symbols

Native Commands

Native commands are all Windows NT commands that have been made executable on the 32-bit subsystem. These commands take advantage of the operating system to its fullest extent. The majority of MS-DOS 6.x commands are native commands. Commands such as **dir**, **type**, and **copy** are all native commands. The command **net start alerter**, which starts the Alerter service, is an example of a new Windows NT command available from the Command Prompt.

Subsystem Commands

Commands for other protected subsystems, such as 16-bit OS/2 1.x commands and older commands for MS-DOS not implemented in 32 bits, are called subsystem commands. POSIX commands also fall into this category. Some examples of older MS-DOS commands are **debug**, **edit**, **mem**, and **share**.

Configuration Commands

Configuration commands are commands to configure your MS-DOS system to retain compatibility. Statements such as **Buffers=10** in a **config.sys** or **config.nt** file are considered configuration commands. Other examples are **devicehigh**, **dosonly**, and **install**.

Utility Commands

You can use utility commands for TCP/IP (Transmission Control Protocol/Internet Protocol) if it is installed on your machine. TCP/IP is a network protocol used with many UNIX installations, and Windows NT can run it to enable you to communicate with the UNIX world. A set of useful commands is associated with TCP/IP, including **telnet**, **ftp**, **ping**, **rcp**, and **finger**.

Command Symbols

Windows NT has a set of symbols that are used to filter input and output of MS-DOS commands. You can redirect output of a program with the > symbol. You can pipe output to another command, such as **more**, using the pipe symbol, |. These are command symbols.

COPYING AND PASTING DATA FROM THE COMMAND PROMPT

You can take information in a Command Prompt window and copy it to another application that's running in another subsystem. You can take the output of an MS-DOS program running in a Command Prompt window, for example, and copy the information to a Windows NT WordPad file. The easiest technique is to use the Quick Edit mode. To enable this mode, click on the Control menu of the Command Prompt. Select **Edit, Mark**. Using the mouse, select the information you want to copy (see Figure 9.8). Then select **Edit, Copy**. Switch to the target application and paste the previously selected text using **Edit, Paste** or **Ctrl-v**.

```
Select Command Prompt                                         _ □ ×
Copies files and directory trees.

XCOPY source [destination] [/A | /M] [/D[:date]] [/P] [/S [/E]] [/V] [/W]
                          [/C] [/I] [/Q] [/F] [/L] [/H] [/R] [/T] [/U]
                          [/K] [/N] [/Z]

  source       Specifies the file(s) to copy.
  destination  Specifies the location and/or name of new files.
  /A           Copies files with the archive attribute set,
               doesn't change the attribute.
  /M           Copies files with the archive attribute set,
               turns off the archive attribute.
  /D:m-d-y     Copies files changed on or after the specified date.
               If no date is given, copies only those files whose
               source time is newer than the destination time.
. /P           Prompts you before creating each destination file.
  /S           Copies directories and subdirectories except empty ones.
  /E           Copies directories and subdirectories, including empty ones.
               Same as /S /E. May be used to modify /T.
  /V           Verifies each new file.
  /W           Prompts you to press a key before copying.
  /C           Continues copying even if errors occur.
  /I           If destination does not exist and copying more than one file,
               assumes that destination must be a directory.
-- More --
```

Figure 9.8 Selecting text in Quick Edit mode.

N O T E

For Quick Edit to work, you must have the Command Prompt in window layout and not full-screen. To toggle between these two displays, press **Alt-Enter**.

To copy a graphic bitmap (a picture of your Command Prompt screen), press the **Alt-Print Screen** keys. A bitmap (**.bmp**) file of the active window—which should be your Command Prompt window—will be made. You can paste this bitmap file into any Windows NT application, such as Paint, that accepts it. Paste the image into the application you choose, paying attention to the current position of the insertion point.

COMMAND HISTORY

The command history is a popup box that lists the commands you've recently used. In the Properties dialog box, you can specify the number of commands stored in History buffer. To invoke the command history popup, press **F7**. The popup appears as shown in Figure 9.9.

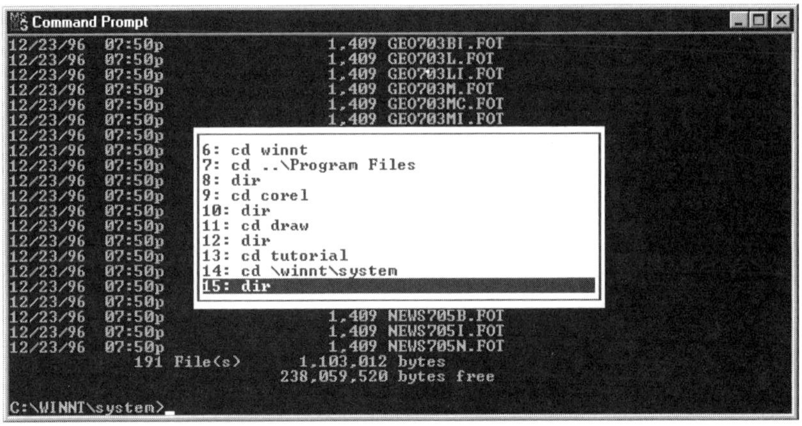

Figure 9.9 *The Command History pop-up.*

Use the arrow keys to select the previous command you wish to execute again and press **Enter**. The command appears in the Command Prompt window and is executed.

SUMMARY

The Command Prompt in Windows NT is a command-line environment you can use to run MS-DOS as well as Windows NT commands. You can also run commands from other subsystems and, and you can copy and paste from a Command Prompt window to other applications running in Windows NT.

CHAPTER 10

WordPad

You might have used Windows Write in a previous version of Windows or Windows NT. For Windows NT 4.0, Write has been replaced with a program called WordPad. As with Write, you can use WordPad to create documents with many different fonts, styles of characters, and page formats. WordPad now lets you open, edit, and save documents in the old Write format, Rich Text Format, or Word 6.0 for Windows format. You can also preview documents before you print them. WordPad is a little easier to use than Write, and it has much better support for embedding objects, a capability that opens a new world of possibilities.

In this chapter you will learn about:

- Editing features
- Putting graphics and objects into your documents
- Searching and replacing text
- Formatting features
- Printing and saving your documents

INTRODUCTION TO WORDPAD

Windows NT WordPad is a word-processing program that allows you to create documents, reports, letters, memos, resumes—almost any short document. WordPad does not have a spell-checker, a thesaurus, or many of the fancy features of the heavy-duty packages such as Microsoft Word or even the word processor in Microsoft Works. Nevertheless, WordPad is a capable tool with a wide array of fonts, styles, and features for creating and editing documents. It is provided with Windows NT 4.0 at no additional cost.

To start WordPad, click on the **Start** button on the Taskbar, and select the **Programs** folder, then the **Accessories** folder, and then **WordPad**. You will see the WordPad window, as shown in Figure 10.1.

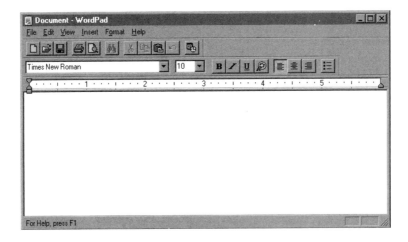

Figure 10.1 The WordPad window.

The menu bar at the top of the window has a few standard application menu items. Immediately below the menu bar are two rows of icons: the Toolbar and the Format Bar. A Ruler below the toolbars indicates the horizontal position and the left and right margins, and it displays tab stops, if any are defined. A Status Bar at the bottom of the window indicates the status of the **Caps Lock** and **Num Lock** keys and other useful information. When your text wraps beyond the bottom of the screen, a vertical scroll bar appears at the right side of the window. When the margins extend beyond the sides of the window, a horizontal scroll bar appears at the bottom of the window. The interface is pretty basic, but it's a major improvement over the interface in Windows Write.

NOTE

Windows Write did not have toolbars or a ruler, and it did not allow you to preview documents. It was limited in its support of embedded objects, and it did not have a direct connection to Microsoft Exchange. WordPad has these capabilities and more. WordPad not only was designed to be even easier to use than Write, but it also added some nice features. However, Write had some features that are not duplicated in WordPad, such as support for headers and footers and automatic page numbering.

EDITING FEATURES

You create a document by entering text, making corrections, perhaps moving paragraphs around, and inserting pictures or other objects—whatever you need in your document. The editing features you will use in Windows NT WordPad are similar to those found in other programs.

Entering Text

As soon as you open Windows NT WordPad, you are ready to enter text. You will get the same blank screen if you click on **New** under the File menu (to create a new document). A straight line symbol, called the *insertion point*, marks where you are about to enter text. The size of the line tells you the size of the selected font. (You will learn more about fonts in the section on formatting.) You can see this insertion symbol in the document displayed in Figure 10.2, which is a copy of this paragraph.

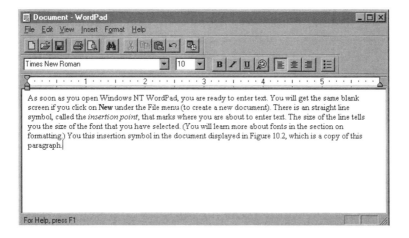

Figure 10.2 Entering text.

Adding Text

Add text by clicking the mouse at the spot you want to insert the text; then start typing. When you point in the WordPad window, the cursor looks like an I-beam. This shape makes it easy for you to point to spaces between characters. You are always in Insert mode. In Insert mode, characters that you enter replace any existing characters as you type. In Figure 10.3, notice that new text was added to the text in the previous figure.

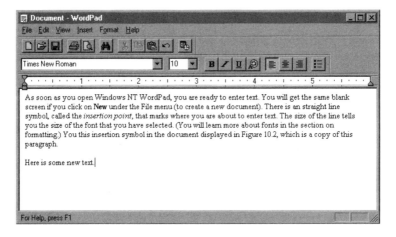

Figure 10.3 Adding text.

Word Wrap

WordPad enables you to change the way lines of text in your document wrap to the next line. If you select **Options** under the View menu, you see the dialog box pictured in Figure 10.4.

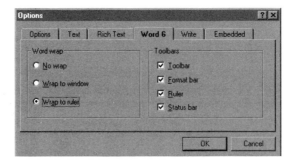

Figure 10.4 The Options dialog box.

You can set word-wrap options for each text format in which you save the document: Text only, Word 6, Microsoft Write, and Rich Text Format (RTF). The wrapping options affect only how text appears on your screen. When printed, the document uses the margin settings specified in **Page Setup** (under the File menu).

With word wrap turned on, you should continue typing text freely until you reach the end of a paragraph. At that point, press the **Enter** key to mark the beginning of a new paragraph. Whenever you press **Enter**, you force WordPad to end one paragraph and start a new one.

Selecting Text

You can select text several ways in WordPad. The first way is the click-and-drag method. Highlight text with the mouse by clicking with the left mouse button at the start point; then drag the mouse to an endpoint. The block of text through which you swept with your mouse will be highlighted, as shown in Figure 10.5.

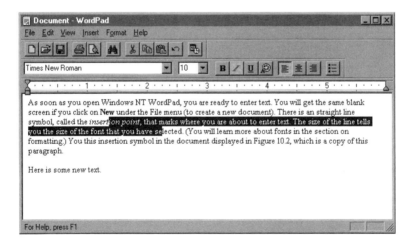

Figure 10.5 *Selecting a block of text by dragging with the mouse.*

You can also select text without dragging with the mouse. If you put the I-beam cursor anywhere over a word you want to select and then rapidly double-click the left mouse button, you select that word. It becomes highlighted, as shown in Figure 10.6.

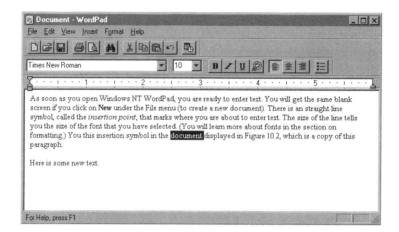

Figure 10.6 *Selecting a word by double-clicking.*

You can select an entire paragraph by rapidly triple-clicking within the paragraph. To select the entire document, choose **Select All** from the Edit menu.

SHORTCUT

The area to the left of the text is called the *selection area*, as shown in Figure 10.7. A special arrow cursor that points toward the top right part of the window appears when the cursor is in the selection area. If you click the left mouse button with the selection cursor next to a line, the entire line gets selected. If you double-click next to a paragraph, the whole paragraph gets selected. If you click while holding down the **Ctrl** key in the selection area, the entire document gets selected.

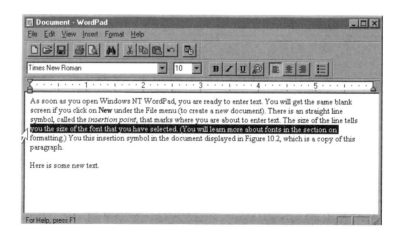

Figure 10.7 *Using the selection area.*

Deleting Text

Once you have a block of text selected, you can delete it by clicking the **Cut** option under the Edit menu, by right-clicking and choosing **Cut** from the pop-up Context menu, or by selecting the **Cut** icon from the Toolbar. If you find you made a mistake in deleting, that's not a problem; choose **Undo** under the Edit menu, or select the **Undo** icon from the Toolbar. You can also delete text to the right of the insertion point using the **Delete** key. You can erase characters behind the insertion point with the **Backspace** key.

Moving Text: Cutting and Pasting

Using the **Cut** command, you can move text around. First, select the text you would like to move; Figure 10.8 shows an example portion of text that needs to be moved. Cut this text, as shown in Figure 10.9. Place the insertion point where you want the text to be moved by clicking your mouse there. Finally, use the **Paste** option in the Edit menu to paste the text at the new location (Figure 10.10). (If you look at the Edit menu before you cut anything, the **Paste** option is grayed out, meaning that it is unavailable.) Choosing **Paste** will place the text at the insertion point, as shown in Figure 10.11. That's it. You have moved text from one place to another.

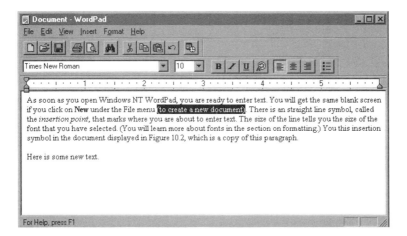

Figure 10.8 *Selecting text to be cut.*

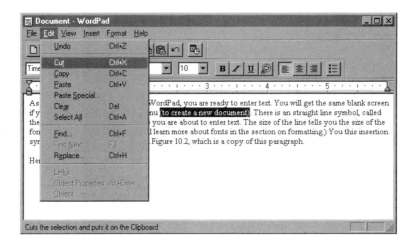

Figure 10.9 *Cutting the selected text.*

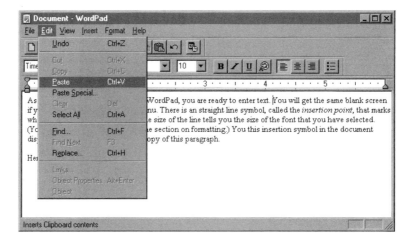

Figure 10.10 *Pasting text in a new location.*

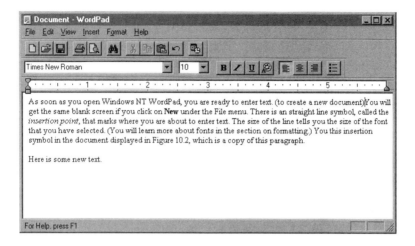

Figure 10.11 *After pasting the text.*

SHORTCUT

WordPad supports the Windows standard keyboard shortcuts for **Cut**, **Copy**, and **Paste**. The keyboard shortcuts are listed on the Edit menu, as illustrated in Figures 10.9 and 10.10.

SHORTCUT

You can continue to paste the last item that was cut. If you use the **Paste** option again, the same item will be placed at the current insertion point. This option is useful, for instance, when you need identical text or formats in various places in your document.

Copying Text: Copying and Pasting

Copying text is similar to cutting and pasting. But instead of cutting your highlighted text, you copy it using the **Copy** command. Select the text you want to copy and then use the **Copy** option under the Edit menu. Finally, select the **Paste** option at the new insertion point, and you have a new copy of the original. The original remains in its place, untouched.

Graphics in Your Documents

The Windows NT native drawing program, Paint, is a tool for creating colorful graphics images. You can take the files you generate with the Paint program (or any other graphics program) and embed them in your WordPad documents. Here's how: Cut or copy the portion of the graphics file that you want. This portion will be stored temporarily on Windows NT's Clipboard. The Clipboard is a storage area that enables different Windows NT applications to share data. (You will see more on the Clipboard in Chapter 16.) The next step is the same as pasting text; after placing your insertion point, choose the **Paste** option under the Edit menu. The drawing will appear next to the insertion point you indicated, as illustrated in Figure 10.12. (You will see examples of this process in Chapter 13 on Windows NT Paint.)

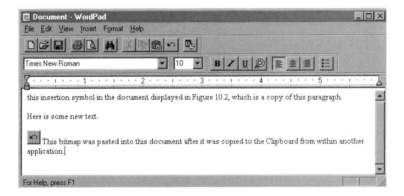

Figure 10.12 *Pasting graphics in your document.*

Objects in Your Documents

WordPad supports object linking and embedding (OLE). With OLE, graphics objects and other objects copied from the Clipboard and pasted in your document are *embedded* objects. OLE is probably the neatest feature in WordPad. You can insert any object made with any application that's registered in Windows NT to support OLE. WordPad will then allow you to edit that object—within the application it is associated with—by simply double-clicking the object. When you edit an OLE object, the application you are running transforms to the application associated with the object. For example, if you embed a Microsoft Works spreadsheet object into a WordPad document, the object appears as a simple graphic in WordPad. However, when you select the object, WordPad becomes the Microsoft Works spreadsheet application, where you can modify the object. When you are finished, click outside the object—in this case, in the WordPad document's text—and you are back in WordPad.

You can insert objects in several ways. The easiest way is to paste the object from the Clipboard after you copy the object to the Clipboard from within the application used to create that object.

You can also insert objects by selecting **Object** from the Insert menu. You'll see the dialog box shown in Figure 10.13.

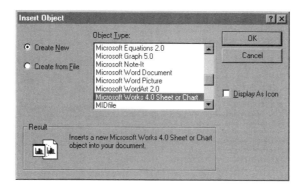

Figure 10.13 Insert Object dialog box.

This dialog box enables you to create a new object by launching the application from within the list of supported object types, or to create an object from a file. After you create the object, the object will appear in WordPad after you close the application associated with the object.

Let's look at editing an inserted OLE object. In this example, let's create a simple spreadsheet chart using Excel or Microsoft Works. After creating the chart, copy it to the Clipboard and then paste it into WordPad. You can paste the object in the usual way or choose **Paste Special** from the Edit menu, which enables you to *link* the object to its source. Any changes to the source will automatically be reflected in the WordPad document. When you double-click the object in WordPad to make changes to it, the source application runs, loading the associated document, rather than transforming WordPad. The spreadsheet chart appears as a graphic in WordPad, as illustrated in Figure 10.14.

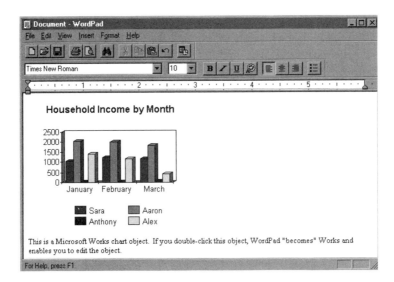

Figure 10.14 *WordPad with an embedded chart object.*

If you pasted the object into WordPad using **Paste**, when you double-click this object, WordPad changes its toolbars and menus to reflect the capabilities in the application used to create the object—in this case, Microsoft Works. This option is illustrated in Figure 10.15. You can now edit the object. If you linked the object using **Paste Special**, double-clicking the object runs the source application in a separate window, giving you full editing capabilities.

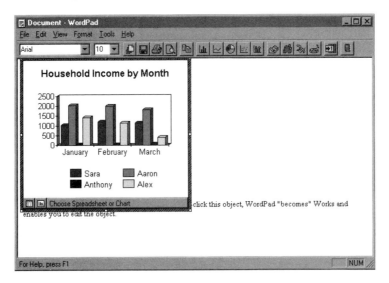

Figure 10.15 *Editing an embedded object from within WordPad.*

SEARCHING AND REPLACING

As you work with documents, you will often find yourself searching for text. If you have a long document and want to find the places where you used a particular word, an automatic search is the way to go. Scrolling line by line and searching manually takes too long.

Replacing one or many instances of text is another frequent task. You might, for instance, need to change all instances of the words *soda pop* to the word *cola*. An automatic search and replace feature helps when you need to make the same change over and over or when you want to change only a few of the occurrences, as long as there is a prompting feature to ask you whether to change a given occurrence. How do you perform these operations in Windows NT WordPad?

Search

To search, click on the **Find** option under the **Edit** menu. The dialog box you encounter, as shown in Figure 10.16, has a text box for you to enter the search pattern. You can click on two options: You can specify that you want a whole-word match only, and you can ask for the case to match exactly. A whole-word match on the word *to* would find only those instances of *to* followed and preceded by a space. If you did not click on this option, the words *too* and *top* would also show up as matches.

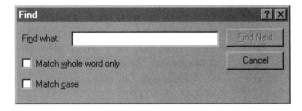

Figure 10.16 *The Find dialog box.*

When you're ready to search, click on the **Find Next** button. If you get a match, the matched text is highlighted in your document, as shown in Figure 10.17, and the Find dialog box remains waiting for your input. You can click **Find Next** again to get the next match, or you can click **Cancel** to close the Find operation.

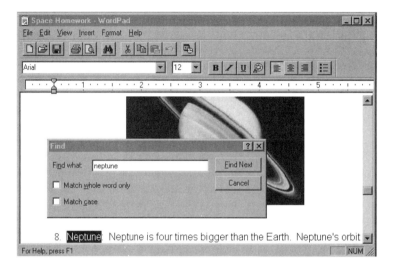

Figure 10.17 Successful find.

Search and Replace

To search and replace, you follow a similar procedure. Select **Replace** under the Edit menu and then fill in a dialog box, as shown in Figure 10.18, with the text string you're searching for and the one you want to replace it with. Choose the **Match whole word only** and **Match case** options, as appropriate, and then click **Replace**. This action will highlight the first match found in your document. To accept the replacement of the highlighted instance and move to the next match, click **Replace** again. You are ready now to accept the replacement of the next occurrence by clicking **Replace** again. You can repeatedly do this through the document if you need to replace only certain occurrences of the match. If you want to replace all of them, click **Replace All** at any point in the process. The **Find Next** button is provided for you to search for the next occurrence without replacing it.

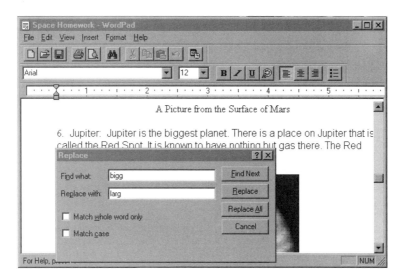

*Figure 10.18 Using **Replace**.*

N O T E The Find dialog box sometimes gets in the way of your ability to view the whole document. It's a good idea to move the Find dialog box to a place on the screen where it doesn't cover a large part of the document. This will make it easier for you to search and replace, because you will be able to see all matches readily.

FORMATTING FEATURES

Windows NT WordPad's format capabilities can make your document look impressive. You can format characters, bullets, paragraphs, and the whole document. You can change characters to italics or bold, choose from a number of fonts, and modify the line spacing and indentation. For document formatting, you can change margins.

The formatting options are accessible from the Format Bar and from the Format menu, both of which are illustrated in Figure 10.19.

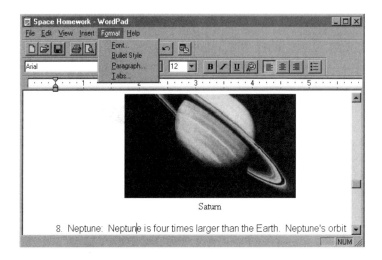

Figure 10.19 *The Format Bar and Format menu.*

Character Formatting

With Windows NT WordPad, you can underline, italicize, make bold, or strike out characters. These choices are more limited than those offered by a word-processing program such as Word, but they are adequate for many personal and business documents. In addition, a wide array of fonts is available. To change the format of characters, click on the Format menu and select **Font**, as shown in Figure 10.20.

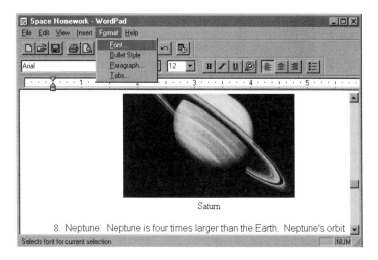

Figure 10.20 *Selecting **Font** from the Format menu.*

Formatting a Selection

You can apply formatting options to existing text by highlighting the text and clicking on any of the options in the Format menu or on the Format Bar. (This method also applies to Paragraph formatting.)

Formatting New Characters

If you have not selected any text, the formatting option you've chosen will apply to any new text you enter at the current cursor location. If you move the insertion point to an area that has a different format and start typing, the characters will share the format of the new context. This feature allows you to jump to any part of your document, regardless of its format, and type or edit as you please. The existing format of the text prior to your insertion will determine the format of any new characters you enter.

Fonts

Fonts come in many shapes and sizes. Select the **Font** option in the Format menu. You will see a Font dialog box, as in Figure 10.21. On the left side is a list of the names of the fonts available. In the middle of the dialog box is a list of the font styles you can choose. On the right side is a list box with all the supported sizes for a given font family. A **Sample** box below shows the highlighted font family along with the style and size options you have chosen. The message area in the lower-left part of the dialog box tells you whether the selected font family is a TrueType font. Fonts in the scrolling list area preceded by the double-T symbol are also TrueType fonts. For a TrueType font, the font you see on screen is displayed exactly as it will look when printed. The font selection available is the complete set of fonts you have installed for use with Windows NT.

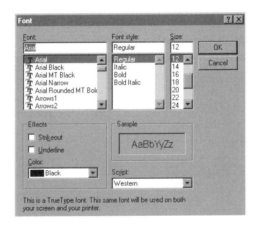

Figure 10.21 The Font dialog box.

Paragraph Formatting

Now that we've looked at character formatting, let's move on to paragraph formatting, which allows you to change the look of entire blocks of text. To change paragraph indentation and alignment, select **Paragraph** on the Format menu. The Paragraph dialog box, as shown in Figure 10.22, displays. You can apply these formats to existing text by highlighting the text and clicking on the option. If you set up an option with no highlight, the option will remain valid for all subsequent text you type in.

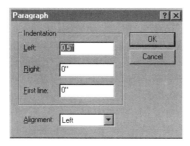

Figure 10.22 *The Paragraph format dialog box.*

Indentation

You can indent a paragraph's first line using the **Tab** key. An alternative is to use the indentation features in WordPad. To use this, type text in a paragraph without using any carriage returns (that is, without pressing **Enter**). WordPad does the line-feeds automatically with its word-wrap feature. When you press **Enter**, you start a new paragraph and the program uses the indentation settings in the Paragraph dialog box.

Figure 10.22 illustrates the paragraph indentation options. You can set the first-line indent in inches or centimeters (whichever is used in Control Panel). You can also set left and right indents, which amount to extra margins on the left and right side of your page. (You could use these indents to inset quotations, for example.)

You can also set the indentation using the Ruler. A small triangle at the top edge of the Ruler represents the first-line indentation of a paragraph, as illustrated in Figure 10.23.

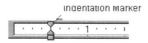

Figure 10.23 *The first-line indentation marker.*

You can change the first-line indentation for any paragraph by first clicking in the paragraph and then clicking on this marker and sliding it to the desired first-line indentation. This is illustrated in Figure 10.24.

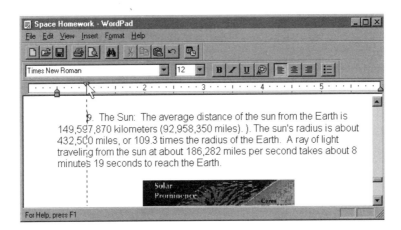

Figure 10.24 *Setting the first-line indentation.*

The two triangles at the bottom of the Ruler are also used to set indentations. The one on the left sets the left indentation of the paragraph for all lines after the first. The triangle at the right end of the Ruler sets the right indentation for the Ruler. The little square below the left triangle is used to set the left and first line indentations simultaneously.

Text Alignment

Text can be aligned with either margin. In addition, you can center-align text, which is useful if you are, for example, entering your name and address at the center of the top of a resume. If you choose the conventional left-margin alignment, your text will look jagged on the right edge. If you choose right-margin alignment, text will be aligned with the right margin. Click on the choice you want in the drop-down menu selection in the Paragraph dialog box (shown in Figure 10.22): **Left**, **Centered**, or **Right** alignment. The alignment options are also included on the Format Bar, as illustrated in Figure 10.25.

Figure 10.25 *The alignment options on the Format Bar.*

Document Formatting

With document formatting, you can select options that apply to the whole document. You can set and clear tabs and margins and choose the page orientation.

Margins and Page Orientation

To define the top, bottom, left, and right margins and set the page orientation, choose **Page Setup** from the File menu. The Page Setup dialog box (illustrated in Figure 10.26) displays.

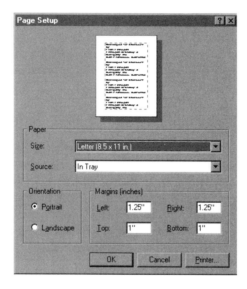

Figure 10.26 *The Page Setup dialog box.*

Use this dialog box to define the left and right margins and set the page orientation. You can also specify the paper size and printer page source and select the printer.

Tab Settings

Click on the **Tabs** option in the Format menu. The Tabs dialog box opens up, as shown in Figure 10.27. In the **Tab stop position** entry box, you list where you want tabs. After entering the tab stop position, click on **Set** to set the position and add it to the list of entries.

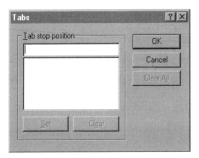

Figure 10.27 *Changing tab settings.*

Set tab stops for one inch and two inches and click **OK**. Notice the L-shaped character that appears on the Ruler at the 1-inch and 2-inch marks, as illustrated in Figure 10.28. This is the tab stop character for the Ruler. You can reposition these tab stops by clicking on them and moving them with the mouse.

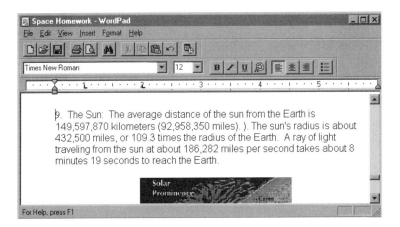

Figure 10.28 *The tab stop characters on the Ruler.*

SHORTCUT

You can also add or remove tab stops on the Ruler by using the mouse. To add a new tab stop, click on the Ruler at the desired tab stop location. A new tab stop character appears there. To remove a tab stop, click on it and drag it off the Ruler onto the page and release the mouse button. The tab stop disappears from the Ruler.

PRINTING AND SAVING DOCUMENTS

Before you print your document, you should save it. To minimize wasted paper, you should also preview your document to make sure that you get what you want on the printed page.

Saving Documents

To save documents in WordPad, choose the **Save** or **Save As** option under the File menu. A fairly standard Windows NT Save dialog box, as illustrated in Figure 10.29, displays.

Figure 10.29 *The Save As dialog box.*

Click on the **Save in** drop-down menu if you want to save the file in a location other than the current directory. Enter the name of the file in the **File name** entry box. Click on the **Save as type** drop-down list box to select the format or type for the document. The choices are **Word for Windows 6.0**, **Rich Text Format (RTF)**, **Text Document** (standard ASCII), and **Text Document - MS-DOS Format**. After making all your selections, click the **Save** button. Your file is saved with the name and in the file type and location you specified.

Previewing Documents

To preview your document, select **Print Preview** under the File menu. The WordPad window changes to allow you to preview your document as it will appear when printed, as shown in Figure 10.30. The margins are denoted with broken lines (they don't appear on the printout).

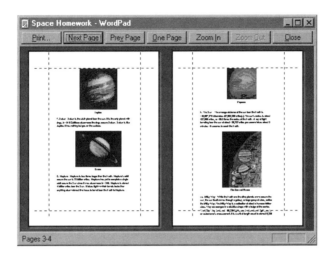

Figure 10.30 *The Print Preview window.*

A button bar at the top of the window contains the controls for the Print Preview window. This window lets you change the page you are viewing using the **Next Page** and **Previous Page** buttons. It also enables you to view one page of the document or two pages side by side using the **One Page/Two Page** toggle button. You can zoom in on an area of the page to see more detail. When you are finished previewing your document, you can send it to the printer with the **Print** button. To close the preview and go back to the normal WordPad view, use the **Close** button.

Printing Documents

To print a document from Windows NT WordPad, choose the **Print** option under the File menu. The Print dialog box, which is standard within most Windows NT applications, displays, as shown in Figure 10.31.

You need to select the range of pages to print. You can print to a file, for later printing. You can select multiple copies by typing in the number of copies in the **Copies** area. If you do not want to print to the default printer listed at the top of the dialog box, click on the **Printer Name** drop-down list box and select an alternative printer. Click **OK** after your options are set.

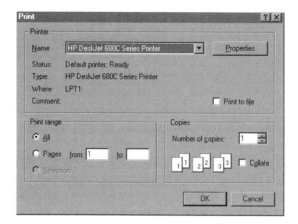

Figure 10.31 *The Print dialog box.*

SUMMARY

Windows NT WordPad is a word-processing program that's useful for drafting personal and business documents quickly. Although you won't find many fancy options, you can use the vast array of fonts available to Windows NT as well as some simple formatting options. You can format documents at the character, paragraph, or document level. You can change the style of characters from boldface to italics, and you can also change their size. At the paragraph level, you can change line spacing and the indentation and justification of paragraphs. At the document level, you have options to set margins. You can import graphics or objects from programs such as Windows NT Paint or copy in text from any text file. You can save your document in Word for Windows 6.0, RTF, or as an ASCII text file without formatting. Before you print your documents, you can preview the printed page.

CHAPTER 11

Internet Explorer

Internet Explorer is Microsoft's successful entry into the competitive world of Web browsers. Web browsers allow users to view specially formatted information from all parts of the globe via the Internet and the World Wide Web. The Internet is a huge network of computers that can communicate with one another. The World Wide Web, a subset of the Internet, allows access to information stored in HyperText Markup Language (HTML) documents. This information may include text, images, sound and video clips, programs, and even 3-D virtual reality environments. Internet Explorer, which is bundled with Windows NT 4.0 and Windows 95, provides a simple and attractive interface to the Web.

In this chapter you will learn how to:

- Get started with Internet Explorer
- Use the Internet Explorer interface

- Find your way around the Internet
- Fine-tune Internet Explorer

BEFORE YOU START

You will need to check a few things before you start exploring the World Wide Web. First, check that the Internet Explorer icon is on your desktop. The icon looks like a globe under a magnifying glass and is usually titled **The Internet**. If the icon is not present, you can install it through Windows NT's Add/Remove Programs applet. You will find this applet in the Control Panel. Once the Add/Remove Programs dialog box has appeared, click on the **Windows NT Setup** tab. Select **Accessories** from the components list and click on the **Details** button. Internet Explorer is part of the Internet Jumpstart Kit. Select the kit and press **OK**. Select **OK** in the Add/Remove Programs dialog box, and Windows NT will install Internet Explorer for you.

The next thing you will need is an Internet connection. Double-click the **Internet** icon on your desktop. Until you have successfully set up a connection, opening this icon runs the Internet Connection Wizard (Figure 11.1). If you have another browser, such as Netscape, on your computer, you can use the same connection for Internet Explorer. Select **Current**, which imports your current settings into Explorer. If you do not have another browser, you can follow the **Automatic** route to set up an account with the Microsoft Network (MSN) or choose **Manual** to select your own account.

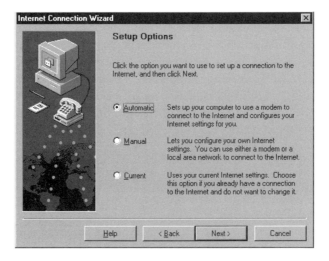

Figure 11.1 The Internet Connection Wizard.

To set up an Internet account, you will need Internet access either through an Internet Service Provider (ISP), a provider such as Microsoft Network, or via a local area network (LAN). If you want to access the Internet using an Internet service provider, you must contact the ISP and set up an account. ISPs include national networks, such as Netcom or PSINet, or they may be available locally. Write down all the account information your ISP provides you, such as your user name, password, SMTP and POP addresses, and the phone number for the connection. If you are connecting over a LAN, talk to your network administrator about how to configure your system to access the Internet. If you want to access the Internet using MSN, the Wizard will help you set up an account or connect to an existing account.

The Wizard walks you through the process of setting up Internet Explorer to surf the Internet. This chapter will not discuss the specifics of what you will see in the Wizard, because it differs depending on the kind of connection you are using.

STARTING INTERNET EXPLORER

After you've set up the Internet connection using the Wizard, you are ready to start using Internet Explorer. To start it up, double-click the **Internet** icon. If you are accessing the Internet over a LAN, Internet Explorer will start up and connect to your home page immediately. If you are dialing an ISP or service such as MSN, Internet Explorer will open your Internet connection dialog box. Clicking on **Connect** will cause your modem to initialize and dial your Internet service provider. Once the modem has completed the connection, Internet Explorer will load its designated home page, usually the Microsoft Internet Explorer page. You can specify a different home page through a procedure we will discuss in a minute.

After Internet Explorer has loaded its home page, you should see a screen that looks something like Figure 11.2.

If your screen looks somewhat different, it is probably because you are not using the latest version of Internet Explorer (as of this writing, the newest version was 3.01). Having the latest version will certainly increase your enjoyment of the Web, but it is not crucial. Most of the menus and buttons will function similarly, because the language of the Web (HTML) is designed to be fairly backward-compatible. If you would like the latest version, we will discuss how to download it from Microsoft at the end of the chapter.

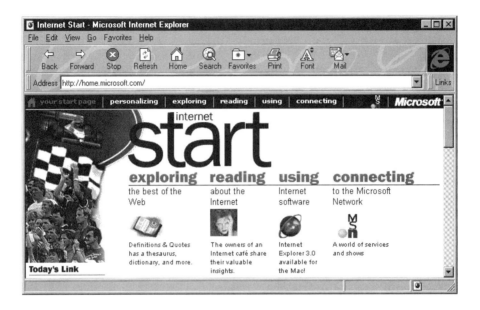

Figure 11.2 *The Internet Explorer home page.*

THE INTERNET EXPLORER WINDOW

The Internet Explorer window is divided into two parts: browser controls and the Page View. It is important to distinguish between the parts, because they have very different functions. The browser controls include the Menu Bar, the Toolbar and the Address Bar (Figure 11.3).

Figure 11.3 *The Browser Controls.*

The browser controls govern which page Internet Explorer loads into the Page View area and determine how that page is displayed. Because many Web pages have minimal formatting, you may want to adjust things such as font size, background color, and text color. (Some pages define the text and background colors, and you can't override them.) You can also save or print pages, view a page's HTML source code, and set passwords using the browser controls.

The Page View area is where Internet Explorer interprets and displays the content of each Web page (Figure 11.4). Through helper applications, called plug-ins, Internet Explorer can display a wide array of content, ranging from static text to animations, sound clips and short movies.

Figure 11.4 The Page View showing a page containing many links.

Web pages also contain controls called *hypertext links.* Hypertext links are normally designated by underlined and highlighted (colored) text but can also appear as images or buttons. When you click on a hypertext link, a new page usually starts to load in Internet Explorer. However, some links initiate file downloads, others run animations or play sounds, and still others activate special page controls that allow you to fill out forms and send information to a remote site. Many types of links are possible in the millions of Web pages on the Internet. With some links, your mouse cursor changes to a hand when it is hovering over the link.

The Browser Controls

Each browser control has a set of functions to help you get around.

The Menu Bar (Figure 11.5) contains the typical Windows menus File, Edit, and View. It also contains menus particular to browsers: **Go** and

Favorites. **Go** provides a list of navigation options, and **Favorites** allows you to access a list of your favorite Web pages. The Help menu provides information about various features.

Figure 11.5 The Menu Bar.

The Toolbar, shown in Figure 11.6, provides shortcuts for many of the menu options.

Figure 11.6 The Toolbar.

When you hover over a button with the mouse cursor, Internet Explorer raises the button and changes its color. The first two buttons, **Back** and **Forward**, allow you to load pages you've viewed previously. This feature is especially helpful when you are viewing a series of related pages, such as a catalog of products or online software documentation. The next three buttons allow you to stop the current page from loading, reload the current page, or go to your home page. **Search** takes you directly to Microsoft's Search page, and **Favorites** displays a list of your favorite sites. The **Print** button prints the current page, the **Font** button changes the page's font size, and the **Mail** button activates Microsoft's Internet Mail or Microsoft Exchange, depending on how you access your electronic mail.

The Address Bar allows you to type in Internet addresses (also known as Uniform Resource Locators, or URLs) or click on several selected sites, such as Microsoft's Search and Best of the Web pages. The Address Bar has two settings, which you can toggle by depressing the vertical double bar at the left of the Links area or Address area. For one toggle, the URL of the Web site fills almost the entire width of the window, and only the word *Links* of the Links area is visible. For the other toggle, the links area is visible, revealing a series of predefined Links that Microsoft thinks you might enjoy checking out. You can also grab the vertical double bar to the immediate left of the Links area and slide it to the left and right to reveal a combination of the URL address and the predefined links. You might prefer leaving a smaller address area that enables you to see all the predefined links, as shown in the bottom view in Figure 11.7.

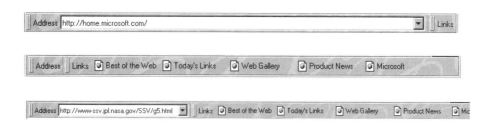

Figure 11.7 Three modes, or views, of the Address Bar.

In the address text area, you can enter any valid URL for registered Web pages, such as *www.pepsi.com*, and the browser will attempt to connect to that Web site. For many companies, you can guess the name of the Web page and often get it right. You can also click on the pull-down menu button at the right end of the text area and select previously entered addresses.

If you select any of the links buttons, such as **Best of the Web** or **Web Gallery**, you'll see a link to one of Microsoft's predefined pages, where you'll find useful information and tools, as shown in Figure 11.8.

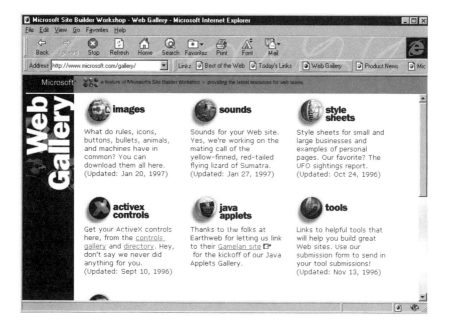

Figure 11.8 The Microsoft Web Gallery page, a predefined link on the Address Bar.

The Page View Controls

The Page View controls are inherent to the Web. The founders of the Web organized it around a technology called hypertext, which links the contents of one page to a series of other pages (Figure 11.9). In Internet Explorer, you can cause a related page to load by clicking on its highlighted hypertext reference in the current page. For example, to load a page about Henry VIII in a page about England, you would click on the text that reads Henry VIII. Page designers might also indicate links through images, buttons, menu bars, and pick lists. If you are new to the Web, this arrangement might seem confusing at first. However, with experience, you will be able to readily identify links from nonlinks.

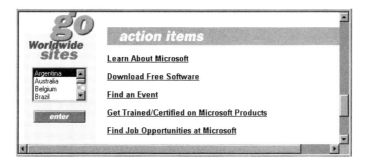

Figure 11.9 *Nearly everything on this page is a link.*

At the bottom of the Page View is the Status Bar, which provides feedback on page links. For example, if you placed the cursor over the **Learn About Microsoft** link, the Status Bar would display the link's address, such as **Shortcut to** *www.microsoft.com/mscorp*. While you're loading a page, the Status Bar indicates the page's progress using a blue bar at the right corner, as shown in Figure 11.10. When the bar is completely blue, the page has finished loading.

Figure 11.10 *The Status Bar.*

GOING PLACES

Now that you are familiar with Internet Explorer's interface, it is time to start going places on the Web. If you know the address of a page, it is often easiest to type that address into the box on the Address Bar and press **Enter**. You can also choose **Open** on the File menu. This action will display the Open dialog box, shown in Figure 11.11.

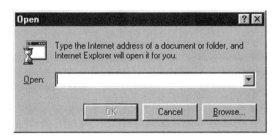

Figure 11.11 *The Open dialog box.*

Type in the address and press **OK**. Note that it is important for you to type the address exactly as it reads. Web servers are not forgiving of extra spaces or missing characters.

After you arrive at the desired page, you can follow its links to other pages. To click on a link, move the cursor over the link until it becomes a hand. Depressing the left mouse button loads the linked page. If you load the wrong page or wish to return to a previous page, press the **Back** button on the Toolbar. Keep pressing the **Back** button until you load the desired page. You can also move forward through the list by pressing the **Forward** button. Or you can go to a previously viewed page directly by selecting it from the History list on the Go menu, as shown in Figure 11.12.

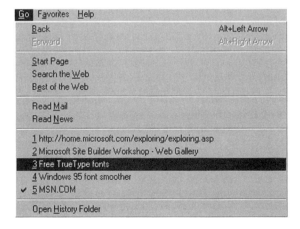

Figure 11.12 *The History listing on the Go menu.*

If you do not know an address, the Internet provides many ways to search for it. Some of the most popular search engines include Yahoo, Lycos, and Alta Vista. Microsoft gives you an easy way to use these search engines by providing a general Search page (Figure 11.13). You can reach this page by pressing the **Search** button on the Toolbar.

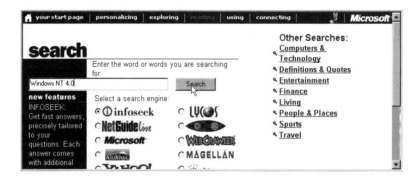

Figure 11.13 The Microsoft Search page.

Type in a few words that describe what you are looking for and click the **Search** button. The search engine will bring up an index of pages related to the words you entered.

Favorite Places

If you often visit certain places on the Internet, you will not want to repeatedly type or click your way there. Internet Explorer provides an easy way to add an Internet site to your desktop. With a favorite location loaded into the Page View, click on the **Create Shortcut** option on the File menu. Internet Explorer will inform you that a shortcut for the page has been placed on your desktop. Clicking on this shortcut will start Internet Explorer and go directly to the page.

If you also have Netscape Navigator on your computer, Internet Explorer will import your Netscape bookmarks and make them available. You can add a page to your bookmarks by selecting **Add Favorites** using either the **Favorites** button or the Favorites menu, as shown in Figure 11.14.

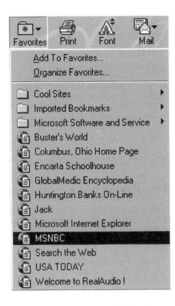

Figure 11.14 The Favorites menu and Toolbar pull-down menu.

SAVING PAGES

If connection time is at a premium, you can save Web pages and view them later offline. When a page you wish to save is in the Page View, select **Save as File** on the File menu. A dialog box will ask you where you wish to save the file. Give the file a name and click **OK**. When you are offline, click on the **Internet** icon but do not connect to the Internet. Internet Explorer will continue to load. Return to the File menu and choose Open. In the Open dialog box, enter the path to your saved file or use Browse to locate it. Internet Explorer will load the saved file into the Page View. Unfortunately, you cannot save images when you save a page as a file, so the page will look somewhat different. However, you can now read it at your leisure.

VIEWING A PAGE'S SOURCE CODE

If you are interested in Web page design, viewing a page's source code is an excellent way to learn the latest tricks. Select Source from the View menu. Internet Explorer will open a Notepad window to display the code, as shown in Figure 11.15. You will need to know a little about HTML to understand what everything means. Of the many good sources for HTML information on the Web, try the World Wide Web Consortium (W3). You can find it at *http://www.w3.org/pub/WWW*.

Figure 11.15 *Viewing a Web page's source HTML file.*

CONFIGURING INTERNET EXPLORER TO SUIT YOUR TASTES

One of the most interesting aspects of Internet Explorer is the amount of control you have over its operation. Internet Explorer allows you to select a desired level of security, add new helper applications, and change your home page. You can even change the color of the text, background, and links of pages you load. You make these changes using the Options dialog box or the Internet Properties applet.

To view the Options dialog box, select **Options** on the View menu. You access the Internet Properties dialog box, which is exactly the same as the Options dialog box, by clicking on the **Internet** icon in the Control

Panel. The dialog box has six tabs labeled **General**, **Connection**, **Navigation**, **Programs**, **Security**, and **Advanced**. We will discuss each in turn.

The General Tab

The **General** tab (or page) lets you make cosmetic changes to your browser (Figure 11.16). The **Multimedia** options let you choose to stop videos, images, or sounds from playing. This option can be useful if your connection is slow. Changing link, text, and background colors can be fun, but with the multitude of Web page styles, it can sometimes lead to confusion. At the bottom of the page is a button labeled **Font Settings**. This button takes you to the Font dialog box, where you can change the font that your pages will use. As a default, most pages use Times New Roman or Arial. If you dislike the default font, you can change it without much harm.

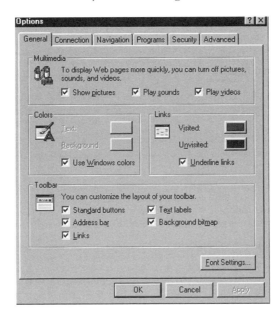

*Figure 11.16 The **General** tab.*

The Connection Tab

This page displays the current settings for your Internet connection. If your connection is up and running, you usually need not change anything here. However, if you can't get connected, the problem may be on this page. If you

are connecting to the Internet using an Internet service provider, make sure
that the IP address, account name and password are correct. You can check this
information by clicking the **Properties** button to view the connection specifics.
You may have to contact your ISP for help. If you are connecting via a LAN, you
can check the settings by clicking on the **Settings** button on this page.

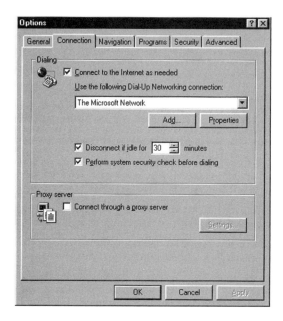

Figure 11.17 *The* ***Connection*** *tab.*

The Navigation Tab

The **Navigation** tab (Figure 11.18) allows you to change your start page and
set as many as five quick link pages. You can change or specify a page by clicking **Use Current** when the desired page is loaded into your Page View, or you
can type in the address yourself. The default pages for Start and Search are
Microsoft's. The bottom of the page lists the number of days to store a record

of sites that you've accessed. These files are stored in the History directory under your *%System Root%* directory for NT, usually WINNT\History. If you use Internet Explorer often, you might want to decrease the number of days that pages are kept. You can also view or clear the history list.

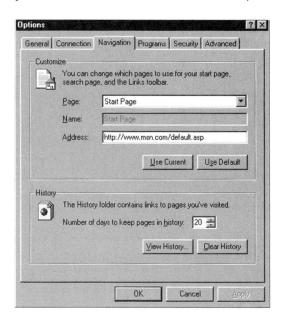

*Figure 11.18 The **Navigation** tab.*

The Programs Tab

This page lists the mail and news reader you have selected to work in conjunction with Internet Explorer (Figure 11.19). In the **Viewers** section, you can set up new viewers to handle different file types. You need to know a bit about the viewer before you attempt to do this. Fortunately, Internet Explorer includes almost all the viewers you will ever need.

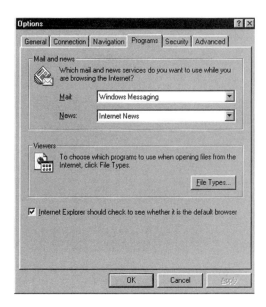

Figure 11.19 The *Programs* tab.

The Security Tab

The **Security** page (Figure 11.20) is divided into three sections: **Content advisor**, **Certificates**, and **Active content**. The **Content advisor** lets you screen users, such as your children, from violence, profanity, and nudity. The feature includes a password so that users cannot circumvent the restrictions.

The **Certificate** section provides a level of security when you're viewing information or sending information from or to secure Web sites. The virtue of the certificate scheme is that transmissions include a security certificate. If the certificate does not match the certificate in the certificate database, you are warned that the transmission is not secure. You can change the settings so that insecure transmissions are not allowed, and that provides significant security. This feature is useful if you send your credit card number or other personal information over the Web.

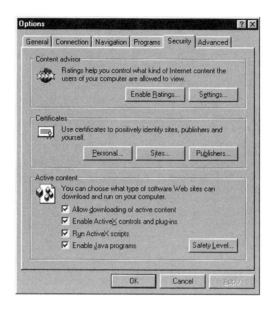

Figure 11.20 The Security tab.

Active content refers to Internet programs that become active when you load a page. Examples are Java and ActiveX controls, plug-ins, and applications. The plug-ins are automatically installed whenever you encounter one on the Web that you don't already have. Enterprising hackers use plug-ins as an opportunity to damage your system. Unless you are an expert or confident of the sites you visit, you will want to keep these features active and the **Safety Level** set to **High**, which is the default.

The Advanced Tab

The final property tab is a collection of miscellaneous features (Figure 11.21). Because most Internet connections are unsecured, Internet Explorer will warn you if you are putting private information at risk. You can also view the temporary Internet page file from this page.

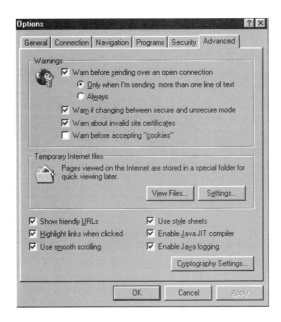

Figure 11.21 The Advanced tab.

UPDATING YOUR BROWSER

If you do not have the latest version of Internet Explorer, it is a good idea to update it. To see which version you have, click **About Internet Explorer** on the Help menu.

Almost every aspect of the Internet and the World Wide Web is constantly improving. Using an older version of Internet Explorer may prevent you from enjoying the new features. Moreover, it is easy to update your browser. To do so, go to *http://www.microsoft.com/ie/default.asp* and click on the **Internet Explorer** button. The links will lead you the rest of the way. You'll simply download a program that will be stored in the location you specify. After the download has completed, exit the current version of Internet Explorer and execute the program you downloaded. The new version installs itself.

FREE STUFF FROM MICROSOFT

In addition to the Internet Explorer, which Microsoft gives away for free, Microsoft hands out a variety of applications for you to try at no cost at www.microsoft.com. For example, you can obtain Microsoft FrontPage, a full-blown HTML Web page toolkit, for free. You can also access the Microsoft Network at www.msn.com, and sign up to preview MSN for one month at no charge. If you decide to try MSN, Microsoft sends you a CD-ROM that includes a free version of the MSN application, which works in much the same way as Internet Explorer (Figure 11.22). In fact, it works with the Internet Explorer, although it is more than a browsing tool. It's an online service and content provider, much like America Online and CompuServe. It offers forums, chat rooms, and special services such as Encarta (a multimedia encyclopedia) online. The MSN software enables you to access the content provided by MSN only to its members.

Figure 11.22 The MSN browser.

Summary

Internet Explorer is a browser that's used to navigate among Web sites on the Internet. You get started with Internet Explorer by running the Connection Wizard, which launches the first time you run Internet Explorer. Depending on how you are connecting to the Internet, you may have to contact an Internet service provider or the system administrator of your local area network for information about setting up Internet Explorer. If you opt to connect to the Internet using the Microsoft Network, the Wizard walks you through the process of setting up an MSN account. If you have a browser, such as Netscape Navigator, installed on your system, Internet Explorer will use the same settings to make your connection to the Internet.

The major components of Internet Explorer's user interface are the Menu, the Toolbar, and the Status bar. Links contained in HTML documents enable you to navigate around the World Wide Web. Certain navigation tools are built into the Internet Explorer, such as the **Back**, **Forward**, **Search**, and **Favorites** buttons. You can use the Address Bar to connect to Web sites by entering a URL such as *www.compaq.com.*

Internet Explorer lets you save pages for offline viewing as well as view the HTML source code for a Web page.

You can fine-tune a variety of Internet Explorer settings to meet your tastes or to correct problems. You can change the font and font size along with text and background colors. You can turn on security features to ensure that your vital information doesn't end up in the wrong hands and prevent users of your system from accessing certain areas of the Web. You can also define the default home page and decide how long to store previously connected links on your local hard drive.

It's easy to update your browser as well as obtain free software from Microsoft.

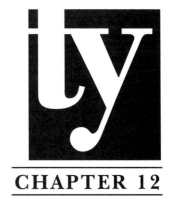

CHAPTER 12

HyperTerminal

Windows NT, like Windows 95, has a simple communications program called HyperTerminal. You can use HyperTerminal with a modem connected to one of your PC's communication ports (COM ports). In this way, you can access other computers over a telephone line, call up an incredible variety of bulletin boards and news retrieval services, and transfer data from your computer to anywhere there's a telephone, modem, and computer. HyperTerminal is not a sophisticated program, but, in the spirit of other Windows tools, it gives you basic functionality.

In this chapter you will learn how to:

- Open HyperTerminal
- Configure HyperTerminal
- Use the HyperTerminal menu items

GETTING STARTED WITH HYPERTERMINAL

To open HyperTerminal, click on the **HyperTerminal** icon in the Accessories menu. As shown in Figure 12.1, the first time the program starts, it presents a dialog box where you enter a name for the connection. You also choose an icon for the connection.

Figure 12.1 *The HyperTerminal window with the connection dialog box.*

Enter a name and select an icon, as shown. Then click **OK** (see Figure 12.2).

Figure 12.2 *The Connection Description dialog box.*

A new dialog box prompts you to enter the phone number for the connection. Enter the phone number and press **OK** (see Figure 12.3).

Figure 12.3 The Phone Number dialog box.

Still another dialog box prompts you to make the connection (see Figure 12.4).

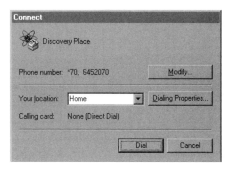

Figure 12.4 The Connect dialog box.

If you click the **Dial** button, HyperTerminal dials the number you specified and tries to complete the connection. If everything works, you will see the login screen of the bulletin board or service to which you are connecting, as shown in Figure 12.5.

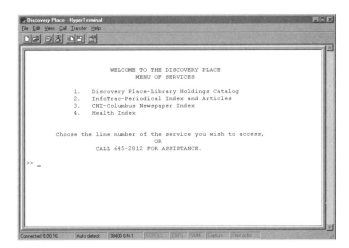

Figure 12.5 *The connection screen of the service dialed.*

That's how simple it is to connect to a BBS or other service using HyperTerminal. Connecting to a service is an easy task, but there's more to using HyperTerminal than that. Sometimes the default configuration used by HyperTerminal doesn't work. So let's look at this application in a little more detail, starting with the HyperTerminal window.

THE HYPERTERMINAL WINDOW

The HyperTerminal window has a menu bar with **File**, **Edit**, **View**, **Call**, **Transfer**, and **Help** options. The File menu saves and opens HyperTerminal setup files. Once you define a setup file for a particular bulletin board, for example, you just read that file and dial the number to connect. All your settings, including the phone number, are stored in the file. The File menu also includes a **Properties** option that enables you to change the default terminal emulation, modem settings, and the amount of screen information saved in the scrollback buffer. The File menu also enables you to print the contents of the HyperTerminal window. The Edit menu lets you copy text from a HyperTerminal session so that you can paste it into another application. The View menu lets you specify whether the Toolbar and Status Bar are visible and lets you change the font that appears in the window. The Call menu lets you connect or disconnect. The Transfer menu allows you to perform file transfers between computers and capture screen text, and Help displays the help information on HyperTerminal.

We'll look at these menu items in more detail later, but, for now, let's look at some of the configuration changes that modify the default behavior of HyperTerminal.

CONFIGURING HYPERTERMINAL

The File Properties menu item, also accessible from the **Properties** icon (shown in Figure 12.6), opens a dialog box that offers a variety of options. These selections determine how HyperTerminal controls a modem and presents information to you.

Figure 12.6 The Properties toolbar button.

Phone Number

When you select the File menu **Properties** item or select the **Properties** button, the dialog box shown in Figure 12.7 displays. It opens with the Phone Number page displayed.

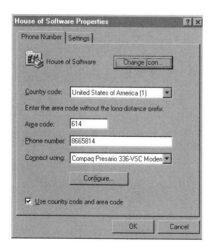

Figure 12.7 The Phone Number properties page.

Using this dialog box, you can change the icon for the current connection and specify the country code, area code, and phone number. You can also select and configure the modem if you are using a modem to connect to remote locations.

Connection and Modem Commands

If you are using a modem to connect, it is displayed in the **Connect using** pull-down list. If you select the **Configure** button, you will get a dialog box like the one in Figure 12.8. Normally, you define most modem settings using the Modems applet on the Control Panel, but HyperTerminal uses settings that many other applications, such as Internet Explorer, do not need to use. This dialog box displays five pages, or tabs, of settings that can be changed. You should know what you are doing before you change any of them.

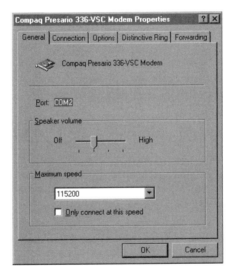

Figure 12.8 *The Modem Properties dialog box.*

You probably won't need to change any of these settings, because the defaults were set for use with your modem when you installed the drivers for it in NT. Also, if your modem is not working properly, you can usually fix the problem using the Modem Troubleshooter in Windows NT Help or by consulting the documentation that came with your modem. Many of the options you can specify with this dialog box are not related to your modem but instead have to do with special services you may be using through your phone company.

HyperTerminal Emulation

By default, HyperTerminal attempts to detect the type of terminal emulation supported by the BBS or service you are connecting to. However, you can specify the terminal emulation used by HyperTerminal. Select the **Settings** tab of the Properties dialog box, as shown in Figure 12.9.

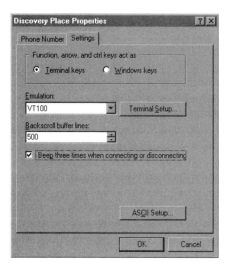

Figure 12.9 *The Settings page of the Properties dialog box.*

By selecting a terminal type from the **Emulation** pull-down list box, you can specify that HyperTerminal behave like some of the popular terminal types. The default is for HyperTerminal to detect the best terminal type to emulate. You probably won't want to change this setting unless the default terminal type does not work properly.

On this page, you can also specify the number of lines that HyperTerminal stores in its scrollback buffer. To minimize memory use, you might want to reduce this number from the default value of 500 lines.

Terminal Setup

If you decide to select the terminal emulation for HyperTerminal, you can change settings for that terminal package by clicking the **Terminal Setup** button. You'll see a somewhat different dialog box pop up depending on the terminal you chose to emulate. Figure 12.10 illustrates the Terminal Settings dialog box for the VT100 terminal emulation.

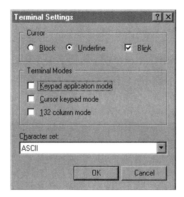

Figure 12.10 *The VT100 Terminal Settings dialog box.*

In this dialog box, you can change several terminal settings, including the default character set.

ASCII Setup

Clicking the **ASCII Setup** button on the **Settings** page of the Properties dialog box (illustrated in Figure 12.9) displays the dialog box shown in Figure 12.11.

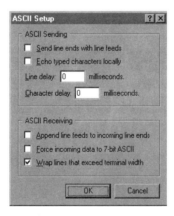

Figure 12.11 *The ASCII Setup dialog box.*

This dialog box enables you to change the behavior of how ASCII data is sent and received. **Wrap lines that exceed terminal width** cuts off long lines automatically and wraps them onto the next line. **Echo typed characters locally** types your input immediately without waiting to get a response from the remote system. If all characters are appearing twice in your HyperTerminal session—if you see HHyyppeerrTTeerrmmiinnaall, for example—then turn off this option. You can also choose to have carriage returns translated to carriage returns and line feeds for inbound text or outbound text (or both). If incoming lines of text are overwriting the same line, check this option.

HYPERTERMINAL MENU OPTIONS

The HyperTerminal menu bar contains File, Edit, View, Call, Transfer, and Help options. Let's look at these menu items in detail.

File Menu

The File menu, illustrated in Figure 12.12, enables you to create new connections, open saved connections, and save the current connection. Current connection settings are saved with the **.ht** extension (for HyperTerminal).

Figure 12.12 The File menu.

If you want to open a previously saved connection, click **Open**. The Open dialog box displays, listing your previously saved connections, as shown in Figure 12.13.

Figure 12.13 *The Open dialog box.*

Select the connection to open and click **Open**. The Connect dialog box (illustrated in Figure 12.4) displays. Click **Dial** to have your modem dial this service or BBS.

Other options on the File menu enable you to set up and print the HyperTerminal window contents. The **Properties** option enables you to change the current configuration, as discussed earlier.

Edit Menu

The Edit menu contains standard Windows NT options for selecting, copying, and pasting text.

View Menu

The View menu contains entries for toggling the Status Bar and Toolbar off and on. It also contains an entry for changing the font displayed in the HyperTerminal window, as shown in Figure 12.14.

Figure 12.14 *The Font item on the View menu.*

If you select the **Font** option, you will see a dialog box that enables you to change the current font displayed in the HyperTerminal window. This dialog box lists the constant-width fonts installed on your system.

Call Menu

The Call menu lists options for connecting and disconnecting from the current BBS or service.

You will find that the remote system will often hang up automatically after you log off. However, if it doesn't hang up the connection properly, use the **Disconnect** option on the Call menu.

If your modem is not dialing out correctly, try issuing a **Disconnect** command to clear the modem.

SHORTCUT

Transfer Menu

You can transfer files from a bulletin board to your computer or from your computer to a friend's computer. When you get a file from a remote system onto your computer, you *download* the file. When you post a file on a remote computer, you *upload* the file. You will often encounter these terms in dealing with bulletin board systems. There are two types of transfers: text and binary.

The Transfer menu, illustrated in Figure 12.15, enables you to send and receive files, capture the text that appears in the HyperTerminal window, or send the text in the window directly to the printer.

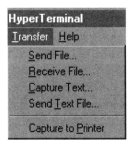

Figure 12.15 The Transfer menu.

Text Transfers

You use text transfers for regular ASCII files—that is, files that have no special characters. You can save a plain ASCII file from most word processors. (A Microsoft Word **.doc** file can be transferred as a binary file.) To send this type of file, you need to prepare the other computer to receive a text file. How you do this depends on the system and software that is running. Usually, a series of menus leads to preparation for file transfers. Under HyperTerminal's Transfer menu, select **Send Text File**. To receive a text file, issue the **Capture Text** command under the Transfer menu; then signal the remote computer to begin its transfer.

Binary Transfers

If you are transferring nontextual information, you can classify the file as *binary*. There's an important advantage to binary file transfers: they use error-checking and correction programs, so you can have a high degree of confidence in the quality of the data even in the presence of phone-line noise. There are protocols for transferring binary files in HyperTerminal. A *protocol* specifies how information is packaged and transmitted. Choose a protocol supported by the computer with which you are exchanging files.

Binary transfers are similar to text transfers. You first prepare the remote computer either to send or to receive a binary file, as appropriate. Then, under the Transfer menu, select **Send File** (to upload a file) or **Receive File** (to download a file). Be sure that the protocols on both ends match; otherwise, the transfer will never begin.

HyperTerminal automatically detects the protocol used when you are downloading a file.

NOTE

Capturing Text to the Printer

HyperTerminal also enables you to print the contents of the current window as it updates. Selecting **Capture to Printer** sends all screen updates to your printer.

The **Capture to Printer** option is a toggle. As long as it is selected, all screen updates will be printed. You must deselect it to turn it off.

NOTE

Help Menu

The Help menu displays the HyperTerminal help. The built-in help is most notable for its Modem Troubleshooter feature, as illustrated in Figure 12.16. Use this help if you can't get your modem to respond.

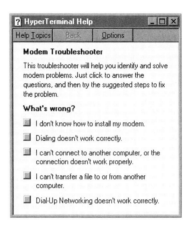

Figure 12.16 *The Modem Troubleshooter in Help.*

SUMMARY

Windows NT HyperTerminal is a simple utility program that makes your PC a gateway to information sources. You can use HyperTerminal to dial news-retrieval bulletin boards or to exchange files with a friend. The numerous HyperTerminal settings allow you to choose the look, feel, and other parameters of your communications. You can save all your settings in **.ht** session files.

CHAPTER 13

Paint

Paint is a graphics application provided with Windows NT 4.0 that enables you to create simple graphics images using various tools. You can paint with many colors, which can be brushed on finely or filled in with a spray can or bucket of paint. You can also create shapes composed of different line widths and colors. The resulting image file can be used in other Windows NT programs, such as WordPad.

For Windows NT 4.0, the Paint program is new. It replaces the program called Paintbrush that was included with all previous versions of Windows. Paint is similar to Paintbrush, but it has been improved.

In this chapter you will learn about:

- Using Paint
- Cutting and pasting
- Selecting effects
- Establishing and saving file formats
- Printing your images

USING PAINT

Start Paint by clicking on **Paint** in the Accessories submenu. (To do this, click on the **Start** button on the Taskbar, select **Programs**, then **Accessories**, and then **Paint**. You can create a shortcut for Paint and place it on the desktop or at the top level of the Start menu.) You will see a Paint window like the one in Figure 13.1. Let's look at everything in this window.

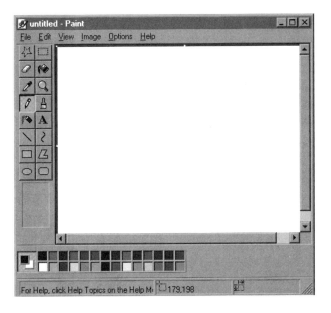

Figure 13.1 The Paint window.

On the left side of the window is a tool box that contains icons for the graphical actions you can perform and the objects you can create. These icons represent objects called *tools*. When you hold the mouse cursor over a tool for about a second, a ToolTip appears, telling you the name of the tool. At the bottom of the Paint window is a color box, which contains all the colors available for drawing. The middle of the screen is the drawing area. To make a picture, first choose a tool, and then choose options such as color and line size and start drawing with your mouse. To create an object, click on the mouse's left button in the drawing area and release the button. At the bottom of the window is the Status Bar, which displays information about the current tool, the coordinates of the upper-left-hand corner of any object, and the size of that object. You can remove the tool box, color box, or Status Bar by deselecting it in the View menu.

Opening a File

You can open an existing drawing by clicking on the **Open** option under the File menu and selecting a file name. To create a fresh drawing, click on the **New** option under **File**; your background color will fill the Paint window.

Drawing

Paint starts with the Pencil as the default tool. Experiment in the drawing area by clicking and dragging your mouse. The Pencil tool does not define an object; rather, it works much like a real pencil. Wherever you move the mouse (while holding down with the left mouse button), the Pencil leaves a mark. The marks defined by your movements will be the same color as the foreground color you selected. The Pencil tool is useful when you zoom in on a part of your drawing; it's good for detail work.

A tool that works much like the Pencil tool is the Brush tool, which is next to the Pencil tool.

You will experiment with other tools and options as you read further.

Setting Brush Shapes

The shape of the tip of the brush can be changed. When you select the **Brush** tool, you will see the Brush tip box appear immediately below the tools area, as shown in Figure 13.2. Choose a tip shape by selecting it with the mouse's left button. If you resume drawing with a brush, you can see the effect of a new brush stylus.

Figure 13.2 *Choosing a brush tip.*

Using Colors

By default, all the available colors are shown on the bottom of your Paint window in the color box. Click the mouse's left button on a color to make it the active foreground color. Click the mouse's right button on another color to make it the active background color. These selections will show up in the window adjacent to the Color palette.

To turn off the color box, deselect it from the View menu.

Setting Line Width

To change the line width of the tool you are using, select the **Line** tool or the **Curve** tool. The Line size box appears below the tool area. Click on a new line width in the Line size box. The line size you select becomes highlighted. Now draw some more shapes in the drawing area to see the effect of your selection. When you switch to one of the object-drawing tools, the line size you just selected is retained.

Erasing

To erase small areas in the drawing window, use the **Eraser** tool. This tool has two modes: eraser and color eraser. You use the **Eraser** tool in eraser mode by clicking and dragging with the left mouse button. This erases everything underneath your cursor no matter what color, replacing it with the background color selected. Clicking and dragging with the right mouse button erases only the current foreground color, replacing it with the current background color. Choose this tool and experiment on your drawing by erasing part of what you have drawn. Click on the mouse's left button for the eraser or the right button for the color eraser, and rub your drawing as you would with a real eraser.

Lines

Paint provides a Line tool for drawing straight lines. Make lines by clicking on a starting point, dragging, and then clicking on an endpoint. A perfectly straight line will connect the two points you defined, as shown in Figure 13.3. Remember to change the line width as necessary in the Line size box.

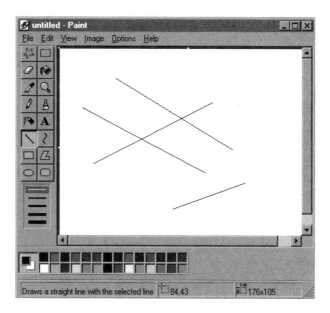

Figure 13.3 *Creating a straight line.*

Curved Lines

The tool adjacent to the Line tool lets you draw curved lines. Draw a line with two points, just as you did with the Line tool; then, with the cursor still active, enter a third point (by clicking and holding, then dragging to see the effect) that distorts the line into a curve. The farther away the third point is from the line, the sharper the curve in the original line. You click a fourth time to distort your line even further. Experiment with this by using the tool in your drawing window, as shown in Figure 13.4.

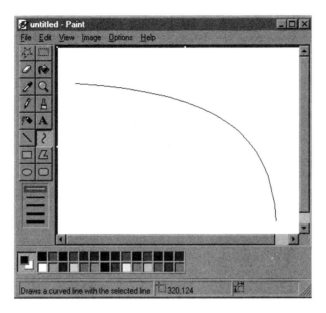

Figure 13.4 Creating a curved line.

Spray Can

You can use the Spray Can—sometimes called the *airbrush* tool—to spray paint onto your drawing area. (Graffiti artists will surely like this tool.) Click on the tool that looks like a spray can, choose a color, and start spraying by clicking the mouse's left button. The longer you hold the spray at a point, the darker and more dense the color will be. An example is shown in Figure 13.5.

Figure 13.5 *Using the Spray Can tool.*

Defining and Filling Shapes

Most of the other tools define shapes. You can define circles, ellipses, squares, and many irregular shapes. These shapes can be filled or unfilled. You can make a donut, for example, by combining filled and unfilled circles. Here's how: Select the **Ellipse** tool, as shown in Figure 13.6. Then select the **fill with no border** fill selection in the Fill box area under the tools. Draw a large circle, constraining the ellipse to a circle by holding down the **Shift** key as you drag. Next, select a new foreground color. Finish your donut by drawing a smaller filled circle (hold down **Shift** while dragging) inside the larger one.

Figure 13.6 *Making a donut out of two filled circles.*

You can also fill regions or objects in your drawing using the **Fill** tool, which resembles a paint can spilling its paint. When you select this tool, the mouse cursor changes to the paint can. The hot spot for this cursor is the bottom of the dripping paint. When you place the bottom tip of the dripping paint inside an object and click with the mouse, the current foreground or background color fills the object. The left mouse button (for right handers) fills with the foreground color; the right mouse button usually fills with the background color.

Most of the shape tools require a single click-and-drag to define a shape. Most of them also enable you to draw a regular shape, such as a square or circle, by pressing down the **Shift** key as you drag. This is true for the Ellipse tool, the Rectangle tool, and the Rounded Rectangle tool. The fourth shape tool, the Polygon tool, can be used to define arbitrary shapes by entering points, clicking and dragging with the left mouse button. The final point must coincide with the first one to complete the shape. When you have placed the last point, terminate the shape by clicking with the right mouse button. You can enter as many points as needed to define the shape. An example of an unfilled arbitrary shape is shown in Figure 13.7. The shape in this example is about to be closed by placing the final point on the first one.

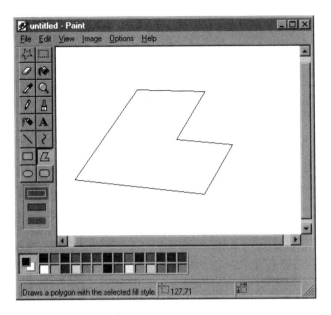

Figure 13.7 *Using the Polygon tool.*

Entering Text

Documents often require that text accompany graphics. Paint makes this easy. The Text tool icon has an **A** in it; click on it. Click your mouse in your drawing to define your insertion point. You can also drag an insertion region, or *frame*. Paint creates a text frame on your drawing that includes an insertion point, and it pops up a Font selection dialog box somewhere on your screen. If you start typing, you will get characters inside the text frame that are the size and font of those displayed in the Font dialog box. The frame expands as you continue typing. You can also resize the frame or move it by holding your mouse on the edges of the frame and waiting for the mouse cursor to change. If you place the mouse over one of the eight resizing nodes, the mouse cursor changes to a double-headed arrow. You can click and drag on these nodes to change the shape of the text frame. If you hold the mouse over the text frame line, but not on top of a node, the mouse cursor changes to an arrow. You can then click and drag the text frame and place it anywhere on your drawing.

NOTE

In Paint, text is made up of graphics characters. In other words, you have painted characters onto the screen with dots, which are called *pixels*. Where as a text program such as Notepad saves characters by ASCII values, a graphics program such as Paint can't distinguish points that belong to a sphere from points that belong to a letter *A*. Paint saves the whole bitmap. (A *bitmap* is an array of points.) You can therefore erase portions of characters with the Erase tool.

SHORTCUT

You can use the **Backspace** key to erase any text you have just entered. If you move the insertion point, however, you will no longer be able to erase text this way. You must use cutting tools in this case.

You can customize some aspects of your fonts. The Font dialog box enables you to select a font, font size, and font attributes. A few of these styles are shown in Figure 13.8.

Figure 13.8 Text style options.

To change the size or family of fonts, click the list box on the Font dialog box and select among the families of fonts, just as you did for Windows NT WordPad or any other Microsoft text application.

CUTTING AND PASTING

You have two tools available to cut portions of your drawing. Both of them are displayed with dotted outlines at the top of the tool box. The rectangle tool is useful for cutting out rectangular shapes from your drawing. The other tool shows a starlike shape; it allows you to define the shape of cuts using your mouse. Just click and drag the mouse in the shape desired, and then end your shape on the starting point. Once you define a shape with this tool or with the rectangular cut tool, the area to be cut is highlighted with a dotted line.

Figure 13.9 displays a drawing that is about to have a cut made in it. Here the rectangular cut tool is used to define the area to be cut, which is highlighted by a dotted line (around the word *Varied*). You can move this cut region by clicking on it and dragging it to a new location. Try this. Now choose the **Cut** command from the Edit menu. The cut region is now erased.

Figure 13.9 *Defining a cut region.*

You can paste the cut area anywhere on your drawing. Choose an insertion point and select the **Paste** option from the Edit menu. You can paste the selected region to another application, such as WordPad. The cut region will reside in the Windows NT Clipboard for possible reuse.

Copying Areas of Your Drawing

If you chose the **Copy** command instead of **Cut**, your original cut region will be left intact. You can still paste a copy of that region elsewhere on your drawing or into another application.

Copying Areas of Your Drawing to a File (Cropping)

If you choose the **Copy To** item on the Edit menu, Paint brings up the Save dialog box, enabling you to save the selected region as a file. This is useful for cropping images or drawings. When you open the file that you saved using **Copy To**, it is sized exactly to the edges of the region you selected.

Effects: Inverting Colors, Flipping, and Rotating

Once you have a cut area defined, other special effect options are available. Use the Image menu, as shown in Figure 13.10. You can select a flip, rotation, or inverse image of your selection. Try each of these selections to see their effects.

Figure 13.10 *The Image menu for effects.*

Effects: Stretch

Using the Image menu, you can stretch or reduce the size of a cut region. Once you've defined a cut region, select **Stretch/Skew**. The Stretch and Skew dialog box displays, as shown in Figure 13.11.

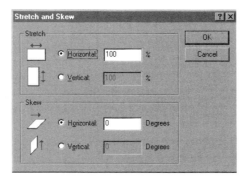

Figure 13.11 *The Stretch and Skew dialog box.*

You specify how much you want to stretch the selected region as a percentage of the current size. First select the direction in which you will stretch the selected region, either **Horizontal** or **Vertical**. The text window next to the selected direction becomes active. Next, enter the new size as a percentage of the current size. To make the object larger, enter a value greater than 100%. To make it smaller, enter a value smaller than 100%. Finally, click **OK**. Note the change in the size of the selected object. To enlarge or reduce an object in both directions, repeat the process, selecting the other direction. Figure 13.12 illustrates an object that has been stretched several times. It was originally a filled square. Can you tell how it was stretched?

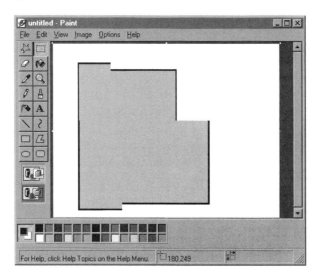

Figure 13.12 *An object that has been stretched.*

Effects: Skew

The Skew option is similar to **Stretch**. Select the region you want to skew, or tilt. As for Stretch, define a cut region and then select **Stretch/Skew** from the Image menu. In the Stretch and Skew dialog box, specify how many degrees and the direction in which to skew the selected region. An example in which characters are skewed vertically is shown in Figure 13.13.

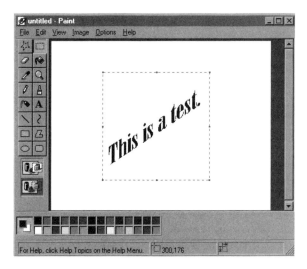

Figure 13.13 *Characters skewed vertically.*

Zooming In and Out

To display details of a drawing, use Paint's **Zoom** feature. You can zoom in on objects two ways. The first way is to redefine your view using the View menu. Click on **Zoom** under the View menu, and a submenu lists several magnification levels for your drawing. You can select **Large** or **Custom** magnification. Either way, you will probably have to scroll horizontally or vertically to find the part of your drawing you want to view at this greater magnification level.

A more useful way to zoom in on part of an image is to use the Magnifier tool in the tool box. When you select this tool, the cursor changes to a magnification rectangle and several magnification levels are listed below the tool box. You can select the level of magnification you want, but this has the same effect as choosing **Zoom** from the View menu. It's probably easier to just select the **Magnifier** tool, place the cursor, which changes to a magnification rectangle, over the area that you want magnified (Figure 13.14), and click on it. That area will be shown at high magnification, as in Figure 13.15. To revert back, choose the **Magnifier** tool again and then click in your drawing.

Figure 13.14 *The magnifier rectangle.*

Figure 13.15 *Effect of zooming in.*

FILE FORMATS AND SAVING

When you have completed a picture, save it by clicking on the **Save** or **Save As** option under the File menu. In the Save dialog box, select a computer and drive on the network in which to save your file by browsing or selecting them from the **Save in** list box. Type a file name in the **File name** text area. The Save As dialog box is displayed in Figure 13.16.

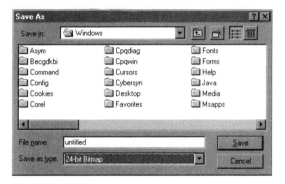

Figure 13.16 *The Save As dialog box.*

You can choose from a few different file formats in the **Save as type** list box. These formats are listed in Table 13.1.

Table 13.1 File Formats for Graphics Files

FORMAT NAME	EXTENSION	DESCRIPTION
Monochrome bitmap	**.BMP**	A black-and-white file format. Small in size. Colors are converted to black-and-white whenyou save with this option.
16-color bitmap	**.BMP**	The standard Paint format; it contains 16 colors only. Storage is 4 bits per pixel.
256-color bitmap	**.BMP**	This option is useful for transferring a file to a program that uses more than 16 colors.Storage is 8 bits per pixel.
24-bit bitmap	**.BMP**	This option is useful for transferring a file to a program that uses 24-bit images ("true color images"). Storage is 24 bits per pixel.

The default file format is based on the number of colors you are currently displaying.

Making Wallpaper

To save your drawing as wallpaper, select one of the two **Set As Wallpaper** options on the File menu (Figure 13.17). One option centers your drawing on the desktop; the other selection tiles multiple copies of your drawing.

*Figure 13.17 The **Set As Wallpaper** selection.*

You must save your drawing or picture before you can specify that it be set as wallpaper. However, if you haven't saved it before you select one of the two **Set As Wallpaper** options, Paint is "smart" enough to invoke the Save dialog box so that you can save the image first.

PRINTING

Printing is simple using Paint. From the File menu, select the **Print** option. You will see a fairly standard Windows NT Print dialog box, shown in Figure 13.18. You can choose a few options here, such as the number of copies to print or whether to send the output to a printer or to a file. When you've selected the options, click **OK** to start printing.

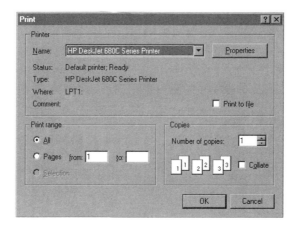

Figure 13.18 *Choosing Print options.*

SUMMARY

Windows NT Paint is a basic and intuitive graphical toolkit for creating images. You can create and manipulate colors, shapes, and text. You use a tool box to select tools for a variety of operations or to create several objects. Paint includes versatile tools, such as the Ellipse tool to create ellipses and circles as well as two cutting tools to cut out portions of an image. You can add text in many fonts, sizes, and colors. Some special effects are available: You can flip, invert, rotate, skew, enlarge, and reduce images. The result of your Paint session can be saved and copied to other programs. For example, you can place a Paint image into a WordPad or Word file or a PowerPoint presentation.

CHAPTER 14

Other Accessories

In addition to the utilities covered so far, the Accessories submenu includes a number of handy utilities: a simple text editor called Notepad, a general-purpose calculator, a clock and a phone dialer, among others. Even some games are available. All these accessories are optional, meaning that you choose which of them you want on your system at initial installation. You can also add or remove them later using the Add/Remove Program applet in the Control Panel.

In this chapter you will learn about:

- Notepad
- Calculator
- Clock
- Phone Dialer
- Imaging
- Games

Several of the accessories are not listed here because they are covered elsewhere in this book. WordPad is covered in Chapter 10, HyperTerminal in
Chapter 12, and Paint in Chapter 13. The Clipbook Viewer is described in
Chapter 16, and the Multimedia accessories are covered in detail in Chapter
18. Several accessories are not described in this book, because they are rarely
used and the Help provided with those tools is a good source of information.

You can see these accessories by clicking the **Start** button and selecting
the Programs menu. The Accessories submenu is usually the first item listed,
as shown in Figure 14.1.

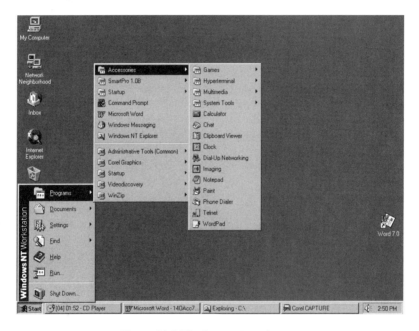

Figure 14.1 *The Accessories submenu.*

NOTEPAD

Often you need to use a plain ASCII text editor to look at a file. Windows NT
provides Notepad for this purpose. This simple text editor is similar to the one
used in WordPad, discussed in Chapter 10. You can select text by using your
mouse to click and drag. You can cut, move, and paste text in the same way
you do in WordPad. To start Notepad, select the **Notepad** icon from the
Accessories submenu. You will see a screen like the one in Figure 14.2. There
is a menu bar and a window for entering and editing text.

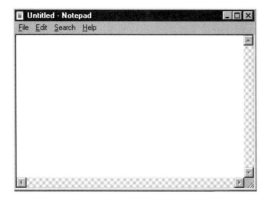

Figure 14.2 *The Notepad screen.*

File Functions

If you click on the File menu, you'll find familiar menu options. You can open an existing file by clicking **Open**. You will see the dialog box shown in Figure 14.3. Here you can search through the drives and directories on your Windows NT network to find the file you want. You need to make sure it is a text file, though—otherwise, your screen will be garbled with binary codes.

Figure 14.3 *Opening a file.*

You can save files with **Save** (for existing files) or **Save As** (for new files.) The Save As dialog box also has a check box enabling you to save the document as a Unicode file, as shown in Figure 14.4. Unicode is an international standard for character sets. Basically, it allows you to use international fonts and characters within your document. By default, Notepad saves your file as an ASCII text file containing no font or formatting information. If you save the file as a Unicode document, any special Unicode characters you enter into the file are stored with the file. You must use a Unicode-compatible font to see these characters.

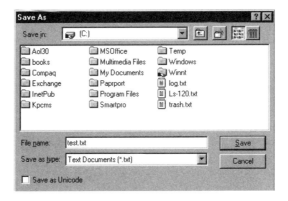

Figure 14.4 Saving a file.

Edit Functions

The main window is for entering text. As shown in Figure 14.5, you enter text freely into Notepad. You can change the default wrapping behavior in Notepad by selecting the **Word Wrap** option in the Edit menu (shown in Figure 14.6). The wrapping is not stored in the document when you save it; it is used only to force text to wrap within the Notepad window. You need to take this into account, because many programs will not recognize lines of ASCII text longer than 256, 1025, or 2048 characters. Be aware that you must force line breaks in your document.

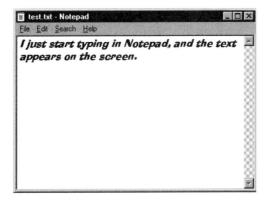

Figure 14.5 Entering text into Notepad.

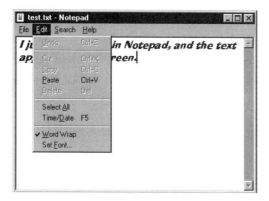

Figure 14.6 *The Notepad Edit menu options.*

You can set the font to use for your file using the **Set Font** option in the Edit menu. If you want to cut and paste text, select the text with your mouse and choose the **Cut** option under the Edit menu. With your mouse, place the insertion point where you want to paste; then click the **Paste** option, also under the Edit menu. You can also paste ASCII or Unicode text from other applications as well, such as the HyperTerminal program.

Search Functions

You can look for character strings in Notepad by using the **Find** option under the Search menu. This command is similar to its counterpart in WordPad. As shown in Figure 14.7, you type in the string you are looking for in the **Find what** text box. Indicate whether case matching is important—that is, whether Fred and FRED should be distinguishable. You can also determine whether you want to search up or down from where your insertion point is. Click on the appropriate radio button under the **Direction** heading. Click on **Find Next** to start the search. If a match is found, it will be highlighted and presented onscreen, as shown in Figure 14.8. You can continue looking for further matches by clicking on **Find Next**.

Figure 14.7 *Typing a string into the **Find what** box.*

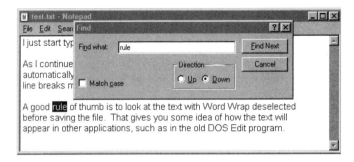

Figure 14.8 A highlighted match.

CALCULATOR

Open the Calculator by selecting the Calculator icon in the Accessories sub-menu. Windows NT has a simple calculator and a fairly capable scientific calculator wrapped up in one package. To see the two types, click on the appropriate switch in the View menu. The Standard switch gives you the calculator face shown in Figure 14.9. You get the four arithmetic operators: / (division), * (multiplication), – (subtraction), and + (addition). You can also use the square root function (**sqrt**) and percent (**%**). There is one memory register that can be cleared (**MC**), added to (**M+**), stored into (**MS**), and recalled (**MR**).

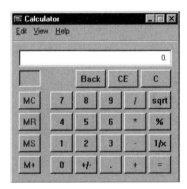

Figure 14.9 Standard calculator face.

Scientific Calculator

In Scientific mode, the calculator presents a larger number of keys, as shown in
Figure 14.10. In this mode, you can do arithmetic in different number systems:
decimal (the default), binary (0 to 1), octal (0 to 7), and hexadecimal (0 to 9, a to
f). For numbers in binary, octal, and hexadecimal, you can use logical operators,
such as And, Or, Xor, and Not. You have trigonometric functions (sin, cos, tan),
as well as their inverses and hyperbolic functions (Inv, Hyp check boxes). You can
obtain a description of the keys and what they do by right-clicking the key and
selecting the What's This option, as shown in Figures 14.11 and 14.12.

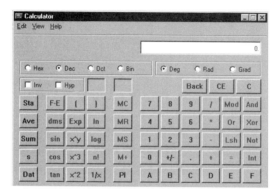

Figure 14.10 *Scientific calculator face.*

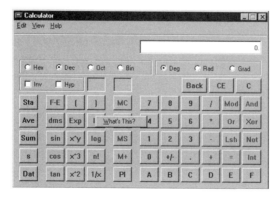

Figure 14.11 *The right-click What's This pop-up.*

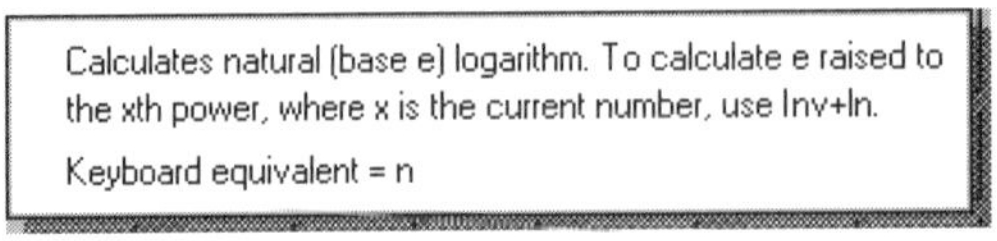

Calculates natural (base e) logarithm. To calculate e raised to the xth power, where x is the current number, use Inv+ln.
Keyboard equivalent = n

*Figure 14.12 A description of the natural log (**ln**) key.*

CLOCK

If you select the **Clock** icon in the Accessories submenu, you will see a time display in a window, as shown in Figure 14.13. You can change the look of the clock in several ways. Choose between analog and digital displays by selecting the **Analog** or **Digital** option under the Settings menu. You can remove the menu bar and title altogether by choosing the **No Title** option. The result is shown in Figure 14.14. You can also choose fonts for the digital display and specify that the clock remain on top (this option is on the Control menu in the upper-left corner), no matter what other windows are open. For the digital display, you can choose whether the clock displays seconds and the date.

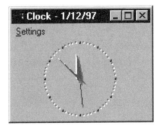

Clock - 1/12/97
Settings

Figure 14.13 Clock.

23:55:22
1/12/97

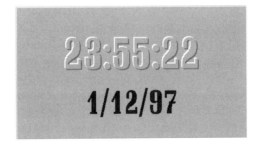

Figure 14.14 Digital clock with no menu.

GAMES

The Games submenu contains two games from Windows 3.x—Minesweeper and Solitaire—and two new games: FreeCell and Pinball. Choose any of these games by clicking the **Start** button and then **Programs**, **Accessories**, and **Games**. You can obtain complete rules for a particular game by choosing the Help menu in the game's menu bar.

THE PHONE DIALER

The Phone Dialer is designed to operate the same way as your speed dial functions on your expensive phone. You can store as many as eight phone numbers that can be dialed with just a press of a button, as shown in Figure 14.15.

Figure 14.15 *The Phone Dialer.*

To store a phone number, click an empty phone number slot located on the right side of this dialog box. It will prompt you to enter a name and a phone number. Select **Save** to add it to your Speed Dial list, or **Save** and **Dial** to save it and dial the number immediately. There is also a place to enter a number without storing it, and a drop-down list of the last numbers dialed. To use this program, you will need a modem.

IMAGING

If you work with scanned images, the Imaging program lets you view and edit your image. It also works as the interface software to your Twain-compatible scanner. You can use the Imaging accessory to view a variety of graphics files, make annotations on files or scanned images (see Figure 14.16), and print them.

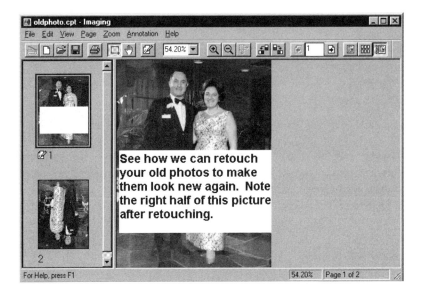

Figure 14.16 *A scanned image with an annotation.*

SUMMARY

Windows NT has several handy accessories. The Notepad program is a simple ASCII text file editor that uses the same kinds of editing tools you have seen in other Windows NT programs. Clock is a basic utility that displays the current time on your screen in either analog or digital format. You can use the Calculator for simple arithmetic and for scientific calculations and relax with several games included in Windows NT. The Phone Dialer enables you to dial remote locations using your computer. Finally, the Imaging program is the application interface program that works with Twain-compatible scanners, and it also enables you to view and annotate a variety of graphic file formats.

CHAPTER 15

System Administration Tools

This chapter describes tools you can use to administer Windows NT Workstation, to control disks and handle the needs of local users. If you're running Windows NT 4.0 Workstation on a network, many of these tasks will be handled by your system administrators. You probably won't have the right to make changes related to the security of the network or the right to monitor network resources, so this chapter might not be applicable to you. If you want to understand how to use some of NT's monitoring and diagnostics tools—such as Performance Monitor and Event Viewer—to isolate performance problems, the information in this chapter can help you get started. If you're running Windows NT 4.0 Workstation on a machine or small network at home, you are the administrator, so this chapter is valuable.

A golden rule of system administration is, "If it ain't broke, don't fix it." That rule certainly applies to Windows NT 4.0 Workstation, a highly sophisticated operating system. When your system is working well, don't make changes haphazardly to see whether you can make things better. Unless you understand the impact of your changes, they will probably have a negative impact.

Windows NT 4.0 Workstation has one shortcoming that complicates system administration of hardware: lack of Plug and Play support. This means that NT may not recognize your new hard drive or new modem if the device is not on Microsoft's Hardware Compatibility List (HAL). The ultimate solution may be to buy a different device, because Microsoft and your computer manufacturer may not have drivers to support the device for Windows NT 4.0 Workstation. So don't try to use Control Panel applets described in Chapter 5 or the system administration tools described in this chapter to fix a problem for which there is no good solution. Windows NT 5.0 Workstation will support Plug and Play, and that will make life much easier when you're adding new hardware.

In this chapter you will learn about:

- System administration on Windows NT
- The User Manager application
- Event Viewer
- Disk Administrator
- Performance Monitor
- The Diagnostics tool

AN OVERVIEW OF WINDOWS NT'S SYSTEM ADMINISTRATION

System administration keeps your Windows NT workstation running efficiently. A Windows NT network consists of computers that are connected in some way. If one or more of the machines in the network are down, the resources on those machines are unavailable to other users. You will find that administering a Windows NT system, however, is far less difficult and cumbersome than it is on a UNIX system. Almost all the functions of system administration are handled through the Windows NT graphical user interface.

To set up software and hardware, you use the applets in the Control Panel, shown in Figure 15.1. The Control Panel applets are covered in more detail in Chapter 5.

Figure 15.1 The Control Panel.

To perform system administration tasks, such as performing backups, administering disks and user accounts, and monitoring performance, you use the administrative tools, which are accessed through the **Programs** menu item on the Start menu, as shown in Figure 15.2.

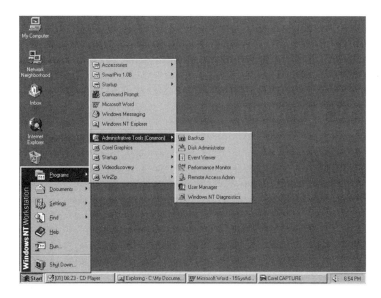

Figure 15.2 The administrative tools.

Administering Operating System Services and Devices

Service

Device

The operating system provides many services, including Alerter, RPC, and others. You manage and monitor these services in the Control Panel using the Services applet. The software for controlling devices is managed using the Devices applet. You will rarely use these two applets, because a hardware device or service is usually configured properly when it is installed.

Performance Monitoring

You can monitor the performance of hardware, the operating system, and its components with the Performance Monitor tool. Normal system administration requires that you sometimes monitor system performance and bottlenecks. You cannot change any parameters with this tool, but you can display, graph, and set up alerts for the parameters.

Security and Account Administration

System administrators are responsible for adding new user accounts and determining their access rights. With the User Manager tool, you will create groups of users for security purposes. You can use built-in groups and built-in security rights to take care of most of your user-security requirements. The User Manager tool is covered in detail later in this chapter.

Archiving and Retrieval of Data

For any operating system, especially one that serves multiple users, you must have a reliable and easy-to-use tape-archiving system. The Windows NT Backup utility allows you to archive, and back up, and restore files. You can do full, incremental, or differential backups, and you can use Backup in batch mode.

To use Backup, you use the Tape Devices applet in the Control Panel to install the drivers for your tape devices. After installing the tape backup device, you use the Backup utility on the System Administration Tools menu to perform the backups (and to restore files if needed). The Help included with Backup should be sufficient for you to use it effectively.

Hardware Maintenance

One of the duties of system administration is hardware maintenance. The Control Panel has a set of applets to configure and maintain hardware devices. Table 15.1 summarizes those devices and lists the applets you use to add or change configuration settings.

Table 15.1 Hardware Devices and Corresponding Control Panel Applets

DEVICE	CONTROL PANEL APPLET
Keyboard	Keyboard
Mouse	Mouse
Video	Display
SCSI	SCSI Adapters
PC Cards	PC Card (PCMCIA)
Network Adapters	Network
Tape	Tape Devices
Modem	Modems
Sound Cards, MIDI	Multimedia
Printers	Printers
COM (Serial) Ports	Ports
Uninterruptible Power Supply	UPS

Prepare emergency disk.

The Control Panel applets are discussed in more detail in Chapter 5.

Repairing Your System with the Emergency Disk

Windows NT has a number of system files that are needed to keep the system operating. If any of these files becomes corrupted, you can try to repair the system files using the emergency disk that you created when you installed Windows NT. Each computer can use only the emergency disk created for it.

To repair corrupted system files, insert the first (boot) disk of your Windows NT Emergency Repair disks in drive **A** and then start your computer. In the first Setup screen, type R, for repair, and follow the instructions, inserting other disks as needed. If the operation is successful, remove the emergency disk and then press **Ctrl+Alt+Delete** to restart your computer.

You can create the emergency repair disk when you install NT or any time later using the **RDIDSK** command

N O T E

N O T E

If you don't have your emergency disk and your system doesn't function, you may have no choice but to reinstall Windows NT from the installation disks or CD-ROM.

THE USER MANAGER

Anyone can use the User Manager in some capacity. Highly privileged groups, such as the Administrator group, fully use the User Manager to manage existing accounts and create new ones. If you are running NT Workstation at home, you can create accounts for family members, specifying the rights and permissions of each person.

Opening the User Manager

To start the User Manager, open the Start menu and select **Programs, Administrative Tools, User Manager**. The window pictured in Figure 15.3 will appear on your screen.

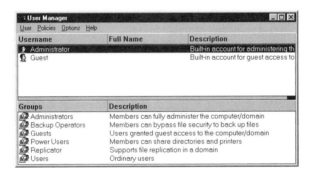

Figure 15.3 *The User Manager window.*

Every Windows NT workstation has predefined accounts and associated privileges. An *account* consists of a user ID and a password as well as other information maintained about the user and the configuration of the account. Table 15.2 shows the built-in accounts.

Table 15.2 Built-In Accounts

BUILT-IN ACCOUNT	DESCRIPTION
Administrator	The Administrator user is part of the Administrator group and cannot be removed from it. In the case of the Administrator group, privileges are the maximum available. If you are logged on as Administrator, you can change all aspects of your Windows NT configuration. You set up the password for the Administrator account when you install Windows NT.
Guest	A Guest account is provided to allow a visitor to gain access to your machine without having to create a user ID for the person. This user account has membership in the Guest group. You can set permissions on files for restricting a Guest's access.

Most of the built-in groups in Windows NT are shown at the bottom of Figure 15.3.

The Administrator account is a member of the Administrator group, which has the broadest set of rights for a workstation. If you are running NT Workstation at home, you should have access to the Administrator account. If you installed NT, you set up the account then. A member of the Administrator group can configure all aspects of the workstation. If you are running NT Workstation on a network at work, you probably won't have access to the Administrator account. In that environment, you will not be able to add new accounts or modify policies.

Adding New Users

If you are running Windows NT 4.0 Workstation at home and find that your children change things when they use the computer, you can create new accounts for them and limit their rights and permissions. With their own account they get to make some changes, so they can set their own colors and wallpaper and even have their own shortcuts on the desktop.

To set up a new user account, click the **User** menu and select **New User**. The New User dialog box, shown in Figure 15.4, appears.

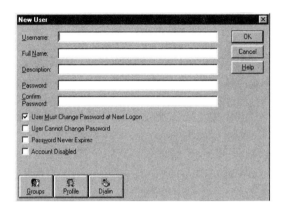

Figure 15.4 *The New User dialog box.*

You'll need to fill out this dialog box to create the new account. The account name for this user goes in the **Username** field. You must enter the password correctly twice and select the appropriate password options toward the bottom of the dialog box.

To assign this user to a predefined or local group, select the **Groups** button at the bottom of the page. The Group Memberships dialog box displays, as shown in Figure 15.4.

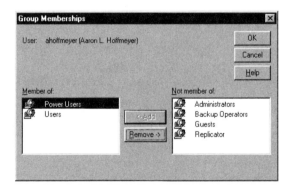

Figure 15.5 *Making a user a member of a predefined group.*

Use this dialog box to specify the groups of which user is a member. Each group has unique rights and privileges. Members of the Administrator group have unlimited access to the resources on the local workstation. Power Users have a lot of access, but they can't take control of resources in the same way that the members of the Administrator group can. Members of the Guest group have the most limited access. After assigning the group or groups to this user, click **OK** to go back to the New User dialog box.

The other two buttons in the New User dialog box enable you to assign a local or network profile directory for the user and specify whether the user has dial-in rights.

The *profile* is a directory where the user's specific login files are stored. If you want each user of this workstation to be able to configure his or her own desktop with his or her own tools and backgrounds, you'll need to specify where these files are to be stored. If you are on a network and are setting up an account for a user who may access the network from any workstation, you should specify that the user's home directory is on a shared network directory. That way, that user will be able to maintain the same desktop on many machines. The account mentioned above is a *roaming account.*

Adding a New Local Group

If you are using NT 4.0 Workstation at home and you have young children, you might want to create a new local group to specify what your children can access. You could also limit their access by making them members of a predefined group, such as Guests, and that would give them fairly limited access. For this or other reasons, you might want to create a new local group. To do so, click on the **User** menu and select **New Local Group**. The dialog box shown in Figure 15.6 displays. Complete the dialog box and click **OK** to create the new group. You can define the rights of this group using the Policies menu, as you'll see later.

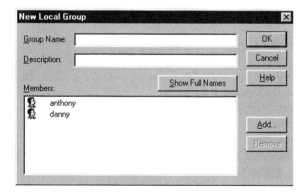

Figure 15.6 Creating a new local group.

Defining Policies

In addition to setting up new user accounts and creating and defining group memberships, the User Manager enables you to control three aspects of the system: account policies, user rights, and audits.

Account Policies

You can define policies for the accounts on your local workstation. To do this, select **Policies**, **Accounts**. The dialog box shown in Figure 15.7 displays. As you can see, this dialog box enables you to control many aspects related to passwords and logging on.

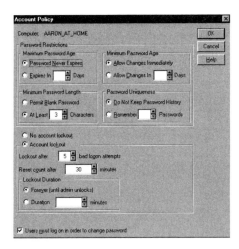

Figure 15.7 *Defining account policies.*

User Rights Policies

To specify the rights of groups and users, access the User Rights Policy dialog box (shown in Figure 15.8) by selecting **Policies, User Rights**.

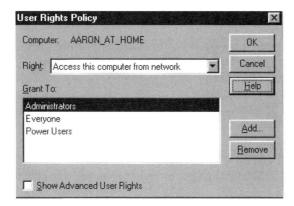

***Figure 15.8** Defining user and group rights.*

This dialog box enables you to select specific rights from the pull-down scrolling menu labeled **Right**. You can then define which groups or users have access to the selected right. To give a user or group a specified right, click the **Add** button and select the user or group in the resulting dialog box. If you click the **Show Advanced User Rights** option, advanced administration rights become selectable in the **Right** pull-down menu.

Audit Policies

Using the User Manager you can define which user-related events are audited by the system. *Events* are actions that occur within Windows NT—for example, successfully logging on, failing to delete a file, and opening a file. When you audit events, whenever the event occurs, NT generates an event listing for the system log. The event will then appear in Event Viewer, which is covered in more detail in the next section.

To define the user-related audits, select **Policies, Audit**. The dialog box shown in Figure 15.9 appears.

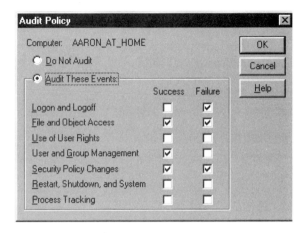

Figure 15.9 *Defining user audits.*

EVENT VIEWER

Event Viewer is a Windows NT tool for monitoring and logging events that occur on a Windows NT system. An event can be security-related—for example, a failed logon attempt—or application-related, such as an error received when a file cannot be opened. You can also get a system-related event such as a power supply failure. In all these cases, Windows NT allows you to keep track of and view events using Event Viewer.

Event Viewer enables you not only to view event logs on the current workstation but also to access the event logs on other computers running Windows NT. It can be useful for system administrators trying to troubleshoot problems with computers across a LAN, even when the other computer is at a remote location.

If you are running NT Workstation at home, you might use Event Viewer to find out why something is not working. It can often give you enough details to point you in the right direction. The information stored in the event logs is particularly useful if you contact Microsoft, your computer's hardware manufacturer, or an application development company for technical troubleshooting. Often, an error message stored in Event Viewer points directly to a solution, if one is available.

Using Event Viewer

Open Event Viewer by clicking on the **Event Viewer** icon in the Administrative Tools menu. You will see the Event Viewer window, shown in Figure 15.10.

; Event Viewer - System Log on \\AARON_AT_HOME					
Log View Options Help					
✓ System	Source	Category	Event	User	Computer
Security	Service Control Mar	None	7001	N/A	AARON_AT_HOME
Application	Service Control Mar	None	7024	N/A	AARON_AT_HOME
	RemoteAccess	None	20032	N/A	AARON_AT_HOME
Open...	Serial	None	11	N/A	AARON_AT_HOME
Save As...	Serial	None	24	N/A	AARON_AT_HOME
	EventLog	None	6005	N/A	AARON_AT_HOME
Clear All Events	Serial	None	24	N/A	AARON_AT_HOME
Log Settings...	Service Control Mar	None	7001	N/A	AARON_AT_HOME
	Service Control Mar	None	7024	N/A	AARON_AT_HOME
Select Computer...	RemoteAccess	None	20032	N/A	AARON_AT_HOME
	Serial	None	11	N/A	AARON_AT_HOME
Exit Alt+F4	Serial	None	24	N/A	AARON_AT_HOME
2/25/97 1:41:11 PM	Serial	None	24	N/A	AARON_AT_HOME
2/25/97 1:41:11 PM	Serial	None	24	N/A	AARON_AT_HOME
2/25/97 1:41:03 PM	EventLog	None	6005	N/A	AARON_AT_HOME
2/25/97 1:41:11 PM	Serial	None	36	N/A	AARON_AT_HOME

Figure 15.10 *The Event Viewer window.*

If you open the Log menu, shown in Figure 15.10, you will see three types of event logs: **System**, **Security**, and **Application**. The column headings, which remain the same from one log to another, are **Date**, **Time**, **Source**, **Category**, **Event**, **User** and **Computer**. You can select any of the three types of events (system, security, and application) to view the event for that type.

> You must be logged on as a member of the Administrator group to be able to view security log information. You do not need special rights to view the other two types of logs (application and system).

N O T E

Information about Events

The columns in Event Viewer have the following meanings:

- **Date**. The date that an event occurs.
- **Time**. The time that an event occurs.
- **Source**. An application name or the name of a component of the system.

- **Category**. A classification of the type of event by source. In many cases, you will see "None" listed.

- **Event**. The unique identification number of the event.

- **User**. The user who was logged on the machine when the event occurred. An entry of **N/A** means that this information was not available to the source.

- **Computer**. The computer on which the event occurred.

Icons

Icons are shown on the left of the list of events. These icons are listed and described in Table 15.3.

Table 15.3 Event Viewer Icons

ICON	NAME	PURPOSE
	Warning	Sometimes an indication of possible future problems, but usually not a serious issue. (For example, a printer's queue is purged).
	Error	A serious problem that requires attention.
	Information	Used when your computer has success fully completed an event (such as when the event log starts).
	Success Audit	Successful security events (for example, successfully logging on).
	Failure Audit	Failed security events (unsuccessfully attempting to log on).

Updating the View

You can update the log you're viewing by clicking on **View**, **Refresh**. The log files are updated automatically, but the Event Viewer display does not reflect the latest information until you update the display manually. You can also update the display by pressing **F5**.

Getting Details About Events

To view more-detailed information on any event, double-click on the event. A dialog box like the one shown in Figure 15.11 appears. In the **Description** text box, you'll see details about the source of the error or event. Debugging information is presented the **Data** box. This information is useful to a technician or developer who is helping you correct a problem. If you want to see the detailed description of the next or previous events without switching back to the Event Viewer display, you can click on **Next** or **Previous**.

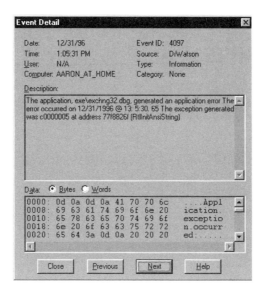

Figure 15.11 *Detailed view of an event.*

DISK ADMINISTRATOR

Disk Administrator enables you to create and delete partitions on your hard drive(s) and to add volume and stripe sets. (These terms will be explained in the following sections.) It's most useful if you have purchased a new hard drive and you want to set up that disk with a primary NT File System (NTFS) partition. NTFS volumes are more efficient and faster than DOS's old FAT (File Allocation Table) volumes. NTFS also supports compression of volumes and file security.

Managing Hard Disks and Partitions

Click **Disk Administrator** in the Administrative Tools menu to see the Disk Administrator window shown in Figure 15.12. Your disks are shown as colored bars, with partition and size information displayed. The primary partition is displayed with a dark blue border around the bar for that partition. A logical drive is displayed with a bright blue border. At the bottom of the Disk Administrator window is a status bar that tells you about the currently highlighted partition. Above the status bar is a legend of the color display.

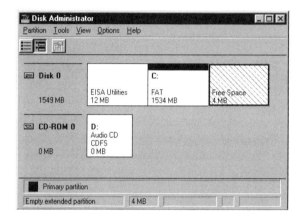

Figure 15.12 *The Disk Administrator window.*

Partitions

You create *partitions* on a hard disk to organize regions of your disk. For example, if you use Windows 95 as a second operating system, you'll need at least one FAT partition (and hopefully at least one NTFS partition). Different file systems must reside in different partitions.

Volume Sets

You can combine free space on different disks into a single entity called a *volume set*. You organize a volume set to fill the free space on one disk before starting to fill the next disk and so on. As many as 32 disks can be used in the creation of a volume set. Create a volume set by selecting two or more areas of free space on one to 32 disks. Click on the first area, click on each subsequent selection with the **Ctrl** key depressed and then choose the **Create Volume Set** option from the Partition menu. A dialog box will display the minimum and maximum size you can choose for the volume set. Select the size you want and click **OK**. A single drive letter is assigned to the volume set.

Creating a New Logical Disk: A Simple Walk-Through

If you purchased a computer with Windows 95 already installed, the primary hard drive (**C:**) was formatted using FAT. Because of the limited number of clusters FAT supports, there is usually some free space at the end of the disk that remains unformatted. If you purchase a new disk to format as NTFS so that you can take advantage of the NTFS capabilities, you can consolidate the free space on your first drive with a volume on your new drive.

The Disk 0 pictured in Figure 15.12 has 4 MB of free space. This is a small piece of disk real estate, too small to use as part of a volume set (because volume sets must be the same size on each disk). So we'll define it as an NTFS logical drive. To do so, we first partition it. Select the free space and then select **Partition**, **Create**. The dialog box shown in Figure 15.13 displays.

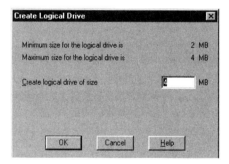

Figure 15.13 *Creating a new logical drive from free space.*

Specify the size of the partition and then click **OK**. The next available drive is assigned by default. If you want to change the drive letter, select **Tools**, **Assign Drive Letter**; then select the desired drive letter in the resulting dialog box. Now the partition will appear in the Disk Administrator window, as shown in Figure 15.14.

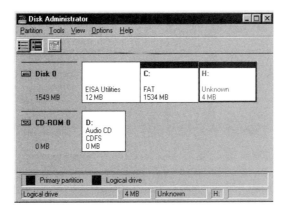

Figure 15.14 *A new, unformatted drive at the end of Disk 0.*

Now the drive needs to be formatted. However, before you can format the drive, you must commit to the partition changes you've made; select **Partition, Commit Changes Now**. A dialog box may display that contains some important disk information. Make sure you write down and do what it tells you to. After you've committed the new partition, it's ready to format. Select **Tools, Format**. The dialog box shown in Figure 15.15 appears.

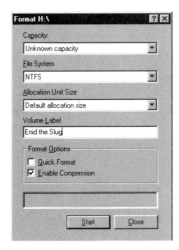

Figure 15.15 *Formatting a new partition.*

In the Format dialog box, specify the capacity, file system, allocation unit (cluster) size, volume label, and whether you want to enable compression (available only on NTFS). Don't select Quick Format; it bypasses flagging bad sectors, which you want to do if there is even a remote chance that there are bad sectors on the disk partition you are formatting. After you've set your options, click **Start**. After the formatting is complete, you'll see the formatted drive in the Disk Administrator, ready to access and use, as shown in Figure 15.16.

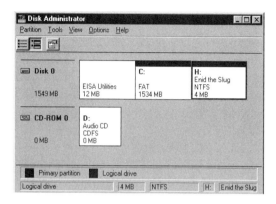

Figure 15.16 *A new, formatted logical drive.*

Viewing and Changing Drive Properties

Disk administrator also lets you view and change the properties of any formatted drive on your system. Select the drive and then select **Tools**, **Properties** (or click the **Properties** icon on the Toolbar). The drive Properties dialog box displays, as shown in Figure 15.17. This is the same Properties dialog box you see when it is invoked from My Computer or Explorer.

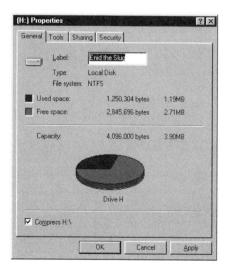

Figure 15.17 *The drive's Properties dialog box.*

This dialog box has three or four tabs, depending on whether the drive is formatted using FAT or NTFS (the **Security** tab appears only for NTFS drives). The **Security** tab enables you to define permissions and audits for the drive.

PERFORMANCE MONITOR

There may come a time when you are using NT and you sense that something is not right. The system is not as responsive as it once was. You're not sure why, and you can't pinpoint the source of the bottleneck. NT provides Performance Monitor for those times. Performance Monitor enables you to log and record data on a variety of processes and objects. Having data about your system can help you figure out why an application is not behaving the way you expect. You can localize the problem to an application, the operating system, or the hardware.

To use Performance Monitor, choose data that you want to view and then set up the format and frequency of updating for the data. You can also specify a log file to view the data later. There are four formats for Performance Monitor:

- The Chart view presents a chart of the items you choose to monitor. It displays the data in real time or from a recorded session.
- The Report view summarizes the data for inclusion in written reports.
- The Log view keeps data records so that you can examine them later.
- The Alert view lets you know when minimum performance criteria you set aren't being met.

All four views have the same window, menu bar, toolbar, and status bar.

Using Performance Monitor

Start Performance Monitor by selecting it from the Administrative Tools menu. The window shows the default Chart view, as shown in Figure 15.18. Table 15.4 lists and describes the icons on the Performance Monitor toolbar.

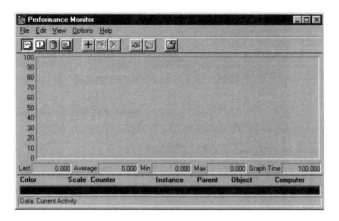

Figure 15.18 *The Performance Monitor window.*

Table 15.4 Performance Monitor Toolbar Icons

ICON	PURPOSE
	View a chart.
	View the alerts.
	View output log file status.
	View report data.
	Add counter. Use this button to add a parameter.
	Modify selected counter. Use this button to change settings for a counter.
	Delete selected counter. You can delete a parameter with this button.
	Update counter data. This logs another interval of data immediately after you select it.
	Place a commented bookmark in the output log.
	Options. Click this button to set up options.

Saving and Restoring Settings

The combination of all four views available in Performance Monitor is called a *workspace*. You can save the settings you make in your workspace in a file with the default extension **.PMW**. You save settings using the **Save Workspace** option available under the File menu. You can restore your workspace by using the **Open Workspace** option. If you want to save settings only in one view, use the **Save Settings** option.

Updating the Display

You can update the display manually or at a periodic interval automatically. The default is to update the display every 10 seconds automatically. Click on the **Options** menu for a particular view.

Using a Chart

Performance Monitor's Chart view presents a colorful display of parameters of interest. By default, Performance Monitor opens in Chart view, as shown in Figure 15.18, but it does not display data until you specify the data you want to see.

Click on the **Add counter** icon in the toolbar. The dialog box displayed in Figure 15.19 appears.

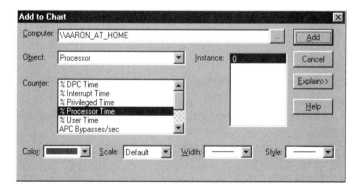

Figure 15.19 *The Add to Chart dialog box.*

When this dialog box opens, it assumes that you want to monitor the performance of the workstation you are currently using. If you want to monitor some other machine in your domain or workgroup, specify it in the **Computer** field. Then you need to specify the objects and metrics for the objects you want to monitor. For example, if you are trying to determine whether you have enough RAM, you might want to monitor memory paging faults. Select **Memory** from the pull-down **Object** list and then **Page Faults/sec** from the **Counter** scrolling list. Click **Add** to add this counter to the display. You can then choose another metric to display. You might then select **Paging File**, **%Usage**. Finally, you could select **Processor**, **%Interrupt Time**. After you've added these three metrics to the display, click the **Done** button to go back to the Performance Monitor window, which updates the display of the data items you selected.

At this point you could open an application and see what happens to the chart. If you have enough RAM, you should see fewer than 50 paging faults per second in the chart. Figure 15.20 shows a chart in which paging faults per second shoot up to more than 600.

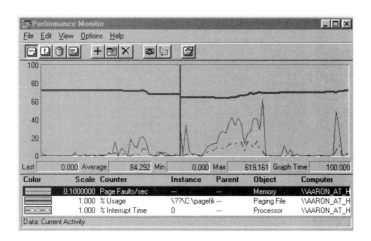

Figure 15.20 *A graph of paging faults/sec, paging file usage, and processor interrupts.*

You can double-click on the chart to toggle the menu bar and title bar off. You can also turn off the Toolbar by deselecting it from the Options menu. In that way, you can create a more picturesque view, one that's better for screen captures.

There are many categories of objects to monitor, and each object has at least two data items. Some data items can reveal short-term problems, and others are better for pointing out long-term issues. To get the most from Performance Monitor, you need to have some idea of what the data should be like—you need to understand what's "under the hood."

Using a Text Report

You go through a similar process in setting up a report. Click on the **Report** icon or select **Report** under the View menu. You will see a blank Report page. Click on the **Add data counter** icon to display a dialog box similar to the Add to Chart dialog box you filled in before. Select the appropriate computer, object, counter, and instance. Then click **Add**. Make further selections if you want to and then click on **Done**. The report will display, as shown in Figure 15.21.

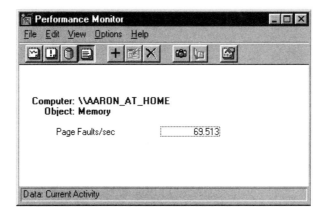

Figure 15.21 *The Report view.*

Log Files and Alerts

The Log file view and the Alert view work in much the same way as the chart and report views. There are some differences, but the basic procedures are similar.

Log Files

One significant difference is that you set up a log file to record data to review later, as opposed to viewing the current activities. After you define the objects for which you want to record data, save these options in a Log File Settings file (**.PML**). Then exit Performance Monitor and start it again. Go into Log view and select **File, Open** to open the log file and start recording data to it. You can leave it open while you put the computer through its paces for a while; then stop recording by clicking the **Options** icon and then clicking the **Stop**

Log button in the Log Options dialog box. Or you can stop logging by exiting Performance Monitor.

Later you can open the saved log file and examine the data in any of the other views. To do that, select the view and then select **Options, Data From**. Specify that you want to view the data from the log file you recorded earlier rather than the current data. Then specify the objects and data items you wish to view. In Chart view, you'll see a graph of the recorded data items for the objects you specified. The chart will not update.

The Alert View

The Alert view works like the Chart and Report views except that when you select the objects and data counters to monitor, you specify a data limit that must be violated (either higher or lower). When the counter for that data item goes outside the boundary you've defined, an alert appears in the window, as shown in Figure 15.22.

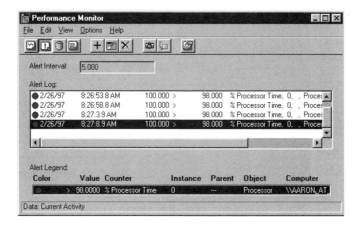

Figure 15.22 *The Alerts view.*

THE DIAGNOSTICS TOOL

The final system administration tool covered in this chapter is probably the least exciting but most useful. The Diagnostics tool contains a library of information on your computer's hardware, NT, and your applications. When you run this tool, the information updates to reflect the current status of everything.

One of the best ways to use the Diagnostics tool is to run it first when everything is working fine or before you make a change to your system. Print the comprehensive listing and hold onto it. Later, if you make a change to the system, such as installing new hardware, or if something stops working properly, you can run the Diagnostics tool again and compare the new information to the original. Unfortunately, the Diagnostics tool is not so robust that it isolates and fixes the trouble or tells you how to fix the problem, but still it's invaluable when you need it.

You access the Diagnostics tool from the Administrative Tools menu. You'll see a dialog box with nine tabs, as shown in Figure 15.23. Each tab presents a different category of information about your setup.

Figure 15.23 *The Diagnostics tool.*

At the bottom of each page are buttons that enable you to refresh the view, see the resource and services properties, and print the current page's information. Some of the pages contain subcategories of information, which you access using additional buttons. The **OK** button closes the dialog box.

The Diagnostics tool does not enable you to change settings or values in any way. It simply reports the facts. You use the Control Panel applets to change these values.

Summary

Windows NT 4.0 Workstation was designed with system administrators in mind. NT gives administrators all the power that they would have in administering the UNIX operating system in an easy-to-use interface. Many of the applications that enable you to make changes to the system are in the Control Panel (covered in Chapter 5).

One set of tools is not included in the Control Panel but is accessed using the Start menu. These administrative tools include Backup, Disk Administrator, Event Viewer, Performance Monitor, User Manager, and NT Diagnostics. Administrators may not use these often, but when problems come up, they can be the most valuable applications in NT.

User Manager is used to create and maintain user accounts, groups, and policies. Event Viewer gives you access to system events, security alerts, and application issues, and you can use Disk Administrator to partition and format part of a hard disk. You can monitor the performance of your system using Performance Monitor, and the NT Diagnostics tool contains a wealth of information about your system.

CHAPTER 16

Object Linking and Embedding

Data is passed between software programs in a number of ways. In the 1980s, Microsoft introduced a standard for passing data between Windows programs. Called object linking and embedding, or OLE, this technology lets you place a *link* to an *object*, such as a graphics file or part of a spreadsheet, inside another file, such as a WordPad or Word document. Whenever you make a change to the linked object (the graphics file or spreadsheet), that change is reflected in the file that contains the link to the original object.

You can also *embed* an object in a document. If you embed a Paint image in a WordPad file, for example, the Paint image becomes a part of the WordPad document.

Treating data and software as objects proved a popular idea, and Microsoft soon updated the original OLE standard calling the new version OLE2. OLE2 was a significant improvement over the original standard, and now most applications use only the new version. The term OLE now usually refers to the OLE2 standard, which is an integral part of almost all applications designed for Windows, Windows 95, and Windows NT.

OLE has continued to evolve. The Common Object Model (COM) standard enables applications to access resources, such as a control for a browser, using OLE. In effect, COM is a subset of OLE that defines how objects relate to one another; it gets the objects talking to one another. A version of the COM specification for accessing resources across the network is the Distributed Common Object Model, or DCOM. The Windows NT Explorer interface integrates the use of local files, directories, applications, shared network directories, domains, and printers as objects, and it uses OLE to manage the relationships among those objects.

You may have heard about Microsoft's introduction of ActiveX in 1996, and you may have heard that ActiveX is merely OLE renamed. Actually, ActiveX is a new name for the part of the OLE specification that used to be called OLE Custom Controls, or OCXs. The big difference is that an OCX, such as a movie viewer embedded in a Web page, tends to consume a lot of resources, because it is always active. But ActiveX controls, despite their name, become *inactive* when they lose the user's focus and consume fewer resources than OCXs. Internet Explorer takes advantage of ActiveX, but so far few other Microsoft products have followed suit. However, ActiveX will be incorporated into Microsoft Office in the near future. It may even play a role in the applications delivered with Windows NT 5.0.

The next version of Windows NT will take OLE to a new level, incorporating OLE into the operating system at the microkernel level. OLE will also spread its wings to encompass network OLE servers; you will be able to browse across the network for services, and network services will appear to be on your computer's desktop. OLE is the standard that will bridge the gap of the client/server environment and leverage the power of distributed computing. It will continue to be much more than pasting objects in a document.

But distributed computing lies in the future. This chapter sticks to the traditional role of OLE, that of linking and embedding objects. In this chapter you will learn about:

- Linking and embedding
- Creating objects
- Editing objects
- The ClipBook Viewer
- Creating a package

LINKING AND EMBEDDING

For you to use it, object linking and embedding technology must be built into applications. Many of the applications included with Windows NT 4.0 Workstation support OLE. The Microsoft Office and Works products all support OLE, and most applications designed for Windows NT or Windows 95 incorporate OLE support. You should check other products' documentation to see whether they support it.

OLE makes transferring data among applications less cumbersome. Suppose you have created a company logo in Paint. You then paste this logo into a mail merge letter you created in Word. You generate the letters and are about to print them when you discover that the logo has a mistake. The brute-force, ugly way to correct this problem is to redo the logo, delete the old version, and paste the new logo to each of the letters. At the very least, you would have to paste the new version into your original mail merge document and regenerate the letters. With OLE, however, you link the logo into the Word document. If you change the logo, the change is automatically reflected wherever it is linked. You need not do anything further. You don't have to regenerate the letters.

Embedding works differently. Suppose you want to create a document in WordPad that includes four different Paint images. It would be convenient to be able to store the images as part of the document, and that is the case with embedding. The images do not exist in any other file except the WordPad document in which they are embedded, and you have a single file that contains all your information. Moreover, you can make a change to any of the images while you are editing the document. Embedding is more than just pasting, because you can double-click an embedded object to start editing it in the original application in which it was created.

An example of a document with linked and embedded objects is shown in Figure 16.1. Here you see a WordPad file, an embedded Paint object, a packaged sound object, and a linked video clip. (We will discuss packaging later in the chapter.)

Figure 16.1 *A document with linked and embedded objects.*

Clients and Servers

Two types of applications are involved in an OLE transfer. The OLE *server* is the application that provides the data you are linking or embedding. The OLE *client* is the application that uses the server's data. In the preceding example, the WordPad application was the client application and Paint was the server application.

Not all applications can act as both a client and a server. Sound Recorder, Media Player, and Paint can act only as servers. WordPad can act as both client and server. Microsoft Word also has this dual capability.

The Clipboard

Whenever you do a cut-and-paste operation, you are using the Clipboard, a temporary storage space used for transferring data within one application or between two or more applications. The Clipboard holds only one object at a time. If you perform a new cut or copy operation, the old data in the Clipboard is written over.

CREATING OBJECTS WITH LINKING AND EMBEDDING

The linking and embedding operation is similar to the cutting and pasting you've done with WordPad or Paint. You need to select special menu commands to get the OLE operations; check your application's documentation for specific commands. Let's look at some typical commands you will encounter.

Applications vary in their level of support for OLE, so you might not see all these commands. Also, some applications may assign different names to some of these functions.

N O T E

Cut and Copy

After selecting or defining a region to be cut, you use the **Cut** command to perform the cut. The data is moved to the Clipboard, ready to be pasted elsewhere. To retain the data in the original document and copy it to the Clipboard, use the **Copy** command.

Paste

Once you have data in the Clipboard, you can paste it into another document or elsewhere in the same document by using **Paste**. This command will not create a linked object. If the client and server support object embedding, this command *may* produce an embedded object. For example, a Paint image pasted inside a WordPad document will become an embedded object.

Paste Special

This command is similar to **Paste** except that when you select it, you get a dialog box that lets you choose the format of the object (if different formats are available). In Figure 16.2, a Paint image is being copied. The **Paste Special** command is then used in WordPad, as shown in Figure 16.3. You see a dialog box, shown in Figure 16.4, that asks you to specify a choice of data types: Bitmap Image, Picture (metafile), or Device Independent Bitmap.

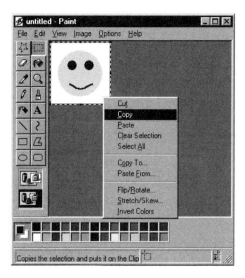

Figure 16.2 *An image to be copied.*

Figure 16.3 *Using the **Paste Special** command.*

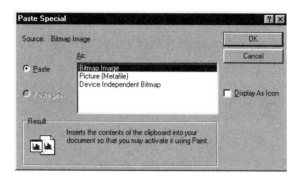

Figure 16.4 Choosing a data type.

Paste Link

The **Paste Link** menu option in some applications permits you to paste an object with linking. When you use **Paste Link**, you are creating a link to the original source document. If the object changes in the original source document, that change can be updated automatically and immediately in the destination document. You can often specify that you update the link manually.

Inserting an Object

When you insert an object, you can either embed or link it. Many Windows applications support inserting objects. In WordPad, for example, open the Insert menu and select **Object**. The Insert Object dialog box displays, as shown in Figure 16.5. Notice the two radio buttons labeled **Create New** and **Create from File**. The dialog box will vary from one application to the next; for example, the dialog box in Word has two tabs instead of two radio buttons. But the basic choices are usually similar to those shown.

You can create objects using any OLE application registered in Windows NT. If you want to create a new object, select the type of object from the scrolling list and click **OK**. You then will see a window for the appropriate application, and you can use it to create the object. You do not need to start the application separately before you copy and paste an object. Here, you create an object while you are editing your destination document.

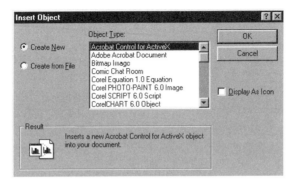

Figure 16.5 *Inserting a new object.*

If you select the **Create from File** radio button (or tab), the dialog box shown in Figure 16.6 appears.

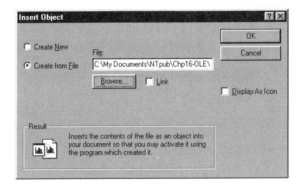

Figure 16.6 *Inserting an existing object.*

In this dialog box, you can browse for the existing file by clicking the **Browse** button. You can specify that the object file exists as a link by clicking the **Link** selection. If you don't specify that the object file is linked to the source, it will be embedded, as explained in the **Result** area at the bottom of the dialog box. The dialog box will also probably contain an option for you to display the object as an icon. If the object is an image or animation, it appears as an image in the destination document or file unless you specify that it be displayed as an icon.

Links

You can use the **Links** command to display any links that are present. You can also edit, cancel, and delete links. As an example, let us look at two linked objects in a Word document, as shown in Figure 16.7. Click on the **Links** command under the Edit menu. You will see a dialog box (Figure 16.8) with a list of the links that are present in the document.

Figure 16.7 *Two linked objects in a Word document.*

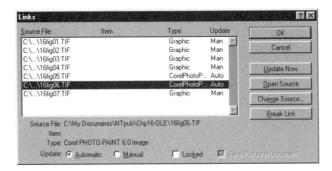

Figure 16.8 *Looking at links.*

The important options in this dialog box are:

- **Update Now**. If you prefer to update manually rather than automatically, choose the **Manual** radio button. Every time you want to update your document, click the **Update Now** button. Sometimes you may find that certain objects don't get updated even though they have been designated for automatic update. Use **Update Now** in these cases to see the changes in the destination document.

- **Open Source**. If you click **Open Source**, you will open a server application window. You can then edit the source object.

- **Change Source**. You can change a link using the **Change Source** button. It opens a dialog box that lets you browse your directories and network for another file that you can link to.

- **Break Link**. To cancel a link, click the **Break Link** button after highlighting the link you want to cancel. Select this option if you no longer want an object that is placed in a document to be updated through a link.

- **Locked/Unlocked**. In some Link dialog boxes, you'll see a radio button or check box to lock a link. This is another way that you can freeze the current state of an object and disallow revision through links. Select **Locked** to make an object unresponsive to changes in a linked source object. Clear this button or box to unlock the link and undo the lock operation.

After completing any changes to the link, you must use the **OK** button for the changes to go into effect.

WARNING

If a server application is performing an action, such as printing, you might get a "server unavailable" message when you try to create or edit an object in the destination document. Wait for some time to see whether the server becomes available. You can also cancel the current operation and then switch to the server application to find out which operation is occupying the server. Cancel or complete the operation. If you are accessing files on a remote computer, make sure that it is running.

Copying a Linked Object

If you copy an object that has links from one document to another, the links to the source document are also copied even if you perform a simple paste operation. If you do not want the links, you can open that document and cancel them.

EDITING AN EMBEDDED OBJECT

You edit an embedded object by double-clicking on the object. For an embedded Paint object in WordPad, the WordPad window switches to a Paint window (the server application), as shown in Figure 16.9. The object is highlighted and ready to edit.

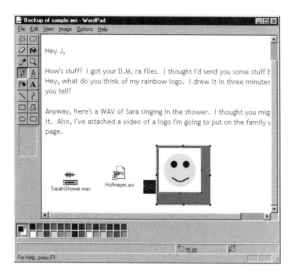

Figure 16.9 *Editing an embedded Paint object.*

Make changes to the object and then click outside the picture frame to switch back to WordPad, as shown in Figure 16.10. For some servers, you may have to exit using the File menu to get back to the client document.

Figure 16.10 *Switching back to the client document.*

EDITING A LINKED OBJECT

Editing an automatically linked object is similar to editing an embedded object. When you double-click on the object in the destination document, you will be editing the source file directly. After finishing your edits, save the object and exit the server application. Your changes are reflected in the destination document automatically. For manually linked objects, use the Links dialog box to open the source file to edit. Make your edits and save the file. To see the update in the destination file, select **Update Now** in the Links dialog box.

THE CLIPBOOK VIEWER AND THE CLIPBOARD

The ClipBook Viewer and the Clipboard are tools that you can use in transferring data. The Clipboard stores any information on which you use the **Cut** or **Copy** command; it holds only one object at a time. When you copy another object, the first object is written over. You can use the ClipBook Viewer to store objects, in *pages*, for further use. The ClipBook Viewer is like a repository; objects can be placed there temporarily or permanently. You can also use the ClipBook Viewer to transfer information between different computers and users.

You can store information in the Clipboard in various formats, so you can transfer information between applications that use different formats.

Opening the ClipBook Viewer

Open the ClipBook Viewer by double-clicking on the **ClipBook Viewer** icon in the Main group of Program Manager. You see the ClipBook Viewer window, as shown in Figure 16.11. It has a menu bar, toolbar, and status bar like those you have seen in other applications. In the active window area, you will see two icons: one for the Clipboard and the other for the local ClipBook (the ClipBook that is on your machine). In Windows NT you can access ClipBooks on remote machines as well as your local ClipBook. The buttons in the toolbar (Table 16.1) are for the most common commands in the menus.

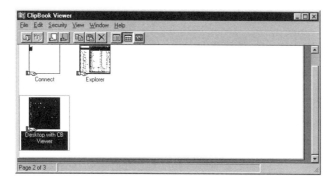

Figure 16.11 *The ClipBook Viewer.*

Table 16.1 Buttons in the Toolbar

BUTTON	FUNCTION	DESCRIPTION
	Connect	Allows you to connect to a ClipBook on anothercomputer.
	Disconnect	Severs a connection with another computer's ClipBook.
	Share	Shares a ClipBook page with other users.
	Stop sharing	Terminates the sharing of a ClipBook page.
	Copy	Copies a selected ClipBook page with this button.
	Paste	Pastes the object in the Clipboard into the ClipBook.
	Delete	Deletes a selected ClipBook page or the contents of the Clipboard.
	Display titles	View the titles of ClipBook pages.
	Display thumbnail pictures	View small thumbnail pictures of your pages in ClipBook.
	Display contents	View the contents of a selected Clipbook page.

Sharing Information

You can transfer data between the Clipboard and the ClipBook page and between the application and the Clipboard.

To transfer data to and from the ClipBook or Clipboard, use the **Cut**, **Copy**, and **Paste** operations. From an application, select the object and then use the **Cut** or **Copy** command from the application's Edit menu. This places the object onto the Clipboard. From there, you can paste the object into another application or onto a ClipBook page.

Sharing a ClipBook Page and Linking an Object from Another Computer

You can specify that you want to have a page shared when you paste into that page. First, click **Share Item Now**. The Share ClipBook Page dialog box will appear. In this dialog box, you can click on an option box labeled **Start Application on Connect**. This will enable users to start links easily. If you do not check this box, users will not be able to connect to a computer if a server application is not already running. An additional button lets you specify permissions for the page. Click this button to define the access privileges for different user groups.

You can share an existing page by selecting the page in the ClipBook Viewer and then clicking the **Share** button; or choose the **Share** option under the File menu.

Because you can access another computer's Clipboard, you can set up linked objects across your Windows NT network. You can have a source document on one computer and a destination document on another. You can copy and paste link an object from the source document to the destination document. You need to use the ClipBooks of both computers to make the transaction work:

```
Source Document ′ Clipboard ′ ClipBook page ′ Destination ClipBook
page ′ Clipboard ′ Destination document
```

You copy from the source document onto computer 1's Clipboard and ClipBook. Then you make the ClipBook page a shared page if it is not already. From the destination computer (computer 2), you copy the page onto your local Clipboard by issuing the **Copy** command. Then you paste link the object into your destination document and save the destination document.

The Clipboard and Formats

The Clipboard supports many different formats; those that are available depend on the server application. You can view the Clipboard by double-clicking the **Clipboard** icon. When the Clipboard window is active, you see a set of format options under the View menu. Depending on the application, one or more formats may be available. There are some internal formats that will show as being unavailable. Click on any of the alternative formats and see the result in the Clipboard windows. You can save the Clipboard in a file by using the **Save As** option under the File menu. You can then reload the Clipboard from the file (using the **Open** option) for pasting into another document.

CREATING A PACKAGE

You can display objects as *package* icons. You can make a package for an object, for a file or part of a file, or for a command. Packages are especially useful in Mail. You can make a file in a shared directory into a package and include the package in a mail message. When the recipient double-clicks on the package icon, the original file will be displayed from the shared directory. In this way, you avoid sending the file in the electronic message to many recipients. You represent nonvisual objects, such as sound files, exclusively with packages when you embed or link these objects. This happens automatically when you copy a sound file to the Clipboard and paste the object in a destination document.

You can create a package using File Manager or Object Packager. The File Manager approach can be quicker, but it does not have as many options as Object Packager.

Using File Manager to Create a Package

There are two ways you can use File Manager to create a package. You can drag and drop a file from File Manager directly into a destination document. The resulting package will be represented by a generic package symbol displayed above the title of the file. The file should have an application associated with it. For example, a **.txt** file has the Notepad application associated with it. Use the **Associate** command under the File menu in File Manager if there is no association.

The other method is to use the File Manager menus. You have the advantage of being able to link an object into a package with this method.

You can create a package for any file, including an executable file (**.EXE**) or batch file (**.BAT**). When you double-click on a package that contains an executable file, you start executing the file.

Using Object Packager to Create Packages

Object Packager lets you create a package for a file, an object on the Clipboard, or a command. With Object Packager you can choose an icon to represent the object and edit the package's contents or label.

Starting Object Packager

To start Object Packager, open a Command Prompt window and type **packager**. You will get the Object Packager window. In the **Appearance** area, choose the icon to represent the package by clicking **Insert Icon**. In the **Content** area, you will see a file name (for a file) or a bitmap (for an image) if you click on the **Picture** radio button. To activate either side of this window, click on the appropriate side. You can paste or paste link from the Clipboard onto Object Packager.

An Example with a Screen Capture

You can copy your screen or the active window on your screen with two keystrokes. By pressing **Shift + Print Screen**, you display the entire screen as a bitmap on the Clipboard. You can paste this information into Paint or any other document. Similarly, you can use the **Alt + Print Screen** button combination to get a bitmap of only the active window.

Let's make an image of the active window into a package. First, open the Object Packager window and then press **Alt + Print Screen**. Open the Clipboard to see the image of your active window. Activate the **Content** side of Object Packager and use the **Paste** option under the Edit menu. Now click on the **Picture** radio button, and you will see the bitmap on the right side. Go to the **Appearance** side, click **Insert Icon**, and choose an icon from the list. Under the Edit menu, click the **Label** option. You will get a dialog box where you type in a label for the icon and click **OK**. Your package is ready for use. Choose the **Copy Package** option under the Edit menu. This copies your new package to the Clipboard. You can paste this package into an application. Finally, the package is pasted in a WordPad document.

Inserting a Command Line into a Package

You can insert a command line into a package by using the **Command Line** option under the Edit menu. Click on this option and you get a dialog box. Here, you type in a command-line argument and click **OK**. The command line becomes the content of your package. When you embed this package, you have an icon representation of the command. By double-clicking, you invoke the command line that you placed in the package.

Linking a File into a Package

You link a file into Object Packager by copying the file to the Clipboard with File Manager, as already discussed, and using the **Paste Link** option under the Edit menu. This approach makes the file a linked object in your package.

Using Packages in Mail

Embed packages in Mail the way you have in other applications. A package can be copied into a new Mail message body by using the **Paste** option under the Edit menu. You could also use the **Paste Special** option, which allows you to choose between a package representation or the full picture representation when you paste.

SUMMARY

Object linking and embedding technology lets you create compound documents that contain elements of documents from other applications. You can have embedded objects or linked objects. An embedded object is saved only in the document in which you have placed it. A linked object is saved in the source document only. You can edit either type of object. You just double-click the object, invoking the application in which it was created. One advantage of a linked object is that changes made to it in the source document can automatically be reflected in all the documents in which it is placed. You can specify that the update be automatic or manual. You can share objects in the ClipBook by placing objects in ClipBook pages. If these pages are designated as shared pages, your colleagues can access them from other computers. In this way, you can create documents with linked objects that reside on other computers in your network. The Clipboard is a scratch-pad area that holds the latest copied or cut information. You overwrite the Clipboard when you perform a new copy or cut. You can save the contents of the Clipboard in ClipBook pages for later use.

CHAPTER 17

Networking

By Nelson King

This chapter is a whirlwind tour of networking: what it is, what it does, and a little bit of how you do it. Installing and configuring a working network (Windows NT, Novell, or any other network) is one of the most difficult and complicated things you can do in computing. People go to school or get special training just to learn the basics, and it often takes years of experience before they become good at it. However, just because you may not personally install a Windows NT network doesn't mean that you shouldn't know how one works and why they're important.

In this chapter we'll cover enough of the basic concepts to give you an overall picture. Specifically, we'll look at the following topics:

- An overview of networking

- Networking in the world of computer products

- The Windows NT network model

- The components of a network: hardware and software

- The elements of installing and configuring a peer-to-peer network

NETWORKING IN A NUTSHELL

Computer networks have been around for almost as long as computers have existed. As soon as there were two computers of the same kind, people figured out how to connect them and a network was born. The question is, why? The answers may seem obvious, but it's important to fully grasp how the motivation behind networks drives the building of networks and why companies are willing to spend millions of dollars to install and maintain them.

The main reason for a network is to share information. If there were only one computer and everyone had to go to it to get information, people would spend most of their time walking to and from the computer (as they do to use the copier machine). If you can put computers or computer terminals where the people are, they can reach the information without needing to move around.

Sharing information is important, because information is valuable. Most modern businesses run on information, and in many cases information *is* the business. Knowing how much revenue a company generates, keeping the names of customers, storing the designs of products, and maintaining access to several million other kinds of information are the essence of making money, being competitive, and running an efficient operation. When a company sees that many of its employees need access to information, it builds a network.

There are many kinds of networks, and you can classify them from several perspectives. From the geographic perspective, there are local area networks (LANs), which are located in a single building or perhaps are connected among buildings in a small area such as a college campus. Other networks span considerable distances—between cities and sometimes between countries—and are called wide area networks (WANs). Then there are huge, dispersed networks of networks—such as the Internet—that cover a country or the world like a spider's web.

Networks are also classified by their structure, the type of hardware and cabling they use, and above all by the protocol they use. A *protocol*, simply put, is the communications language used by a network to signal how information should be handled as it is transmitted. In a sense, it's the language computers use when they talk to each other and say something like, "I want information." "OK, I've got some." "What form is it in?" "Two hundred packets with a thousand words each." This "conversation" gives you a sense of protocols. The real thing is nothing but packets of binary code with embedded instructions.

Protocols introduce new terminology. For example Windows NT supports two very different kinds of networks (see Figure 17.1). In a *peer-to-peer* network, each computer in the network can share its information with any other computer; they are equals, or peers. This type of NT network can use protocols, such as NetBEUI (NetBIOS Extended User Interface) and PPTP (Point-to-Point Tunneling Protocol). A *client/server* network is based on a *server* that coordinates all the other computers (*clients*). This kind of network can use various protocols, such as TCP/IP (Transport Control Protocol/Internet Protocol), SPX/IPX, and also NetBEUI (more on the protocols in a bit).

PEER-TO-PEER NETWORK

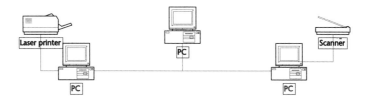

CLIENT / SERVER NETWORK

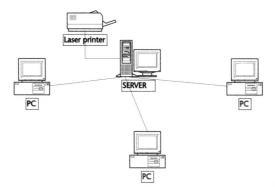

Figure 17.1 *Two kinds of Windows NT networks.*

All networks require specialized hardware, beginning with some kind of cable to connect the machines. Each machine must have a way of attaching the cable and sending transmissions to its processor. This is called a *network interface card*, or NIC. Some kinds of networks require equipment, called *hubs* and *routers*, to organize many computers and their cables. Connecting different kinds of networks requires yet another kind of hardware, usually called *bridges* and *gateways*.

Many networks also require specialized software known as network operating systems (NOS). Windows NT Server is a network operating system, as are Novell's NetWare and Banyan's Vines. Interestingly, the biggest network—the Internet—doesn't have an operating system. It's just hardware and the communications protocol TCP/IP. The Internet relies on software in its member networks to take care of operating system chores such as managing disk drives and printers.

All the parts of a network—computers, cables, interface cards, hubs, routers, operating systems, and so on—have one major goal: moving data from one place to another so that people can share information.

THE WIDE WORLD OF NETWORKING

Over the past decade, many networking schemes have been put into use by various companies. In an effort to establish a common ground for communication among various networks and protocols, the Institute of Electrical and Electronic Engineers (IEEE) and the International Standards Organization (ISO) developed a model that any networking scheme can use for defining its components. It's called the Open Systems Interconnection (OSI) Reference Model and is illustrated in Figure 17.2. At one time it was believed that this would be the way all networks would be defined. That didn't happen, but the OSI Reference Model still remains the best way to describe an overview of networking.

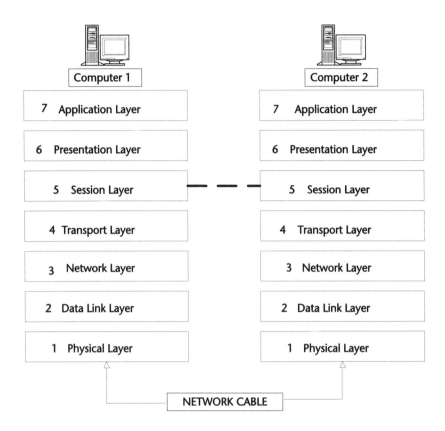

Figure 17.2 The OSI Reference Model.

This model has seven layers that represent different network functions, from the physical connection (in layer 1) to the application that is using networking (at the top in layer 7).   ▽

The layers in the OSI model behave as if they were communicating directly with their counterparts on the other computer. In reality, a layer such as layer 5, communicates with the layer 5 services on the other computer by using services provided by layers 1 through 4 on the same computer to get to the physical connection (the network cable). Then data travels to and from the other computer through layers 1 through 4 on the other computer until layer 5 is serviced. Thus, each layer communicates only with lower layers on the same computer—and also knows only of the services and not the details of the implementation for the lower layers. This means that you could substitute a different layer component as long as you provide the same services. When a layer 5 request passes through lower levels and back up the levels on the destination computer, it is passing through what is called a *protocol stack*. The layer 5 components use the same protocol, or specification of communication. Each of the layers provides a function that is described in the following list; a keyword that summarizes that function appears in brackets:

1. **Physical layer [CABLE].** This layer addresses the specific need to move data between point A and point B. You specify the type of cable required, the number of pins and wires used for transmission, and the technique used for signaling. *Signaling* describes the combination of the electrical characteristics required to communicate (for example, the voltage and logic levels) with the methods to communicate. You must include all the mechanical and electrical specifications needed to interface to the networking cable.

2. **Data link layer [FRAMES].** The physical layer (Layer 1) is concerned only with raw bits. The data link layer is concerned with packaging groups of bits as effectively as possible for error-free transmission. You form packets of bits that are delineated from each other by *framing bits*, markers that convert a packet into a delineated frame. You transfer a frame to another computer's data link layer through the physical layer of each computer.

3. **Network layer [ROUTING].** The network layer "knows" about the network's *topology*—that is, how computers are connected. This layer is responsible for correctly routing communication between point A and point B by specifying the most efficient pathway. This layer is also responsible for dealing with problems related to congestion and traffic on the network and to the limitations of bandwidth or parts of the network. The network layer also handles addresses. For example, you can send a message to a logical address such as the name of a computer, and the network layer translates the logical address to a physical address.

4. **Transport layer [MESSAGES].** The transport layer is responsible for error detection and correction and for dividing messages into packets. Messages that come from the application layer (layer 7) pass through

the transport layer, where they are cut into small packets or combined into larger packets for efficient transmission over the network. Sequence numbers for the packets are assigned to make sure that they are received in the correct order. Upon receipt at the other end, the messages are put back into their original form and an acknowledgment message is sent to the originator.

5. **Session layer [CONNECTION].** The session layer establishes which computer is the talker and which computer is the listener in a communication link. This layer synchronizes and monitors the stream of data.

6. **Presentation layer [FORMATTING].** In the presentation layer, the data is formatted for presentation. At this level attention is paid to issues such as whether lines end in a carriage return or in the combination of a carriage return and a line feed. Data compression may be used in this layer, reducing the number of bits needed to transfer data. The presentation layer also manages security issues by providing data encryption services.

7. **Application layer [INTERFACE].** This layer originates requests for network services. Application software, such as a word processor, can use the services provided on this layer to access network resources such as remote files. The application layer handles high-level security access issues, such as whether a logged-in user has the rights to access a network resource.

Precise matching of software components to this model is often difficult. Some software spans several layers in functionality.

The NT Network Model

Now let's look at the details of how Windows NT performs its networking. In the context of networking, Windows NT has several objectives:

- **To support many networks.** Users must be able to access files on a Windows NT server as easily as on a NetWare server.

- **To support many transport methods simultaneously.** You must be able to use a protocol that supports LAN Manager and NetBEUI at the same time you support a protocol that supports Unix and TCP/IP. You will thereby be able to tie your Windows NT workstation to both networks using the same physical layer and also support multiple transports.

- **To support client/server computing.** You need mechanisms to be able to run parts of applications on local and remote computers and to provide channels of communication between local and remote processes.

To accomplish these objectives, Windows NT uses a flexible system of network components. You can map the Windows NT networking structure to the OSI model, as shown in Figure 17.3. The physical layer is composed of the NICs and cables that tie them to other computers. You can have more than one NIC in your computer.

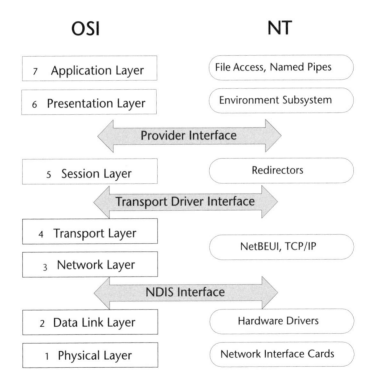

Figure 17.3 *The Windows NT model.*

The data link layer has drivers for the network interface cards. These drivers are loadable (and unloadable) modules and can be removed or added as needed. You can also specify that NT load more than one driver at a time. At the top of the data link layer is the NDIS 3.0 Interface, first developed in 1989 by Microsoft and 3Com to specify the software interface used by transport protocols to communicate with NICs. You can have multiple transport protocols for each NIC that is installed, so you can simultaneously access different network servers using different network protocols, such as the Banyan Vines server and the Windows NT Server.

The next layer is the transport layer. This layer contains transport protocols that are implemented in Windows NT, all of them interfacing to the NDIS interface. The transports included with Windows NT are TCP/IP, NBF, and DLC. TCP/IP is the protocol of the Internet. Because of the vast momentum behind the Internet as well as the local area network equivalent (called an *intranet*), TCP/IP is rapidly becoming the dominant protocol on Windows NT.

The second protocol, NBF, is derived from NetBEUI, the default protocol for Windows NT networking. DLC is designed for use with mainframe computers and the IBM SNA (Systems Network Architecture).

At the top of the transport layer is the transport driver interface, or TDI. The TDI is an interface to networking components called redirectors and servers. A *redirector* is a software component that redirects information requests to the right destination. Suppose an application on your local computer is requesting access to a file that happens to reside on a remote machine. The job of the redirector is to redirect the information request to the correct remote resource. At the receiver end, a software component called a *server* processes the redirector's request for information and furnishes the requested data to the originator.

In the session layer you also have the redirector and server. (Windows NT allows you to have many redirectors and servers.) Each redirector and server addresses a different type of network. Another interface, called the provider interface, is in the middle of the session layer. The provider interface allows you to build software components, called *providers*, that establish connections to remote servers regardless of the type of server, network, or protocol that is required.

Above the session layer is the presentation layer. In Windows NT, the role of the presentation layer is taken up by the protected subsystems in the Windows NT architecture. Each protected subsystem provides a complete environment for processes, including any data-organization requirements for a particular environment.

At the top of the OSI model is the application layer. In Windows NT, this layer corresponds to the programmer-level services that are available for networking. Several networking facilities are available to programmers in their applications.

Networking in Windows NT Server and Windows NT Workstation

One consistent source of confusion is that *both* Windows NT Workstation and Windows NT Server support networking—and you can do networking without one or the other. You can even use Windows NT Server without having a single Windows NT Workstation machine connected to it.

To understand why this is so, let's go back to what was said about the objectives of Windows NT—to provide a highly flexible networking environment. There are many circumstances under which, for example, a Novell network will use a Windows NT Server machine to run applications. Similarly, you can have a Windows NT Workstation computer that connects only to Unix computers on a TCP/IP intranet. Microsoft decided long ago that instead of competing head on with the other systems, it would infiltrate them. This turned out to be a wise choice now that networks are abandoning the "native" NetBEUI protocol of NT in favor of TCP/IP.

When it comes to networking, there are many similarities between Windows NT Server and Windows NT Workstation, but they are not equally endowed. Microsoft never intended the Workstation version to provide more than simple peer-to-peer networking supplemented by limited connectivity to TCP/IP. The Windows NT Workstation doesn't have many of the administrative and monitoring capabilities of NT Server, nor is it optimized to handle high-speed operations with many simultaneous users.

NOTE
In the past couple of years, a controversy has been raised by companies that have depended on the considerable server capabilities of Windows NT Workstation. With version 4.0, Microsoft suddenly limited the number of connections available to the Workstation version. This development negatively affected a number of products, particularly Internet Web servers.

AN OVERVIEW OF NETWORK SETUP

This section will walk you through the configuration necessary for installing a network on a Windows NT 4.0 Workstation computer. This is not a substitute for the complete instructions for doing an installation—that's a subject for several chapters. The intent here is to provide you with the concepts and jargon that surround networks. You may find this information helpful even if you never install a network workstation yourself.

Like most of the technical subjects in working with Windows NT Workstation, this one begins in the Control Panel. You can open the Control Panel through the Start menu, under **Settings**, or in the My Computer folder on the Windows desktop. In the Control Panel folder, locate the **Network** icon and double-click it. You'll see the Network dialog box, which looks like Figure 17.4.

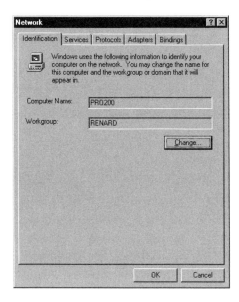

Figure 17.4 Network dialog box, *Identification* tab.

The five tabs in this dialog box (**Identification**, **Services**, **Protocols**, **Adapters**, and **Bindings**) pretty much cover the ground for networking with Windows NT Workstation. Some of the names of the tabs may sound familiar from earlier sections in this chapter. But putting them together with what's necessary to get a network running—that's another matter.

Taking a broad view, here are the steps for installing a network on a Windows NT 4.0 Workstation computer. They correspond to the tabs of the Network Control Panel dialog box.

1. Install a network interface card.
2. Connect the NIC to the network cable.
3. Give your computer a name and membership in a workgroup (or domain).
4. Select additional services for Windows NT (if appropriate).
5. Select the working network protocols and configure them.
6. Bind the protocols to the NIC.

Identification

The first tab, **Identification**, is the easiest to understand. Every computer on a network must have a unique name—an identifier—so that other computers (and their users) know who's on the network and what resources are available. This identifier is entered in the **Computer Name** field. The second field, **Workgroup**, is a little more esoteric. Windows NT (both Server and Workstation editions) supports two methods for organizing the users of a network. One is called a *workgroup*, which is a group of computers and users that more or less work together. Once a computer has been designated as part of a workgroup, it can have specific security and resource rights based on membership in that group. The other method is called a *domain*, which is oriented to network servers. This is the method used by Windows NT to manage a network that has multiple servers and may be geographically dispersed (perhaps all over the country). Domains exist for the same reason as workgroups: to provide a means for identifying security and resource groups.

Keep in mind that when a network supports thousands of users (and computers), it becomes a major problem to keep everything organized. Domains and workgroups are part of the solution. Microsoft will offer the rest of the solution in Windows NT 5.0 with its network directory services.

If you're setting up a simple NT peer-to-peer network—say, four computers in a small office—you will make up a name for your workgroup. If your computer is part of a larger network that uses Windows NT Server, the system administrator (or the equivalent) will give you the name of the domain to use.

Services

Like other services in Window NT, each network service is a collection of capabilities and features. For example, the Workstation service covers all the networking capability of Windows NT Workstation.

The **Services** tab of the Network dialog box, shown in Figure 17.5, will contain different entries depending on which services have been installed. By default, Computer Browser, Server, and Workstation are installed. Any others, such as NetBIOS and Remote Access Service, are installed optionally. The nondefault services may have a number of options to be configured. The options are reached by selecting the service, clicking the right mouse button, and selecting **Properties**.

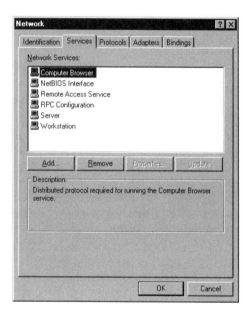

Figure 17.5 *Network dialog box,* **Services** *tab.*

Here is a list of the services that come bundled with Windows NT Workstation:

- **Client Service for NetWare**. Makes this computer a Novell NetWare client workstation.
- **Microsoft Peer Web Services**. Provides connections to a Web server.
- **Microsoft TCP/IP Printing**. Enables a print server service for TCP/IP networks.

- **NetBIOS Interface**. Provides routines to handle old DOS programs networking.
- **Network Monitor Agent**. A basic network monitoring service.
- **Remote Access Service**. Enables dial-up into a Windows NT network.
- **RPC Configuration**. Configures the Remote Procedure Call facility.
- **RPC Support for Banyan**. Special Remote Procedure Call routines for Banyan products.
- **Server**. NT Workstation server routines.
- **Simple TCP/IP Services**. This includes FTP and Gopher services.
- **SNMP Services**. Simple Network Management Protocol monitors TCP/IP networks.
- **Workstation**. NT Workstation networking services.

Protocols

Seven protocols are packaged with Windows NT. The two most commonly used are NetBEUI and TCP/IP. NetBEUI is automatically installed when you set up Windows NT and provides the easiest connections for small local area networks. Using NetBEUI, you can also access other Windows NT workstations and computers running Windows for Workgroups (older versions of Windows). If you want to access the Internet or an intranet, you need to install TCP/IP. Both protocols can be available at the same time, although only one at a time can be used for a network between local computers. Dialing into the Internet with your phone also requires TCP/IP, but that's a different kind of network arrangement.

In addition to NetBEUI and TCP/IP, Windows NT supports the following protocols:

- **AppleTalk**. Support for the major network protocol of Apple computers.
- **DLC Protocol**. Used to connect to IBM mainframe computers.
- **NWLink IPX/SPX Compatible Transport**. Support for Novell networks.
- **Point-to-Point Tunneling Protocol**. A new protocol for private intranet networks.
- **Streams Environment**. Handles flow of data from Unix environments.

These protocols can be added to the active list through the **Protocols** tab of the Network dialog box (Figure 17.6). In most cases, it's necessary to enter additional configuration information, which can be quite involved.

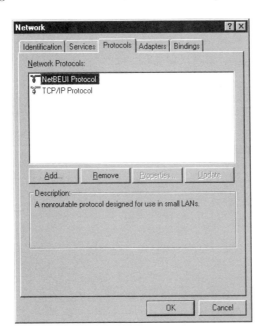

*Figure 17.6 Network dialog box, **Protocols** tab.*

Using the native NetBEUI protocol is attractive, because it's fairly close to Plug and Play. You install network adapter cards, bind the cards to the NetBEUI protocol, and connect the cables. You can buy a number of inexpensive network kits that will take you through the steps.

Adapters

Every computer (server and workstation) requires a network interface card to connect with a network. Over the years there have many different kinds of cards, just as there were many different kinds of networks. There was little compatibility, and configuring the cards could be a nightmare. Fortunately, today the situation is much better. For the most part, networks are now standardized on Ethernet as the topology. There are, however, several grades of Ethernet that follow one rule: more speed, more expense.

When you add a network card to a computer, it must be registered with Windows NT in the **Adapters** tab of the Network dialog box, shown in Figure 17.7. This will install the appropriate *drivers*—software that provides the connection between the hardware and NT—for the type and make of NIC.

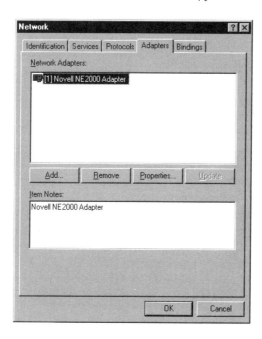

*Figure 17.7 Network dialog box, **Adapters** tab.*

A software driver allows you to use a particular protocol with the NIC, whereas a device driver that you install along with the NIC allows you to control the hardware functions of an NIC. If you want to add network software drivers to your system, choose the **Add** button. You'll see a long list of supported adapters and their protocols. If your adapter isn't in this list, you may need to insert certain Windows NT installation disks or other media (using the **Have Disk** button). To remove an NIC, you highlight the listed NIC in the **Network Adapters** list box and click **Remove**.

Bindings

Once you have installed a network interface card and installed or configured a network protocol, the final step is check the binding of the card to the protocol and network services. *Binding* is programmer jargon for linking information about one object (in this case, the NIC) directly to the use of another object (in this case, a protocol such as NetBEUI and a service such as Server). Bindings are displayed in the **Bindings** tab of the Network dialog box (Figure 17.8).

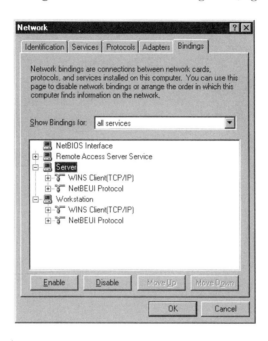

Figure 17.8 *Network dialog box,* **Bindings** *tab.*

This window uses a hierarchical display much like that of Windows Explorer. Click on the + sign to expand the information and the – sign to shrink it. The list box next to **Show Bindings for** lets you see what is bound to each service, protocol, or adapter. The actual binding isn't initiated in this window—that's done when you install the NIC and the protocol—but you can enable or disable any of the bindings.

SUMMARY

Gone are the days when sharing data with another person meant running down the hall with a floppy disk (a sneaker net), at least for companies that want to remain competitive. Computer networks are now common in offices of three or more computers. Even the Internet, with about 70 million users, is a network. Network technology is still loaded with special terminology—words such as *protocol, TCP/IP*, and *drivers*—but the basics, as described in this chapter, aren't very complicated.

Windows NT networking has an open, extended architecture that allows multiple network protocols to run simultaneously with a single network interface card. You can access UNIX workstations over a TCP/IP network while you access other Windows NT workstations with NetBEUI and access Novell NetWare servers with NetWare. Windows NT Server, another product in the Windows family, supplements this capability with domain management features and integrated support for tying into Apple Macintosh computers.

Microsoft has created a network operating system, Windows NT (Server or Workstation version) that is reliable, powerful, and flexible. You'll often hear about NT networking in conversation around the water cooler, especially when the topic is the Internet.

Multimedia

Multimedia is one of the newest and most exciting areas in computing. Windows NT 4.0 offers many improvements to facilitate multimedia devices and applications. In this chapter, you will learn how to use the CD Player to play audio CDs, how to use the Sound Recorder to make your own digital recordings, how to play video files with the Media Player, and how to use the Volume Control to keep the neighbors or family members from complaining.

In this chapter you will learn about:

- New NT 4.0 multimedia features
- The CD Player
- The Sound Recorder
- The Media Player
- The Volume Control
- The Multimedia applet in the Control Panel

MULTIMEDIA FEATURES IN WINDOWS NT 4.0

Windows NT 4.0 has not added many new multimedia features; most of the important capabilities were already present in Windows NT 3.5. But version 4.0 has grouped these features better and enhanced some of them. In brief, the following changes have been made:

- *Better video.* Numerous enhancements have been made in Windows NT 4.0 to greatly improve the playback of video clips. Especially improved is the playback of full-screen videos.

- *Video volume.* The Volume Control on the Taskbar now works along with the video playback so that you can easily control the loudness as the video is being played. In previous versions, you had to stop the video, adjust the volume, and then restart the video.

- *Better sound.* A new version of Audio Compression Manager has been added to improve sound playback.

- *Improved MIDI.* The existing MIDI capabilities have been improved. It's now easier to configure MIDI, and you lose fewer notes in the playback of complex files.

Unfortunately, not every multimedia capability has been added to NT. The following features are still not directly accommodated:

- *Plug and Play.* Although this automatic configuration capability has been around for several years in other Windows operating systems, it is not fully supported by NT. You must manually configure most new multimedia hardware when you add it to a Windows NT system.

- *Joysticks.* Automatic (or native) support for joysticks and other game control devices has not been added. You must manually configure these devices and use the device drivers supplied by their manufacturer. Luckily, most games already have direct support for joysticks.

THE CD PLAYER

In addition to accessing multimedia CD-ROMs that contain software such as games and encyclopedias, you can use your computer's CD drive to play audio CDs as you work. If your system contains speakers, you can play your CDs through them. If you do not have speakers (or if you want your listening to be private), you can use headphones. Most CD drives have a separate headphone jack and volume control on the front panel where you load the CD.

You can also play CDs using the Media Player. Although the Media Player is not as versatile for playing CDs as the CD Player is, if disk space is limited you may choose not to install the CD Player. Using the Media Player to play CDs is covered later in this chapter.

If you use the headphone jack and volume control on the front panel of the CD drive, you may not be able to control the loudness with the Windows Volume Control.

N O T E

Playing an Audio CD

Unless you have a CD player that can play several discs at once, you can play only one CD at a time. If you are using the CD drive to play a CD-ROM such as a game or an application, you will not be able to listen to an audio CD.

The easiest way to play an audio CD is to open the CD Player drawer, put in the disc, and close the drawer. Windows automatically detects the audio CD and starts to play it (by starting the CD Player application). But if you happened to stop the CD Player and want to start playing the CD again, follow these steps:

1. From the Start menu, select **Programs**, **Accessories**, **Multimedia**, as shown in Figure 18.1.

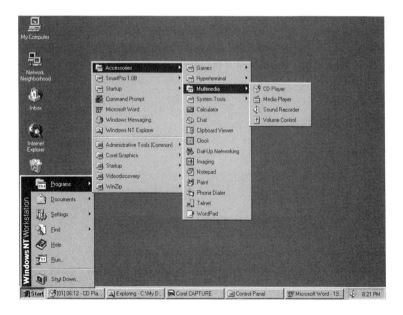

Figure 18.1 *Accessing the CD Player application.*

2. Choose **CD Player** to open the CD Player application.

3. Click the **Play** button in the CD Player window, as shown in Figure 18.2.

Figure 18.2 *The CD Player's main window.*

Using the CD Player Application

The CD Player application that comes with Windows NT 4.0 does everything your home CD player does and more. Like your home CD player, the Windows CD Player has the standard CD player controls, which allow you to play a track, pause on a track, skip ahead to a track, skip ahead within a track, skip back to a track, skip back within a track, stop playing, and eject the CD. These controls are all in the CD Player's main window, which is shown in Figure 18.2.

In addition to the standard controls, the CD Player contains several advanced features that you can access from the menu bar (or toolbar buttons). These features include the following:

*   Setting the play list
*   Setting the view options
*   Setting play options and preferences

Setting the Play List

The CD Player lets you assign the name of a disc, the name of the disc's artist, the titles of the tracks, and the order in which the tracks are played. Setting the play order lets you play the tracks in any desired order and skip any tracks you don't want to hear. To edit the play list for a CD, follow these steps:

1. From the CD Player's main window, select **Disc, Edit Play List** (or use the **Edit Play List** button on the Toolbar). This action displays the Disc Settings dialog box, as shown in Figure 18.3.

Figure 18.3 *The Disc Settings dialog box.*

2. To set the artist and title of the CD, type the appropriate text in the **Artist** and **Title** fields, as shown in Figure 18.4.

Figure 18.4 *Setting the CD's artist and title.*

3. To set the names of the tracks (or songs), select the track from the **Available Tracks** field. Move down to the **Track** name field at the bottom of the dialog box, type in the name of the track, and click **Set Name**. The track's name now appears in the Play List and Available Tracks fields, as shown in Figure 18.5. The track's name will also appear in the **Track** field in the CD Player's main window when the track is playing.

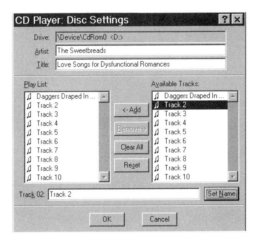

Figure 18.5 Setting the track's name.

4. To remove a track from the play list (for example, to remove track 4), select the track in the **Play List** field and click **Remove**, as shown in Figure 18.6.

Figure 18.6 Removing track 4 from the play list.

5. To play the tracks in a different order, click **Clear All** to clear the **Play List** field. From the **Available Tracks** field, select the desired tracks (one by one) in the order that you want them played and move them to the **Play List** field, as shown in Figure 18.7. To move the tracks from the **Available** list to the **Play List**, either use the **Add** button or drag the selection to the **Play List**.

Figure 18.7 *Setting the play order.*

 To return the play list to its original order, click the **Reset** button in the Disc Settings dialog box.

N O T E

Setting the View Options

The CD Player's View menu allows you to set different display options for the CD being played and for the CD Player itself. By pulling down the View menu from the CD Player's main window, as shown in Figure 18.8, you can display the following information:

- **Toolbar**. This option determines whether the toolbar (set of buttons) is displayed at the top of the CD Player's main window.

- **Disc/Track Info**. This option determines whether the **Artist**, **Title**, and **Track** fields are displayed in the CD Player's main window.

- **Status Bar**. This option determines whether the status bar is displayed at the bottom of the CD Player's main window. The status bar tells you the playing time of the disc and the current track.

- **Track Time Elapsed**. This option displays the elapsed time of the current track in the time counter area of the CD Player.

- **Track Time Remaining**. This option displays the remaining time of the current track in the time counter area of the CD Player.

- **Disc Time Remaining**. This option displays the total remaining time of the entire disc in the time counter area.

- **Volume Control**. This option displays the Windows Volume Control main menu. The Volume Control will be discussed later in this chapter.

Figure 18.8 The CD Player's View menu.

Setting Play Options and Preferences

The CD Player's Options menu allows you to set a disc's play order and some general CD Player preferences. The Options menu is shown in Figure 18.9.

Figure 18.9 The CD Player's Options menu.

The play options can be used in conjunction with each other—that is, you can select both **Continuous Play** and **Random Order**—and include the following capabilities:

- **Random Order**. This option plays the tracks in a random order.

- **Continuous Play**. This option plays the CD continuously in the order selected.

- **Intro Play**. This option plays only the first few seconds of each track in the order selected.

When you select **Preferences** from the Options menu, the Preferences dialog box appears, as shown in Figure 18.10. From this dialog box you can set your general CD Player preferences.

Figure 18.10 *The Preferences dialog box.*

Getting Help on the CD Player

If you need more information on the CD Player, use the online help found under the CD Player's Help menu or the object help associated with the various dialog boxes.

THE SOUND RECORDER

If your system has a sound card, you can use the Windows Sound Recorder to play and record sound (or **.WAV**) files. You can add sound files to your applications, documents, and e-mail. Although sound files are fun and exciting, they require a large amount of disk storage space.

Starting the Sound Recorder

To start the Sound Recorder, select **Programs**, **Accessories**, **Multimedia**, **Sound Recorder** from the Start menu, as shown in Figure 18.11.

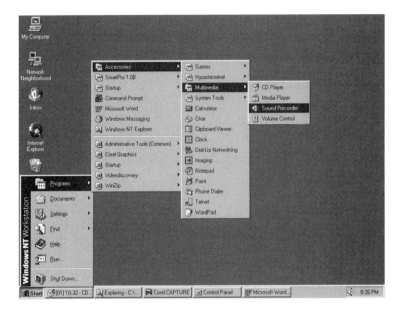

Figure 18.11 *Starting the Sound Recorder.*

When the Sound Recorder starts, it displays its main window, as shown in Figure 18.12. Here you can play prerecorded sound files or record your own.

Figure 18.12 *The Sound Recorder's main window.*

Playing Previously Recorded Sound Files

To play back a previously recorded sound file, you first open the file. To open and play a sound file in the Sound Recorder, follow these steps:

1. Select **File**, **Open**. This action displays a standard Open dialog box.

2. Select the desired sound file and click the **Open** button. This action opens the sound file in the Sound Recorder and updates the main window to display the total length of the recording in seconds and milliseconds.

3. Click the **Play** button to play the recording. As the recording plays, the position and the visual form of the recording are displayed. Notice that the progress bar moves as the recording plays.

Like a regular tape recorder, the Sound Recorder has controls for rewinding, fast-forwarding, playing, stopping, and recording. Using the capabilities of the Volume Control, you can make a recording from the input to your sound card or from a CD or both. The Volume Control determines the source (or sources) of the sound to be recorded. Although the Volume Control will be discussed in more detail later, you can use it now to make a recording from the CD Player.

Recording a Sound File

To make a recording using the Sound Recorder, you need to set up your sources (such as the CD Player), set the *mix*, or relative volume levels, of your sources using the Volume Control, start your sources, and click the **Record** button on the Sound Recorder. To make a recording from the CD Player, follow these steps:

1. Put the source CD in the CD drive, start the CD Player, position it to the desired track (or location in the track), and press the **Pause** button. At this point, the source is now ready.

2. Start the Volume Control by selecting **Programs**, **Accessories**, **Multimedia**, **Volume Control** from the Start menu. This action displays the Volume Control application. Select **Options**, **Properties**, select **Adjust volume for Recording**, and click **OK**. The Volume Control application changes to the Recording Control application, as shown in Figure 18.13. The Recording Control is your *mixing board*.

Figure 18.13 *The Recording Control with the CD Player as the source.*

3. Because you want to record from the CD, select the CD Audio source **Select** button, as shown in Figure 18.13. Make some preliminary recording adjustments by playing the CD and adjusting the volume slider until the graphical equalizer display next to the slider bar never goes into the red. If the graphical display peaks in the red, your recording will be distorted. Now you have set your mix.

4. Set the sound quality to record by selecting **Edit**, **Audio Properties**. At the bottom of the dialog box, select the quality of the recording: CD quality (44K sampling), radio quality (22K sampling) or telephone quality (8K sampling). You can choose the **Customize** button to create your own unique recording settings. You can vary the sampling rate, modulation type, whether the sound is mono or stereo, and whether the sound is recorded as a four-bit, eight-bit, or 16-bit sound. If you have a more powerful sound card, you may even be able to record 32-bit or 64-bit sound files.

5. In the Sound Recorder main window, select **New** from the File menu to create a new recording.

6. Now you are ready to make the recording. With the Sound Recorder, the CD Player, and the Recording Control visible, press the **Record** button on the Sound Recorder and then immediately press the **Play** button on the CD Player. You are now recording.

7. To stop the recording, press the **Stop** button on the Sound Recorder. You may also choose to stop the CD at this time.

8. Now that you have made your recording, you should save it. Select **Save** from the File menu. A standard Save As dialog box appears.

Select the directory and type in a file name for your recording. You can also select the format and attributes of your file by clicking the **Change** button at the bottom of the dialog box. The Sound Recorder saves files as WAV files, but you can change the format to any format supported by your sound card. You may find that your recorded sound file is too large. If you save it again as a 22K stereo file, it will take up half us much space (it also won't sound as good during playback). Click the **Save** button when you are ready to save the file.

9. When you have finished recording, you'll probably want to change the Recording Control application back to the Volume Control application. Select **Options**, **Properties**, and select **Adjust volume for Playback** in the dialog box.

You have just entered the exciting world of digital recording! You're almost an audio engineer now.

If you want to play back your recording, be sure to set the volume of the **Wave** area in the Volume Control, as shown in Figure 18.14. This setting determines the loudness of the Sound Recorder's playback.

N O T E

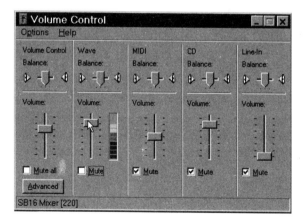

Figure 18.14 The Volume Control set for playback.

If you wanted to record from your sound card's input (perhaps plugging in a microphone), you would use the **Line-In** area of the Volume Control to set the input level. To mix input sources so that you can record from the **Line-In** and **CD**, set the volume levels for both areas in the Volume Control, as shown in Figure 18.15.

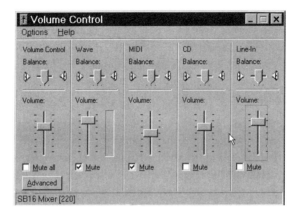

Figure 18.15 *The Volume Control with both the CD Player and the sound card's input as the source.*

Editing Sound Files

In addition to recording and playing sound files, you can perform advanced editing using the Sound Recorder. These capabilities are accessed through the Edit menu:

- **Copy**. This option, used in conjunction with **Paste**, allows you to copy a sound.

- **Paste Insert**. This option inserts a copied sound into a sound file.

- **Paste Mix**. This option mixes or combines two sound files.

- **Insert File**. This option inserts a sound file into another one at the current position of the progress bar.

- **Mix with File**. This option mixes another sound file with the one playing at the current position of the progress bar.

- **Delete Before Current Position**. This option deletes everything in the current sound file up to the current position of the progress bar.

- **Delete After Current Position**. This option deletes everything in the current sound file following the current position of the progress bar.

- **Audio Properties**. This option displays the Audio Properties dialog box, which is shown in Figure 18.16. In this dialog box, you can specify various properties for playback and recording.

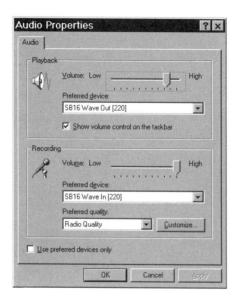

Figure 18.16 *The Audio Properties dialog box.*

Adding Effects

Like any good recording studio technician, you need the ability to add special effects to your recordings. The Sound Recorder provides the Effects menu which includes the following capabilities:

- **Increase Volume (by 25%)**. This option increases the volume of a sound file by 25 percent.
- **Decrease Volume**. This option decreases the volume of a sound file.
- **Increase Speed (by 100%)**. This option increases the speed of a sound file.
- **Decrease Speed**. This option decreases the speed of a sound file.
- **Add Echo**. This option adds an echo effect (or reverb) to a sound file.
- **Reverse**. This option plays the sound file in reverse order.

N O T E

If your sound file is compressed, you will not be able to change its speed or add the echo effect. You can tell whether a sound file is compressed if the green line does not appear in the wave display area of the Sound Recorder's main window. You uncompress a sound file by changing its sound quality under the **Properties** option of the File menu. See the Sound Recorder's online help for more information.

THE MEDIA PLAYER

Although the Media Player is primarily used to play video (or **.AVI**) files, it can also play sound files, MIDI files, and CDs. You select the type of file to play using the Media Player's Device menu.

Starting the Media Player

To start the Media Player, select **Programs, Accessories, Multimedia, Media Player** from the Start menu, as shown in Figure 18.17. The Media Player's main window appears, as shown in Figure 18.18.

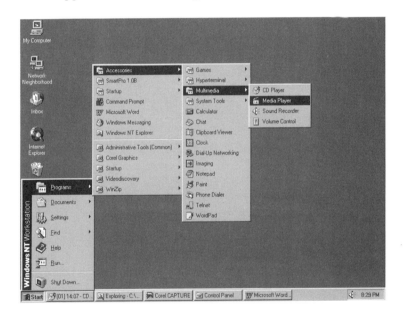

Figure 18.17 *Accessing the Media Player application.*

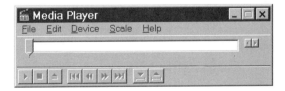

Figure 18.18 *The Media Player's main window.*

Playing a Video, MIDI, or WAV File

To play a video (**.AVI**), MIDI (**.MID** or **.RMI**), or WAV file, you must first open the file. To open and play one of these files in the Media Player, follow these steps:

1. Select **File**, **Open**. This action displays a standard Open dialog box.

2. Select the desired video, MIDI, or WAV file and click **Open**. This opens the file in the Media Player. If the file is a video file, the Media Player creates a separate window for viewing it. The progress of MIDI files, and WAV files is shown in the Media Player's window.

3. Click the **Play** button to play the video or MIDI file. As the file plays, the Media Player's progress bar advances, as shown in Figures 18.19 and 18.20.

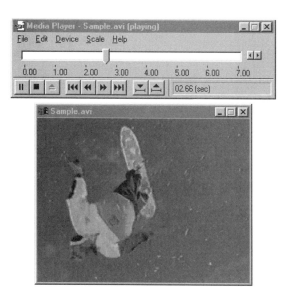

Figure 18.19 *Playing a video (AVI) file.*

Figure 18.20 *Playing a MIDI (MID) file.*

Playing a Video File Using the Full Screen

To play the video in the full screen instead of in a separate window, select **Device**, **Properties**. Choose **Full screen** in the Video Properties dialog box, and click the **OK** or **Apply** button, as shown in Figure 18.21.

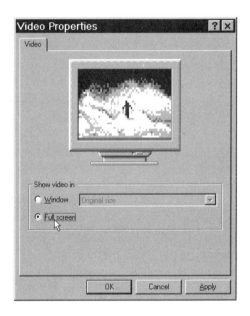

Figure 18.21 *Setting video properties to full screen.*

When you select **Properties** from the Device menu, the Properties dialog box that displays is specific to the device selected in the Device menu. To view video properties when another device is selected, first select **Device**, **Video for Windows** and then select **Properties**. The Properties dialog box shown in Figure 18.21 displays. If one of the other devices is selected, you'll see a different dialog box.

Playing a Music CD Using the Media Player

Playing a music CD using the Media Player is simple. Access the Device menu, as shown in Figure 18.22. Select **CD Music**. If a CD is loaded in the CD drive, the Media Player shows that the CD is loaded. Press the **Play** button and the CD starts playing. Note that Figure 18.22 shows tracks on the CD (the numbers 1 through 4 of a CD), but not the time. You can change what appears in the scale area by selecting **Time** or **Tracks** from the Scale menu. If you want to play tracks individually, select **Scale, Tracks**. This action enables you to switch tracks using the **Next Mark** and **Previous Mark** buttons.

Figure 18.22 *Selecting the device type.*

Getting Help on the Media Player

The Media Player offers many advanced capabilities, such as auto rewind and OLE support. For more information on the Media Player and its features, consult the online help.

THE VOLUME CONTROL

The Volume Control was briefly discussed earlier in this chapter, and now it is time for a closer look. The Volume Control allows you to set not only the overall volume of the sound coming through your speakers but also the mix of the various sound devices (both for sound recording and for playback).

Starting the Volume Control

To start the Volume Control, select **Programs, Accessories, Multimedia, Volume Control** from the Start menu, as shown in Figure 18.23. The Volume Control's main window appears, as shown in Figure 18.24.

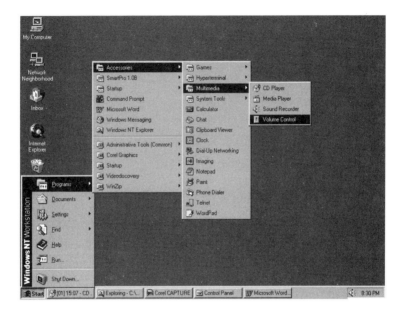

Figure 18.23 *Accessing the Volume Control application.*

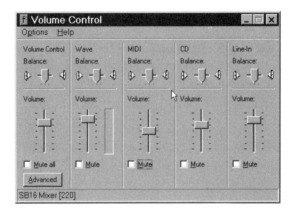

Figure 18.24 *The Volume Control's main window.*

The Areas Controlled by the Volume Control

The Volume Control allows you to set the loudness levels of the various sound devices present in your system. In the Volume Control shown in Figure 18.24, the following areas are controlled:

- **Volume Control**. This area controls the overall, or master, volume of the sound being sent to your system's speakers.

- **Wave**. This area controls the volume of the playback of sound (including video) files.

- **MIDI**. This area controls the volume of the playback of any MIDI (**.MID** or **.RMI**) files.

- **CD**. This area controls the volume of the CD Player.

- **Line-In**. This area controls the volume of the sound card's input line.

Because your sound card is a stereo device, the balance controls adjust the balance of the sound between the left and right speakers.

N O T E

THE CONTROL PANEL MULTIMEDIA APPLET

You may have noticed that each of the applications discussed in this chapter has a Properties dialog box where you can change the properties of each application as you use it. You can also modify these properties, and even load new drivers, using the Multimedia applet in the Control Panel.

Some properties can be changed only in the Multimedia applet. For example, you must use the Multimedia applet to specify that the Volume Control icon appear on the Taskbar next to the time display and to change the drivers and devices. The icon of the Multimedia applet appears in the Control Panel, as shown in Figure 18.25.

Figure 18.25 *The Multimedia applet in the Control Panel.*

When you double-click this icon, you see the dialog box displayed in Figure 18.26.

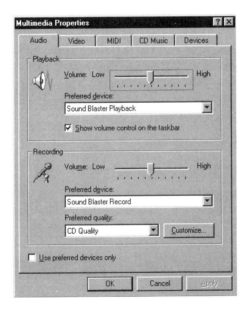

Figure 18.26 *The Multimedia Properties dialog box (**Audio** tab).*

As you can see, the tabbed pages of this dialog box represent the Properties dialog boxes for each of the multimedia devices supported by Windows NT and your sound card. The Properties dialog boxes associated with each individual application let you set properties only for the current session, whereas the Multimedia Properties dialog box enables you to set default properties. In brief, these pages are as follows:

- **Audio** (shown in Figure 18.26). Sets the Playback and Recording volume levels and allows you to select the playback and recording devices. Also lets you specify that the Volume Control display as an icon on the Taskbar next to the clock. For recording purposes, it enables you to set default recording quality by choosing a predefined setting or by creating your own settings using the **Customize** button.

- **Video** (shown in Figure 18.27). Effectively, the **Video** tab is the same as the Properties dialog box that you see when you are using the Media Player as a Video for Windows player. It enables you to specify whether the file plays in a window or full screen.

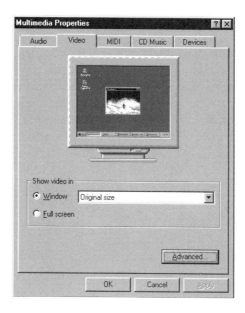

*Figure 18.27 The **Video** tab of the Multimedia Properties dialog box.*

- **MIDI** (shown in Figure 18.28). The **MIDI** page enables you to select the MIDI instrument to use. You can use the sound card or use an external MIDI device (such as a synthesizer attached to your sound card) as the MIDI playback instrument.

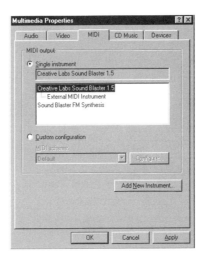

Figure 18.28 *The* ***MIDI*** *tab of the Multimedia Properties dialog box.*

- **CD Music** (shown in Figure 18.29). This page enables you to set the CD-ROM drive as well as the headphone volume (for CD-ROM devices that enable you to set the headphone volume using software).

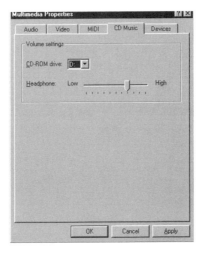

Figure 18.29 *The* ***CD Music*** *tab of the Multimedia Properties dialog box.*

- **Devices** (shown in Figure 18.30). This page shows all the multimedia devices and drivers installed on your system and enables you to add, remove or change the properties of any of them. You can expand the list by clicking on the + icon next to the type of device. The specific device or drivers (or both) will be shown. To change the properties of a specific device or driver, select it and click **Properties**. You will see another dialog box that may or may not allow you to change settings for the device, depending on which one you selected. Some dialog boxes allow detailed settings, and you traverse through several levels of dialog boxes to get to the setting you want to change, as shown in Figure 18.31.

Figure 18.30 *The **Devices** tab of the Multimedia Properties dialog box.*

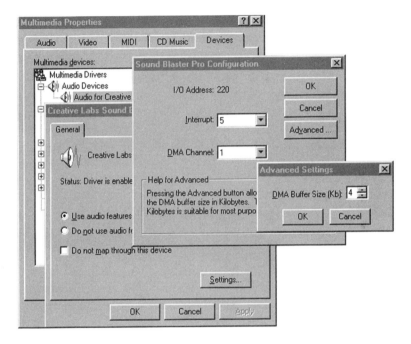

Figure 18.31 *Multiple levels of dialog boxes used to change multimedia device driver settings.*

SUMMARY

Windows NT Workstation 4.0 contains a number of new and enhanced multimedia features. It supports the playback of a variety of media sources: CD music, Video for Windows (AVI) files, MIDI (MID and RMI) files, and WAV files. NT also comes with a Sound Recorder program for recording WAV files.

The CD Player plays audio CDs and lets you enter the titles for the CD, artist, and tracks. These titles are automatically stored on your hard drive, and the CD Player will "remember" them the next time you play that CD. You can enter this information for all your CDs.

The Sound Recorder can be used to record CD-quality, radio-quality, and telephone-quality recordings from a CD source, microphone, or a line input to your sound card. You can save the recording as a WAV file and use it as a system sound or send it to someone via e-mail. This means that you can send voice mail to people.

The Media Player can also play CDs as well as WAV files, MIDI files, and AVI files. It can display AVI files in a window or in full screen mode.

You can use the Volume Control application to change the master volume and the volume settings for any of the devices supported by your sound card. You can also transform the Volume Control application into the Recording Control application and use it as your mixing board while recording sounds with the Sound Recorder.

To change default property settings for all the multimedia devices and device drivers, you use the Multimedia applet in the Control Panel.

INDEX

music. *See also* sound
   MIDI files, 95, 386-87, 394
   playing CDs, 372-79, 388-89
My Computer
   function of, 114-19, 139
   menu options, 119-22
   overview, 113

N

naming computers on network, 123
NDS (Novell NetWare Directory Services), 24
Netscape Navigator, 254
network access, mobile, 27
network integration. *See* integration, network
network interface cards, 360-61, 367-68
Network Neighborhood, 113, 122-23
Network OLE. *See* Distributed COM (DCOM)
networking, 10-11
networks, 3, 353-55, 369-70. *See also*
      Internet; Windows NT 4.0
   configuration of, 77, 106, 363-69
   intranets, 3
   Network Neighborhood, 113, 122-23
   and printers, 152
   schemes
      NT Network Model, 359-62
      OSI Reference Model, 356-59
news retrieval services, accessing, 265
news viewer, 104
notebook computers, 27
Notepad
   editing text, 300-301
   finding text in, 301-2
   overview, 298-99
   saving files, 299-300
   wrapping text, 300
Novell NetWare Directory Services (NDS), 24
NT Explorer. *See* Windows NT Explorer
number formats, 77, 96-97

O

Object Linking and Embedding (OLE),
      335-38, 351
   clients and servers, 338
   copying linked objects, 344
   creating objects for, 341-42
   Cut/Copy commands, 339
   editing
      embedded objects, 344-45
      linked objects, 346
      source objects, 344
   and e-mail, 192
   embedding with Paste command, 339
   image types, specifying, 339-40
   links
      changing, 342-43
      locked/unlocked, 344
      Paste Link command, 341
      updating, 343
   OLE Network (*See* Distributed COM
      (DCOM))
   in WordPad, 228-30
Object Packager, 350-51
objects. *See also* Object Linking and
      Embedding (OLE)
   defined, 36
OLE. *See* Object Linking and Embedding
      (OLE)
online services. *See* Internet
opening
   Control Panel, 75
   files, 47, 128
   folders, 116-19, 128
   Microsoft NT Explorer, 121, 126
   programs (*See* running programs)
operating systems
   microkernel, 7
   subsystems, 7-8
   types of, 16-17
Outbox, 185